INSTIGATIONS

INSTIGATIONS
EZRA POUND AND REMY DE GOURMONT

Richard Sieburth

Harvard University Press, Cambridge, Massachusetts
and London, England
1978

Publication of this book has been aided by a grant from
the Andrew W. Mellon Foundation

Library of Congress Cataloging in Publication Data

Sieburth, Richard.
   Instigations: Ezra Pound and Remy de Gourmont.

   Bibliography: p.
   Includes index.
   1.   Pound, Ezra Loomis, 1885-1972—Sources.
2.   Gourmont, Remy de, 1858-1915—Influence—Pound.
I.   Title.
PS3531.082Z8358   811'.5'2   78-2038
ISBN 0-674-45575-4

ACKNOWLEDGMENTS

I would like to thank the members of the Department of Comparative Literature at Harvard, Harry Levin and Jean Bruneau in particular, for their suggestions and encouragement while this book was still at its dissertation stage. Donald Gallup and Louis Martz of Beinecke Library graciously allowed me access to Pound materials in their collection at Yale. James Laughlin facilitated permission to quote unpublished letters. François Chapon of the Doucet Library in Paris was most kind in permitting me to consult papers of Natalie Barney. I would also like to thank C. F. Terrell of *Paideuma*, where some of these pages first appeared, as well as my editors Joyce Backman, Camille Smith, and Katherine Miller. My greatest debt is to Mary de Rachewiltz, who let me range through Pound's books at Brunnenburg and in general supplied valuable instigation.

I am grateful for permission to quote from the following works of Pound and Eliot.

Reprinted by permission of the New Directions Publishing Corporation and Faber and Faber, Ltd.: Ezra Pound, *ABC of Reading*, copyright 1934 by Ezra Pound. *The Cantos*, copyright 1934, 1937, 1940, 1948, © 1956, 1959, 1962, 1963, 1965, 1966, 1968, 1970 by Ezra Pound; copyright 1972 by The Estate of Ezra Pound. *Personae (Collected Shorter Poems)*, copyright 1950 by Ezra Pound. *Literary Essays*, copyright 1918, 1920, 1935 by Ezra Pound. *Selected Letters (1907-1941)*, ed. D. D. Paige, copyright 1950 by Ezra Pound. *Selected Prose 1909-1965*, ed. William Cookson, copyright © 1973 by The Estate of Ezra Pound; all rights reserved. *Pound/Joyce*, ed. Forrest Read, copyright © 1965, 1966, 1967 by Ezra Pound.

Acknowledgments

CONTENTS

Introduction   1

1   "Amas ut facias pulchram"   28

2   The Problem of Style   50

3   Dissociations   68

4   Flaubert and the Prose Tradition   94

5   The Natural Philosophy of Love   129

Appendix   161
Selected Works by Gourmont   169
Notes   171
Index   193

ABBREVIATIONS OF WORKS BY POUND

ABC   *ABC of Reading* (New York: New Directions, 1960)

G-B   *Gaudier-Brzeska* (New York: New Directions, 1960)

GK   *Guide to Kulchur* (New York: New Directions, 1970)

J/M   *Jefferson and/or Mussolini* (New York: Liveright, 1970)

L   *The Letters of Ezra Pound: 1907-1941*, ed. D. D. Paige (New York: Harcourt Brace Jovanovich, 1950)

LE   *Literary Essays of Ezra Pound*, ed. T. S. Eliot (New York: New Directions, 1954)

P   *Personae* (New York: New Directions, 1926 reprint, 5th printing)

PD   *Pavannes and Divagations* (New York: New Directions, 1958)

P/J   *Pound/Joyce: Letters and Essays*, ed. Forrest Read (New York: New Directions, 1967)

SP   *Selected Prose of Ezra Pound: 1909-1965*, ed. William Cookson (New York: New Directions, 1973)

SOR   *Spirit of Romance* (New York: New Directions, 1958)

References to the *Cantos* give Canto number first, followed by the page numbers in both the 1970 New Directions and the 1964 Faber editions. For example, XXXVIII/189;197. Unless otherwise noted, all translations are my own.

INSTIGATIONS

INTRODUCTION

leading to Remy?
—Canto LXXXVII

"Of all modern critics," observed Eliot in *The Sacred Wood*, "perhaps Remy de Gourmont had most the general intelligence of Aristotle . . . he combined to a remarkable degree sensitiveness, erudition, sense of fact and sense of history, and generalizing power."[1] Pound, who had originally introduced his compatriot to Gourmont's writings,[2] shared the early Eliot's extraordinary esteem for the French man of letters—indeed, between 1912 and 1922 he was to devote more pages of enthusiastic appreciation and translation to Gourmont than to any other single contemporary. It was not to Aristotle, however, but more characteristically, to Confucius that Pound would later compare Gourmont as a civilizing agent. As he explained to the critic René Taupin in a 1928 letter detailing his various debts to French literature, Confucius and Gourmont shared a fundamental common sense that he valued far more than originality; both, moreover, had formulated ideas that, if applied, might contribute to, in his words, the civilizing of America:

> J'ai cité Gourmont, et je viens de donner un[e] nouv[elle] version du *Ta Hio* de Confucius, parce que j'y trouve des formulations d'idées qui me paraissent utile[s] pour civili[s]er l'Amérique (tentatif). Je révère plutôt le bon sens que l'originalité (soit de Remy de G., soit de Confucius).   (L, 217)

> I have quoted Gourmont and have just done a new version of Confucius's *Ta Hio* because I find their works contain formulations of ideas that strike me as useful for the (tentative) civilizing of

1

America. I revere common sense over originality (be it that of Remy
de G. or Confucius).

The contrast between Eliot's and Pound's analogies is illuminating,
capturing as it does both their early affinities and later divergences.
Whereas Eliot tended to view Gourmont almost exclusively as a literary
critic, Pound perceived him as a kind of polymath culture hero whose
scope as poet, novelist, scholar, critic, journalist, philosophe, and naturalist embraced a range of shared interests: Homer, the Latin poets of the
Middle Ages, the troubadours, Cavalcanti and Dante, Stendhal and
Flaubert, the Symbolist movement in France, linguistic and poetic theory, contemporary politics, Mediterranean folklore, and the amatory
customs of butterflies and bees. Taken together, Gourmont's works constituted, according to Pound, "a portrait of the civilized mind. I incline to
think them the best portrait available, the best record that is, of the civilized mind from 1885-1915." They provided "perhaps the best introduction to the ideas of our time that any unfortunate, suddenly emerging
from Peru, Peoria, Oshkosh, Iceland, Kochin, or other out-of-the-way
lost continent could desire" (LE, 344).

When Pound discovered Gourmont's work in 1912, he had himself
only recently emerged from one such lost continent into the civilized
mind of Europe, "seeing he had been born/In a half-savage country, out
of date" (P, 187). In his contributions to such magazines as *Poetry*, the
Egoist, the *New Age*, the *Little Review*, and the *Dial*, the mere mention
of Gourmont soon became a rallying cry of sorts for Pound's campaign
against the provincial stultification of contemporary British and, more
particularly, American letters. He informed Taupin:

> Autre dissociation à faire: quelque fois on apprend, ou subit "influ-
> ence" d'une idée—quelque fois en lutte contre barbarisme, on
> cherche un appui—on s'arme du prestige d'un homme civili[s]é et
> reconnu pour combattre l'imbécillité américaine. (L, 217)

> There is another dissociation to be made: occasionally one learns
> from or is "influenced" by an idea—in one's flight against barbarity,
> one occasionally seeks some sort of support—one arms oneself with
> the prestige of a man both renowned and civilized in order to
> combat American imbecility.

Pound's dissociation is a useful one, indicating as it does the particular
nature of his indebtedness to Gourmont, an indebtedness not so much for
specific ideas (though the very term "dissociation" is perhaps Gourmont's
single most important contribution to Pound's critical vocabulary), as

for a certain manner of holding them, a certain quality of active, limpid mind: "There is nothing more unsatisfactory than saying that Gourmont 'had such and such ideas' or held 'such and such views,' the thing is that he held ideas, intuitions, perceptions in a certain personal exquisite manner. In a criticism of him, 'criticism' being an over-violent word, in, let us say, an indication of him, one wants merely to show that one has himself made certain dissociations" (LE, 343).

"Ideas came to [Gourmont]," Pound observed elsewhere, "as a series of fine wines to a delicate palate, and he was never inebriated. He never ran *amok*," but instead entertained his thoughts with the "absolute fairness" and "absolute openness" of a "man watching his own experiment in laboratory" (SP, 415). Again and again in his various homages to the French man of letters, Pound insisted less on Gourmont's actual works than on the particular texture of the intelligence that informed them—its clarity, its urbanity, its irony, its catholicity, its sensuousness, its imperturbable common sense and aristocratic refusal to allow itself to be stampeded by accepted ideas (*idées reçues*)—qualities, in short, that made of Gourmont "a symbol of so much that is finest in France" (SP, 413) and an appropriate vehicle, as Pound wrote Taupin, to combat American imbecility, "armed with the prestige of a man both renowned and civilized."

The remarkable prestige that Pound and his contemporaries accorded to Gourmont ("Some fames and reputations are like that; Mallarmé is almost a mantram, a word for conjuring": SP, 420) must seem something of a mystery to the reader of today. Highly acclaimed during his own lifetime as doyen of Symbolism and influential editor of the *Mercure de France*, Gourmont has, since the early twenties, undergone a strange eclipse—one recent Gourmont scholar has gone so far as to speak of a "conspiracy of silence" surrounding "the man who, more than any other, played a part in the charter conferred on the 'modernist' spirit in the kingdom of art."[3] Indeed, despite his stature as champion of the literary avant-garde during the early years of the century, Gourmont now receives but scant mention in the French world of letters; in literary histories, he is easily overshadowed by such figures as Jarry, Apollinaire, and Gide, whose reputations his early friendship in part shaped. That Gourmont's intellectual authority should have diminished so drastically in France only a few years after his death in 1915 is perhaps an indication of his extraordinary *personal* presence. Though disfigurement by lupus rendered him a virtual urban recluse, he existed for younger writers, if we are to believe Pound, as "the one man they mentioned with sympathy, the one older man to whom they could look for comprehension, and even for discreet assistance" (SP, 416), as the "final and kindly tribunal where all work would stand on its merits" (SP, 420).

In another sense, however, Gourmont's reputation was a casualty of the First World War: the particular version of humanistic learning he em-

bodied could not survive the disillusionment of those who returned from
the trenches with the sense that they had merely fought

> For an old bitch gone in the teeth,
> For a botched civilization,
> . . . . .
>
> For two gross of broken statues,
> For a few thousand battered books.   (P, 191)

Though his writings had, as Pound remarked, in a way prepared the climate of postwar modernism (LE, 399), Gourmont's elegant scepticism
could not compete with the strident nihilism of the Dadaists; his explora-
tions into the role of the unconscious in literary creation appeared timid
next to the flamboyant nightmares of the Surrealists; his fin-de-siècle
erotic prose and poetry, so provocative in the nineties, seemed merely
obsolete to a generation that had discovered free love and Freud; his rich
sense of the past could not be shared by polemicists suspicious of all tradition; his serene individualism and ideological detachment became a
luxury in a world given over to collective movements in art and politics.
Gourmont's reputation has never really since recovered in France. Although the early sixties saw Karl Uitti's authoritative critical reassess-
ment of Gourmont's work and the reissue by the Mercure de France of
several of his most important books (most notably the *Livre des masques,
La Culture des idées,* and *Physique de l'amour*), Gourmont's forty-vol-
ume oeuvre remains virtually unread in his native country, of interest
only to literary historians.

He has fared somewhat better abroad: in 1966 Glenn Burne, author of
a useful study of Gourmont's influence in England and America, brought
out in English a selection from his works, superseding Aldington's 1928
translations;[4] several of Gourmont's essays have been included in American anthologies of critical writing over the past two decades; and in the
early seventies, Pound's 1922 version of the *Physique de l'amour, The
Natural Philosophy of Love,* went into its second mass paperback printing with an appropriately prurient cover to catch the commuter's tired
eye ("Before Kinsey and before Dr. Reuben there was *The Natural Philosophy of Love* . . ."). On the more scholarly level, Gourmont's impact
on such various Anglo-American authors as T. E. Hulme, T. S. Eliot,
Richard Aldington, and Aldous Huxley has been well documented by
several comparatists.[5] Pound's relation to Gourmont—more complex
than that of any of these authors—has remained relatively unexplored,
however, perhaps because Gourmont himself has, on the whole, seemed
to exegetes a relatively minor component of Pound's particular "ideo-
graph of the good" (LE, 37), a figure peripheral to the central canons of
the *Cantos.*[6]

True, among the French poets that Pound read, Gourmont exerted a far less decisive effect on him than did, say, Gautier, Rimbaud, Corbière, or Laforgue—though the cadences of Gourmont's *Litanies* course through the *Cantos*. His critical influence on Pound was certainly less than Ford Madox Ford's—yet his *Problème du style* provided a theoretical context for Imagism that Ford's writings could never have supplied. It was Ford, to be sure, who introduced Pound to the nineteenth-century prose tradition, but Gourmont's pages on Flaubert proved to be richer in implication. True, Gourmont's essays on language were no doubt less seminal than Fenollosa's meditations on the Chinese written character, his comments on politics or economics had not the statistical persuasiveness of Douglas's, his writings on folklore and mythology lacked the anthropological depth of Frobenius, his *Physique de l'amour* was the book of an amateur entomologist when compared with Agassiz's work in natural science. Yet without Gourmont, Pound would probably not have later assimilated these authors into precisely the same ideogrammic configuration. "My generation needed Gourmont," Pound insisted in 1934; if he did not exactly provide, as Yeats quipped, "a portable substitute for the British Museum" (L, 257), Gourmont nevertheless fulfilled a far more vital pedagogic function. Like all true teachers, he supplied not solutions but rather a series of instigations; he aroused, in Pound's words, "the senses of the imagination, preparing the mind for receptivities" (LE, 345).

Pound was of course not the first to have invoked the works and personal example of Gourmont as instigations "pour civiliser l'Amérique." James Gibbons Huneker, America's foremost importer of contemporary trends in European arts and letters, had in 1895 featured Gourmont in the pages of his *M'lle New York*, a lively fin-de-siècle review dedicated to the dissemination of the latest innovations of the Parisian avant-garde. Two years later Huneker reviewed Gourmont's collection of essays on French Symbolist poets, *Le Livre des masques*, for the *Nation*, protesting that the French critic was unduly neglected in the United States.[7] In 1899 he sent Gourmont some of his own work (a blasphemous short story in the decadent manner of Gourmont's early master, Huysmans) and shortly thereafter the two men entered into friendly correspondence, exchanging books and articles. Huneker's first full-scale study of Gourmont appeared in the *New York Sun* in 1900, and thereafter, as Burne notes, his essays were studded with quotations from the works of the man whom he ranked among Georg Brandes, Havelock Ellis, and Arthur Symons as one of Europe's greatest living critics. Gourmont reciprocated by praising his American colleague's work in the *Mercure de France*; especially impressed by Huneker's *Chopin: The Man and His Music* (1900), he published an article based on the book in the *Mercure* of June of the same year. Huneker in turn dedicated his second volume of short stories, *Visionaries* (1905) to Gourmont; indeed, Huneker seemed all too aware of the latter's pervasive influence on his own rhapsodic prose, for in a later autobiographical novel, *Painted Veils* (1920), Gourmont appeared in a cameo role to chide the young American hero for his lack of originality and to advise him to return back home.

Gourmont's impact on Huneker, however, involved far more than the daring irreverence and erotic explicitness of his now dated imaginative prose. Rather, Gourmont provided Huneker and his collaborators on *M'lle New York* with an exhilarating alternative to the academic stance of such critics as Brunetière, Babbitt, or Paul Elmer More, whose wholesale censure of modern literature placed them at but a short remove from the philistine mob. Champion of the various advanced tendencies in the arts, Gourmont instead embodied the kind of criticism whose primary aim was to encourage innovation, to improve the climate of creation. Combining the journalist's quick eye for the new and noteworthy, the scholar's respect for the past, and the artist's commitment to experiment, Gourmont was a perfect model for Huneker's own attempts to infuse something of the sophistication and excitement of contemporary European art and thought into the provincial American scene. Entitling his own *Promenades of an Impressionist* (1910) after Gourmont's series of *Promenades littéraires*, Huneker emulated the latter's leisurely critical stroll; he lacked the Frenchman's keen sense of direction, however, and allowed himself to be sidetracked too often into polyphonic patches of purple prose. Gourmont's subjective approach to criticism validated Huneker's own impressionistic practice. But whereas Gourmont's literary impressionism was based in a larger epistemological theory (that is, that ideas were only abstracted sensations and hence lacked the authenticity of immediate sense impressions), Huneker's critical pieces were frequently little more than exercises in free association with insights often lost in a welter of arbitrary allusions and synesthetic effects.

Like Gourmont's, Huneker's range was wide; unlike the academic critics, however, he devoted himself almost exclusively to bringing living European artists before the American audience. Trained as a musician, he wrote pioneering essays on Wagner, Strauss, Mussorgsky, Debussy, and Schönberg; as a drama critic, he was an ardent promulgator of the theater of Ibsen, Shaw, Strindberg, and Wedekind; as an art critic, his appreciations of Gaugin, Cézanne, Van Gogh, and Matisse were as influential as his reviews of contemporary American painting—after the Armory Show he advised John Quinn, patron of Pound, Lewis, and Gaudier-Brzeska, on his outstanding collection of modern art. Huneker's excursions into philosophy made him (like Gourmont in France) one of the earliest and most persistent popularizers of Nietzsche in America. Frequently drawing on Gourmont's essays, his literary criticism introduced the wider American public to such French poets as Verlaine, Laforgue, Charles Cros, and Paul Fort (his early collaborator on *M'lle New York*, Vance Thompson, was even more directly indebted to Gourmont: entire pages of his *French Portraits* (1900) were lifted from *Le Livre des masques*). Huneker's first and perhaps most influential collection of literary essays, *Egoists: A Book of Supermen* (1909), contained an examination of Stendhal's life and works which Gourmont thought worthy of translation in the *Mercure de France*, as well as impressionistic studies of Baudelaire, Flaubert, Anatole France, Huysmans, Barrès, Nietzsche, and Max Stirner.

The young T. S. Eliot reviewed *Egoists* for the *Harvard Advocate* in 1909, observing that Huneker, "far too alert" to be American, was French in temperament. Though he chided the critic's style for being "unpardonably hasty, crammed, staccato," he admired its Jamesian "conversational quality" and "informality" which eschewed "all the ordinary rhetorical hoaxes for securing attention." He praised Huneker's choice of subjects ("But the Egoists are all men—French and German—of highly individual, some of perverse and lunary, genius") and was especially drawn to the "critique of Huysmans, the genius of faith."[8] Some four decades later, Eliot recalled that as an undergraduate he had found Huneker's essays "highly stimulating because of the number of foreign authors, artists and composers whom he was able to mention, and whom I had then never heard of. Later it came to seem to me that the actual value of his criticism was slight and the parade of names . . . rather tiresome. But I think his work may have performed a useful service for others as well as myself, in bringing to their attention the names of distinguished contemporaries and men of the previous generation, in the various arts."[9]

Though Eliot seemed unaware of Huneker's substantial debt to Gourmont, he was not alone in his early admiration for America's foremost cosmopolitan critic. Van Wyck Brooks remarked that such collections as *Egoists, Iconoclasts* (1905), *Ivory Apes and Peacocks* (1915), and *Unicorns* (1917) "shoveled into the minds of the young precisely what they did not learn in college." "In the years that I read him, 1914 to 1921," commented Ben Hecht, "I regarded [Huneker] as my alma mater."[10] Huneker's reputation (like Gourmont's) waned after his death in 1921; nevertheless, he provided an extracurricular education in Continental modernism for several generations of American artists and intellectuals. One of the earliest readers of *M'lle New York*, H. L. Mencken, would pursue his mentor's iconoclastic attacks on American democratic and Christian values in the *Smart Set* and *Vanity Fair*. Other early disciples included George Jean Nathan, Benjamin De Casseres (who also wrote on Gourmont), Carl Van Vechten, and Paul Rosenfeld. After the war, the young Kenneth Burke, avid reader of Gourmont as well, would school himself in Huneker's writings—as would Malcolm Cowley and Edmund Wilson.[11]

Huneker was in his heyday as a critic for the *New York Sun* during Pound's university years (1901-1907), but Pound seemed unaware of his existence, preferring the scholarly pursuit of Dante, Villon, the troubadours, and Lope de Vega to Huneker's flashy collection of modernists.

Despite the fact that Pound's college reading included such recent poets as Symons, Dowson, Bliss Carman, and Yeats, he remained relatively ignorant of recent developments in Continental letters. His undergraduate courses at Hamilton had given him a basic grounding in classic French and German literature (in letters to his parents he mentions studying old French verse, Cyrano, Descartes, Pascal, Corneille, and Molière; Goethe and Jean Paul Richter), but with the exception of reading Anatole France's *Mannequin d'osier* in 1905 and writing a review of Péladan's *Origine et esthétique de la tragedie* and *Le Secret des troubadours* in 1906,[12] Pound showed no especial interest in contemporary French literature until he discovered the work of Gourmont in early 1912, that is, some four years after he had left America for Venice and subsequent residence in London.

Pound must certainly have heard of, if not actually met, Huneker while revisiting New York in the fall of 1910, but his published writings make no mention of him—despite the fact that Huneker had written on Yeats for the *Sun* in 1903 and was a good friend of John Quinn, whom Pound encountered for the first time during this same visit. Indeed, Quinn plays an interesting role as intermediary between Huneker, Yeats, and Pound. Yeats met Huneker during his first American lecture tour in 1903, and wrote him later that year to thank him for introducing him to Nietzsche's theories of Dionysian and Apollonian art.[13] Since it was no doubt Huneker who had first exposed Quinn to the German philosopher, he can be said to have exerted an indirect Nietzschean influence on the early Pound through Yeats. Although he was probably unaware of it, Huneker himself was later to owe a more substantial debt to Pound. The intermediary again was Quinn, whom Pound had managed to interest in the work and welfare of James Joyce in 1915; Quinn in turn encouraged Huneker to review *A Portrait of the Artist* upon its American publication.[14] Huneker's literary scoop (it was the first prominent criticism of the novel to appear in America) would almost seem a plagiarism of Pound's early articles on Joyce (for example, the comparisons between Joyce, Flaubert, and Maupassant), were it not for the fact that Huneker had most of his information about the Irish novelist from his friend Quinn.

The series of articles Pound wrote about America after his return to England in early 1911 ("Patria Mia" and "America: Chances and Remedies," respectively published in 1912 and 1913) caught something of the emergent cultural dynamism of New York, but he had not significantly altered his opinion as to the suffocating insularity of the American literary scene—with the notable exception of Mencken, Pound would long remain ignorant of the generation of intellectuals spawned by Huneker's popularizations. Not that Pound's eyes were yet sharply focused on contemporary Continental experiments. His 1911 *Canzoni* were, with few exceptions, decidedly unmodernist in manner: their originality lay rather in how far *back* in the European tradition they went; and "Redondillas," the one long poem that attempted a satirically contemporary tone, was removed from the volume at its page-proof stage.

When he went to Paris in the spring of the same year for a two-month stay with his friend the musician Walter Morse Rummel, Pound still seemed more engrossed in the songs of the troubadours than in the Parisian avant-garde. "I wander about the Blois and the Tuileries," he wrote home to his parents, "and divert my mind with the French classics." Though he did make the rounds of various ateliers and galleries "inspecting the state of Art,"[15] he apparently spent most of his time with Rummel and Yeats. Through Yeats he met Henry Davray, who as redactor of the *Mercure*'s "Lettres anglaises" rubric had reviewed Pound's *Exultations* in 1909. Pound reported home on the meeting:

> Yeats and I went down to Davray's for tea last Wednesday. Davray is a sort of critic here or hereabouts. The place was full of the same. Had a rather good talk with Legouis, one of the professors at the Sorbonne. The crop of poets at present existing in Paris seems a rather gutless lot, given over to description. The picture shows are various. The Salon Indépendent has some very interesting pictures in it and two masterpieces by Dézire. Castellucho and Le Doux also have good things and Matisse's one canvas is well-painted. Freaks there are in abundance.[16]

That Pound should have found the conversation of the English Renaissance specialist Emile Legouis more stimulating than the work of contemporary French poets is indicative of the archaizing bent of his own *Canzoni*. Ford Madox Ford, whom Pound visited in Giessen later that summer (after literary pilgrimages to Sirmione, Verona, San Zeno, the Ambrosian Library in Milan, and Freiburg-im-Breisgau, home of the Provençal scholar Emil Lévy) was to ridicule Pound's volume for precisely this reason. Pound later revealed that

> [Ford] felt the errors of contemporary style to the point of rolling (physically, and if you look at it as mere superficial snob, ridiculously) on the floor of his temporary quarters in Giessen when my third volume displayed me trapped, fly-papered, gummed and strapped down in a jejune provincial effort to learn, *mehercule*, the stilted language that then passed for "good English" in the arthritic milieu that held control of the respected British critical circles . . . that roll saved me at least two years, perhaps more. It sent me back to my own proper effort, namely, toward using the living tongue. (SP, 461-462)

Whether or not Ford's roll on the floor actually produced the apostolic illumination here described, Pound returned to London that fall prepared to modernize both his critical and poetic idiom. He began to see T. E. Hulme again (they had first met in 1909), attended his lectures on Bergson (in which the latter's concept of the "image" was discussed), and was introduced to A. R. Orage, editor of the *New Age*. Through Orage he was introduced into a world hitherto unsuspected, for contributors to the magazine during the next few years included not only men like Hulme, Sturge Moore, Wyndham Lewis, and Rupert Brooke, but others who might have remained completely outside his ken, such as Allen Upward, Middleton Murry, Llewelyn Powys, and Katherine Mansfield.[17]

Orage's *New Age* had long been committed to introducing the best of Continental art and thought into England; Guild Socialist in political tendency, the magazine was open to a cosmopolitan range of intellectual and artistic experiment. From 1908 to 1911 Arnold Bennett (whom Pound had met in Paris in the spring of 1911, though neither seemed very impressed with the other) had served as its specialist in French prose, discussing the work of Stendhal, Anatole France, the Goncourts, Romain Rolland, Gide, and Gourmont (whom he called "the greatest unappreciated writer in France today").[18] Hulme in turn had introduced such French thinkers as Bergson and Jules de Gaultier to *New Age* readers in 1909.

The same year, F. S. Flint, the *New Age*'s commentator on contemporary trends in French vers libre, had published a long review of Paul Delior's *Remy de Gourmont et son oeuvre* (1909). Gourmont's work, Flint observed, "is astounding in its diversity and complexity, in beauty and profundity, in the keen cleavage of old associated ideas and subtle evocation of new." He was particularly enthusiastic about the *Livre des masques*: "They are veritable ambrosia and nectar, and reading them the dry blood of the mind becomes ichor, and one trembles with the penetrating intoxication of novelty." He lauded Gourmont's verse ("poems of a strange musicality, like the clashing of gems"), discussed his novels, theoretical and scientific works, and concluded the survey: "It is impossible to pass through these books without feeling that new eyes and a new understanding are being given to one; old images and metaphors are broken up and made useless; associations that have grown mouldy are crumbled; and fresh with the dew of a new morning the earth again awaits the re-born artist."[19] Although marred by the effusiveness that rendered so much of his criticism ineffectual, Flint's 1909 article was nevertheless the first substantial account of Gourmont's work to appear in England— among the older generation, Arthur Symons had only mentioned *Les Chevaux de Diomède* briefly in an 1897 article for the *Saturday Review*; Gosse was not to publish his eulogy of Gourmont until 1922; and though Havelock Ellis knew Gourmont personally, his account of their friendship would appear only in 1935.[20]

Pound had known Flint and Hulme since the days of the 1909 Poet's Club, but, according to Flint, "Pound used to boast in those days that he was 'Nil praetor [*sic*] Villon et doctus cantare Catullum,' and he could not be made to believe that there was any French poetry after Ronsard."[21] By late 1911, however, Pound was seriously reassessing the direction of his verse and hence was more receptive to modern French importations. His essays of the period, published in the *New Age* between November 1911 and February 1912 under the collective title "I Gather the Limbs of Osiris," clearly reflect the transitional process, for they hearken back to his 1910 *Spirit of Romance* while pointing ahead to the critical formulations of Imagism. It must have been during this period that Pound first began reading Gourmont: the final installments of the "Osiris" series contain a number of peculiarly Gourmontian insights, and in February 1912 we find Pound informing his mother that "Flint, in return for being resurrected has put me onto some very good contemporary French stuff, Remy de Gourmont, de Régnier, etc."[22] What Flint's "resurrection" involved remains uncertain—perhaps Pound alludes to Flint's lapse into temporary obscurity after he ceased writing for the *New Age* in 1910, perhaps to the fact that he had been welcomed into the ranks of the as yet unlabeled Imagist group—but at any rate Pound's debt is clear. He had come to Gourmont late and in a characteristically circuitous manner ("always the long way round to get home," remarks Hugh Kenner echoing Joyce, "In that he was most like Odysseus"),[23] but once he had discovered him, Pound would put Gourmont to use in a way that neither Flint nor Huneker ever could.

The mention of Gourmont in conjunction with Régnier suggests that Pound first began reading Gourmont's verse in early 1912, that is, during Imagism's formative period. T. E. Hulme's *Complete Poetical Works* (later appended to *Ripostes*) appeared in the *New Age* in January of that year; in March, Marinetti stormed through London promoting the first Futurist Exhibition; H.D. and Richard Aldington were beginning to write verse of Hellenic inspiration in the "austere, direct" mode that Pound called for in his February "Prolegomena" (LE, 12); Flint was preparing the survey of contemporary French poetry that would appear in the *Poetry Review* later that year; and Pound himself was experimenting in several metrical directions, integrating his studies of classical quantitative measures, of Anglo-Saxon alliteration, and of Provençal word-music (*motz el son*) with his fresh discovery of contemporary French free verse. Pound's study of current French verse bore quick fruit: one of his first masterpieces in the new manner, "The Return" (published in the June *English Review*), imitates the subtle phrasings of Régnier's *Médailles d'Argile*.[24] And, although he would not allude to them in print until March of the following year, the impact of Gourmont's *Litanies de la Rose* can be felt in the strong anaphoric cadences of "The Alchemist"—

11

first written during this same period, but not included in *Ripostes* until 1920.[25]

These early months of 1912 also saw Pound's initial reading of Gourmont's *Le Latin mystique du moyen âge*, the scholarly source behind the liturgical rhythms of the *Litanies*. Pound had long been interested in medieval and Renaissance Latin verse (the *Spirit of Romance* had contained a final chapter on "Poeti Latini"); in Gourmont's anthology he discovered not only further historical precedents for his own metrical innovations but oblique confirmation of his emergent theory of absolute rhythm (LE, 9). Pound's "Psychology and Troubadours," first delivered as a lecture in the spring of 1912 and published in *The Quest* later that year, in turn adduced *Le Latin mystique* to demonstrate the various medieval Christian prefigurations of the pagan, neo-Platonic cult of Amor in Provence. One of Goddeschalk's visionary erotic sequences in particular (whose "amas ut facias pulchram" Gourmont had singled out as especially Dantesque) would thereafter remain a permanent touchstone of Pound's.

Whereas Gourmont's *Latin mystique* appealed to Pound's postgraduate fascination with the scholarly and the arcane, his *Problème du style* (which Pound also began reading during this period) supplied a crucial theoretical instigation for the modern poetics of Imagism.[26] Though the school had yet to be baptized (Les Imagistes would be first mentioned in the August 1912 appendix to *Ripostes*) and its basic precepts yet to be officially promulgated ("A Few Don'ts" would appear in *Poetry* in March 1913), Pound's essays of early 1912 nonetheless reflect the fundamental themes of *Le Problème du style*, most notably its insistence on a style that would, by the visual immediacy of its images, bring the word "close to the thing," "break up cliché," and "disintegrate these magnetised groups that stand between the reader of poetry and the drive of it" (SP, 41). Hulme's linguistic theory (much of it borrowed from Gourmont and Bergson) had adumbrated similar notions as early as 1909, but Pound's debt to Hulme appears to be minimal: his own particular critical formulations, different from Hulme's in many crucial respects, seem to derive directly from his own reading of *Le Problème du style* in early 1912.

Pound had at this point not entirely abandoned his early Yeatsian admiration for a poetry of "things indefinite, impalpable" with "its powers of vague suggestion" (SP, 33), but he was quickly moving towards a rejection of the quasi-Symbolist aesthetic he had inherited from the British poets of the nineties. He wrote in his "Credo" of February 1912: "*Symbols.*—I believe that the proper and perfect symbol is the natural object, that if a man use 'symbols' he must so use them that their symbolic function does not obtrude; so that *a* sense, and the poetic quality of the passage, is not lost to those who do not understand the symbol as such, to whom, for instance, a hawk is a hawk" (LE, 9). The imprint of

Introduction

Le Problème du style seems evident here, for Gourmont had repeatedly emphasized the importance of exactly presenting the object (visually) perceived rather than the emotion or symbolic association thereby induced. Although Pound wrote Taupin in the late twenties, "Je ne me rappelle rien de Gourmont au sujet de 'symbole' " (L, 218), some decades later he informed another critic that it was precisely Gourmont who had acted as a "liberating influence" from what had been a "traditional symbolism" with fixed values attached to nonvisual symbols.[27] The comment recalls Pound's remarks in his 1914 "Vorticism" essay:

> Imagisme is not symbolism. The symbolists dealt in "association," that is, in a sort of allusion, almost of allegory. They degraded the symbol to the status of a word. They made it a form of metonymy. One can be grossly "symbolic" for example, by using the term "cross" to mean "trial." The symbolist's symbols have a fixed value, like numbers in arithmetic, like 1, 2, and 7. The imagiste's images have a variable significance, like the sign a, b, and x in algebra. Moreover, one does not want to be called a symbolist, because symbolism has usually been associated with mushy technique. (G-B, 84)

Pound is here guilty of a gross misprision of Symbolism, but whatever its critical worth, the passage does underscore what he thought to be the distinguishing features of Imagism.[28] Paradoxically enough, it was in part Gourmont, whose *Livre des masques* has done so much to popularize the Symbolist movement and whose *Litanies* were exemplary of its aesthetic, who provided Pound with the very critical weapons he needed in order to dissociate his poetics from the fin-de-siècle Symbolist practices of such poets as Yeats, Symons, and Dowson.

In May of 1912 Pound visited Paris with H.D. and Aldington. Though he wrote home upon his arrival that he hadn't "found much contemporary art that seems very valuable, bar the regular line, Anatole France, etc.," he returned to England that August from a walking tour in southern France highly enthusiastic about Flaubert ("James and Anatole France infants by comparison") and determined to give himself a "course in modern literature."[29] That August also saw the publication of Flint's survey of contemporary French poetry in the *Poetry Review* (its catalog of recent "ismes" perhaps suggesting Pound's "Imagisme") as well as Pound's appointment as foreign editor of *Poetry*: Imagism now had its semiofficial organ, and Pound was at last in the position to import into America "whatever is most dynamic in artistic thought, either here or in Paris" (L, 10). In September he was suggesting to Harriet Monroe that *Poetry* print the "best foreign stuff" ("one French poem a month"), and by November he was in correspondence with Régnier for contributions.[30]

Meanwhile he and Yeats were "booming" Tagore, the cadences of whose *Gitanjali* Pound compared to Gourmont's *Litanies de la Rose.*

By now the acknowledged *chef d'école* of Imagism, Pound returned to Paris in April of 1913 and met, presumably for the first time, some of the figures grouped around the magazine *L'Effort Libre* (he had probably been put into contact with them by Flint, who had been in correspondence with Romains, the leading exponent of the school of *unanimisme*, in 1912; Pound himself had written a brief review of Jouve for the February issue of *Poetry*). He described the occasion in his 1915 obituary for Gourmont.

> When I was in Paris some years ago I happened, by merest accident, to be plunged into a meeting, a vortex of twenty men, and among them five or six of the most intelligent young men in Paris. I should say that Paris is a place like another; in "literature" the French are cursed with amorphous thought, rhetoric, bombast, Claudel, etc., stale Hugo, stale Corneille, etc., just as we are cursed here with stale Victoriana, stale Miltoniana, etc. The young party of intelligence in Paris, a party now just verging on the threshold of middle-age, is the group that centered about "L'Effort Libre." It contains Jules Romains, Vildrac, Duhamel, Chennevière, Jouve, and their friends. These men were plotting a gigantic blague. A "blague" when it is a fine blague is a satire upon stupidity, an attack. It is the weapon of intelligence at bay; of intelligence fighting against an alignment of odds. These men were thorough. They had exposed a deal of ignorance and stupidity in places where there should have been the reverse. They were serious, and they were "keeping it up." And the one man they mentioned with sympathy, the one older man to whom they could look for comprehension, and even for discreet assistance, was Remy de Gourmont. Remy would send them a brief telegram to be read at their public reading. That is, at first sight, a very trifling matter, but, if examined closely, it shows a number of things: first that de Gourmont was absolutely independent, that he was not tied to any institution, that his position was based on his intelligence alone and not on his "connections" (as I believe they are called in our "literary world"). (SP, 416)

The "gigantic blague" (to which Pound apparently also contributed a congratulatory message) involved the (mock) election and elaborate feting of the "Prince des Penseurs"—a certain Jules Brisset, retired railroad inspector and crackpot author of a volume purporting to prove man's descent from the frog. The mystification, launched by Romains, was aimed at satirizing recent elections by critics and journalists in which

Introduction

Paul Fort and Hans Ryner had, with great pomp, been respectively voted "Prince des Poètes" and "Prince des Conteurs."[33] Pound was quite fond of this proto-Dadaist joke on the Parisian literary establishment, for he returned to it early in the *Cantos* (XXVII/129; 134) and, more nostalgically, in the Pisan sequence:

> when they elected old Brisset Prince des Penseurs,
>   Romains, Vildrac and Chennevière and the rest of them
>   before the world was given over to wars
>   Quand vous serez bien vieille
>   remember that I have remembered,
>   mia pargoletta,
>   and pass on the tradition
>
>   (LXXX/506; 540)

The esteem in which these poets held Gourmont no doubt further fueled Pound's respect for the man who, like Ford Madox Ford in England, seemed the only elder willing to understand and encourage the younger generation (*les jeunes*). Pound apparently attempted to arrange a visit with him, for on his return to London he wrote home that he had been promised a private meeting with Gourmont the next time he visited Paris (L, 21)—he did not foresee that a war would come between them. Pound did, however, make the acquaintance of one of Gourmont's closest friends during this stay in Paris—the American expatriate Natalie Barney, inspirer of Gourmont's *Lettres à l'Amazone*. Miss Barney and Pound would become lifelong friends: when Pound later moved to Paris in the early twenties she lent him the use of her piano while he was composing his opera *Villon;* she financially backed his musical collaborator George Antheil; she cofounded Pound's "Bel Esprit" scheme to provide Eliot with financial independence; and her lively salon on the rue Jacob introduced Pound and other expatriates to a wide variety of French authors and intellectuals.[32] Miss Barney's "Temple à l'Amitié" (a small Doric gazebo in the garden of her elegant town house, which was to have served as the emblem of the "Bel Esprit" project) is memorialized in the Pisan Cantos, as is her particular blend of Gallic and Midwestern verve ("I have got a great deal out of life. Perhaps more than was in it": compare LXXXIV/539; 574).

> The old trees near the Rue Jacob
>   were propped up to keep them from falling
> à l'Amitié
>   . . . . .
>   and Natalie said to the apache:
>   vous etes tres mal élevé

15

and his companion said: Tiens, elle te le dit . . .
  so they left her her hand bag
· · · · ·

  "Entrez donc, mais entrez,
c'est la maison de tout le monde"   (LXXX/505; 539)

Pound and the "Amazone" probably talked of Gourmont's work at length, for upon his return to England Pound arranged the serial publication in the *New Freewoman* of Gourmont's philosophical novel *Les Chevaux de Diomède*—the translation by Mme Sartoris, one of Natalie Barney's friends, had been personally supervised by the author. Later that fall Pound managed to interest Alfred Kreymborg's magazine, *The Glebe* in an American edition and was corresponding with Miss Barney about a possible bilingual version of the work. Neither project apparently succeeded, for as late as 1919 Pound was still trying to get H. L. Mencken to publish the translation in the United States.[33]

The fall of 1913 also saw the publication in the *New Age* of Pound's "Approach to Paris" series. "There are just two things in the world, two great and interesting phenomena: the intellectual life of Paris and the curious teething promise of my own vast occidental nation,"[34] he proclaimed in his first installment—the second, appropriately enough, was devoted to a lengthy discussion of Gourmont's poetry. The six ensuing articles provided a critical survey of recent developments in French verse, focused largely around the works of those poets whom Pound had encountered in Paris that spring: Jules Romains, Charles Vildrac, Laurent Tailhade, Henri Barzun, and André Spire. Although it inevitably touched upon some of the same writers Flint had presented in his "Contemporary French Poetry" of the previous year, Pound's "Approach to Paris" was not merely an indiscriminate inventory of all the latest literary schools, but rather a conscious attempt to select poetic models that might provide new directions for Anglo-American poetics. Nor did Pound restrict himself to the current avant-garde—Rimbaud, Corbière, Paul Fort, and Francis Jammes were also adduced as exemplary of the spirit of serious experiment that characterized modern French verse. Pound summed up the purpose of his "Approach to Paris" in the October issue of *Poetry:*

> If our writers would keep their eye on Paris instead of on London— the London of today or yesterday—there might be some chance of their doing work that would not be demodé before it gets to the press. Practically the whole development of the English verse-art has been achieved by steals from the French, from Chaucer's time to our own, and the French are always twenty to sixty years in advance. As the French content and message are so different from the American content and message, I think the Americans would be less likely to

fall into slavish imitation and would learn hardly more than the virtue of method.[35]

It was in this same series of articles that Pound first invoked the "prose tradition" of poetry—"It is to modern verse what the method of Flaubert is to modern prose . . . It means constatation of fact. It presents. It does not comment."[36] Pound had learned of the Flaubertian aesthetic of constatation from Ford Madox Ford; the latter's dictum, "Poetry must be as well written as prose" would become a permanent axiom of Pound's poetics, as would his insistence that the language of poetry "be a fine language, departing in no way from speech save by heightened intensity . . . Objectivity and again objectivity, and expression: no straddled adjectives . . . nothing that you couldn't, in some circumstance, in the stress of some emotion, actually say" (L, 48). But though it was Ford who first familiarized Pound with Flaubert and the nineteenth-century novel in general, Gourmont played an equally important part in steering the author of *Mauberley* towards "his true Penelope" (P, 187). *Le Problème du style* had devoted a chapter to an analysis of Flaubert's style, comparing his realistic constatation of *moeurs* (manners and morals) to that of the Homeric epics—a juxtaposition that quickened Pound's notion of the prose tradition while pointing towards the later epic techniques of the *Cantos*. Unlike Ford and most contemporary French critics, Gourmont had singled out *Bouvard et Pécuchet* as Flaubert's most revolutionary work. Pound responded by using the *sottisier* technique adumbrated by *Bouvard et Pécuchet*'s "Dictionnaire des idées reçues" in his 1914 contributions to the *Egoist*; in 1917 he would compile an immense Flaubertian inventory of modern stupidity, entitled "Studies in Contemporary Mentality," for the *New Age*. More important than the *sottisier* tactic, however, was the radically encyclopedic mode of *Bouvard et Pécuchet*, which Gourmont had praised. As Pound came to realize in the early twenties, it provided not only a crucial precedent for the formal innovations of Joyce's *Ulysses* but, more significantly, a possible model for the epic inclusiveness of the *Cantos*.

Bouvard et Pécuchet was, as Gourmont finely sensed, the work of a *philosophe*; Flaubert's savage indignation against stupidity (*la bêtise*) placed him in the tradition of Voltaire, whom Pound apparently also began reading around 1914. Imagism had, by this point, given way to Vorticism: under the influence of Wyndham Lewis and Gaudier-Brzeska, Pound's peotics had evolved towards a more dynamic, esemplastic sense of the image as "a radiant node or cluster . . . a vortex, from which, and through which, and into which, ideas are constantly rushing" (G-B, 92). Vorticism, however, entailed more than the kinetic extension of Imagism into the stark geometric abstractions of planes in relation (G-B, 121): it represented, like its predecessor Futurism, an altogether more extreme assault on the stagnant *idées reçues* of contemporary art and culture—

"To the present condition of things we have nothing to say but *merde*," announced Pound in February 1914, auguring the boisterous bravado of that spring's issue of *Blast*.[37] Although his measured voice made him an unlikely ally of Vorticist invective, Gourmont the *philosophe* nevertheless supplied Pound with further weapons with which to strike out at the enemy, in Voltaire's phrase, to *écraser l'infâme*. The most effective of these involved "the dissociation of ideas," a technique of blasting apart received ideas, of disintegrating inert blocks of clichés. Together with Fenollosa's essay on the Chinese written character, Gourmont's analyses of the despotism of abstractions, his investigations into the divorce between words and things (or as he put it, between ideas and images) would provide the basis for Pound's later Confucian notion of *chêng ming*, or the "rectification of names" (GK, 244).

In his *Epilogues* and *Culture des idées*, Gourmont applied his dissociative method to demolish such modern shibboleths as science, progress, reason, revolution, and fatherland—they were merely bloodless abstractions foisted upon the credulous as immutable truths. In the mind's tendency to flee the dynamic contradictions and complexities of immediate experience for the solace of ready-made *idées reçues* Gourmont discerned the source of all tyranny, be it political or linguistic. Like Voltaire, he came to see this tyranny and its attendant evils—superstition, fanaticism, intolerance—as an essentially religious phenomenon. But whereas Voltaire assaulted the Church as the enemy of enlightened Deism, Gourmont rather focused his attacks on Protestant monotheism: the Reformation had destroyed the indigenous polytheistic traditions of Europe still preserved in folk Catholicism, and had substituted a single abstract ideological principle for the sensuous immediacies of the gods. Gourmont's Nietzschean defense of Mediterranean paganism further confirmed Pound's (Swinburnian) rebellion against his own Protestant milieu: in his anticlerical polemics of the mid and late teens he came increasingly to locate the repressive puritan moral (that is, sexual) code and Old Testament monotheism (and its economic corollary, monopoly capitalism) as the root evils of modern Anglo-Saxon culture:

> Christ follows Dionysus,
> Phallic and ambrosial
> Made way for macerations;
> Caliban casts out Ariel. (P, 189)

Gourmont, Pound insisted, had not "mislaid the light of the 18th century" (LE, 340). His "ultimate significance" was not "less than Voltaire's" (SP, 418), because he embodied the essential Enlightenment virtue of cosmopolitanism: against the literary nationalism that had swept France after the 1870 debacle, Gourmont, like Voltaire before him, propounded a more comparative perspective, maintaining that French literature had historically always been at its best when invigorated by fresh infusions from abroad. In such articles as "Provincialism the Enemy," Pound incorporated Gourmont's arguments for a truly international literary perspective into his own campaign against the insularity of Anglo-American letters:

> At present the centre of the world is somewhere on an imaginary line between London and Paris, the sooner that line is shortened, the better for all of us, the richer the life of the world. I mean this both "intellectually" and "politically." France and England have always been at their best when knit closest. Our literature is always in full bloom after contact with France. Chaucer, the Elizabethans, both built on French stock. Translations of Villon revived our poetry in the midst of Victorian desiccation. Contrariwise, the best of French prose, let us say the most "typical," the vaunted Voltairean clarity is built on England, on Voltaire's admiration of English freedom and English writers. And the disease of both England and America during the last century is due precisely to a stoppage of circulation. (SP,200)

He fired off blasts to America, ridiculing editors for their parochial ignorance of contemporary European authors: "There is no culture that is not at least bilingual. We find an American editor . . . who in 1912 or 1913 writes of Henri de Régnier and M. Remy de Gourmont as 'these young men.' The rest of his sentence is to say that this lacuna in his mental decorations does not in the least chagrin him."[38] (Pound did not mention that until early 1912 their work was unknown to him as well.) His old friend, William Carlos Williams, similarly came in for chiding; Pound quoted Gourmont's apology for "literary cosmopolitanism" to him with the admonition, "don't expect the world to revolve about Rutherford" (L, 123). Williams, who was attempting, on the contrary, to forge an intensely local American poetic, later struck back at what he considered Pound's and Eliot's excessive internationalism in the "Prologue" to *Kora in Hell*:

> I do not overlook De Gourmont's plea for a meeting of the nations, but I do believe that when they meet Paris will be more than slightly abashed to find parodies of the middle ages, Dante and Langue d'Oc foisted upon it as the best in United States poetry . . . Imagine an international congress of poets at Paris or Versailles, Remy de Gourmont (now dead), presiding, poets all speaking five languages fluently. Ezra stands up to represent U. S. verse and De Gourmont sits down smiling. Ezra begins by reading "La Figlia che Piange." It would be a pretty pastime to gather with a mental basket the fruits of that reading from the minds of the ten Frenchmen present.

"E.P.," Williams nonetheless conceded, "is the best enemy United States verse has."[39]

Pound was pursuing his campaign for a new Renaissance on many fronts, but he still lacked a magazine that might promote the cosmopolitan artistic and cultural values he was attempting to inculcate into the world of Anglo-American letters. He had resigned from his post at *Poetry* in early 1914; he had installed Aldington as an editor of the *Egoist* (with the result that a great deal of Gourmont got published in its pages, most notably his essay on "Tradition" and his pioneering study of Lautréamont), but his own contributions to the magazine diminished in early 1915. He saw himself progressively excluded from the major British periodicals: for such editors as G. W. Prothero, his association with *Blast* was grounds enough for blackballing him: "It stamps a man too disadvantageously" (LE, 358). Only Orage's *New Age* remained consistently hospitable. As Pound's bitterness towards the "British literary episcopacy" grew, he turned increasingly towards Gourmont's Paris as the model "laboratory of ideas," for it was there that "poisons could be tested, and new modes of sanity be discovered" (SP, 415). He had long admired the *Mercure de France* for its commitment to a wide spectrum of artistic and intellectual experiment, and in early 1914 he proposed to Amy Lowell that she finance an international quarterly modeled on it.[40] The project fell through, but Pound kept casting about for sponsors. When in May 1915 it seemed as if he might be able to take over the editorship of the *Academy*, he wrote fellow-philosophe H. L. Mencken that the proposed magazine would triangulate London, Paris, and America so as to "give the two continents a chance to converse with each other."[41] He apparently wrote Gourmont to the same effect, for the latter graciously responded in early June, offering encouragement and cooperation:

> I have read with pleasure your long letter which so clearly sets forth the need for a magazine which would combine the efforts of the Americans, British and French. I shall help you in this as much as I am able to. I don't think I can do much. My health is poor and I am extremely tired; I could only give you very short pieces, indications of ideas rather than polished pages, but I will do my best. I hope that you will be able to get this little literary endeavour off the ground, and that you find useful assistance on our side. Obviously, if we could bring Americans to a more sensitive appreciation of true French literature and, above all, if we could teach them not to confuse it with all the terribly mediocre works that now abound, this would be a happy result indeed. Are they capable of enough mental liberty to read my books, for example, without being horrified? I think this very doubtful; a long preparation will be necessary. But why not try it? There are in all countries knots of intelligent people, open-minded; one must give them something to relieve them from

the staleness of magazines, something which will give them confidence in themselves and serve as a rallying point. As you say, one must begin by getting them to respect French individualism; the sense of liberty which some of us have in so great degree. They understand this in theology. Why should they not understand it in art, poetry, literature? They must be made to see—if they don't already see it—that French individualism can, when necessary, bend itself to the strictest of disciplines.

To conquer the American is undoubtedly not your only aim. The aim of the *Mercure* has been to permit any man, who is worth it, to write down his thought frankly—this is a writer's sole pleasure. And this aim should be yours. (LE, 356)

Pound's scheme for an international quarterly modeled after the *Mercure* came to naught (it was not until 1917 that Quinn managed to get him editorial control over a section of the *Little Review*), but he remained deeply moved by Gourmont's willingness to collaborate on the project. The various implications of Gourmont's editorial code—"de permettre à ceux qui en valent la peine d'écrire franchement ce qu'ils pensent—seul plaisir d'un écrivain"—came to represent for Pound " the whole civilization of letters" (SP, 420):

"To put down one's thought frankly, a writer's one pleasure." That phrase was the centre of Gourmont's position. It was not a phrase understood superficially. It is as much the basis of a clean literature, of all literature worth the name, as is an antiseptic method, the basis of sound surgical treatment.

"Franchement," "Frankly," is "Frenchly," if one may drag in philology. If, in ten lines or in a hundred pages, I can get the reader to comprehend what that one adjective *means* in literature, what it means to all civilization, I shall have led him part of the way toward an understanding of de Gourmont's importance.

"Frankly" does not mean "grossly." It does not mean the overemphasis of neo-realism, of red-bloodism, of slums dragged into light, of men writing while drugged with two or three notions, or with the lust for an epigram. It means simply that a man writes his thought, that is to say, his doubts, his inconclusions as well as his "convictions," which last are so often borrowed affairs. (SP, 416)

Gourmont's "franchement" can be correlated with the ideal of *sinceritas* which so dominates the *Cantos*—the Confucian 誠 (" 'Sincerity.' The precise definition of the word, pictorially the sun's lance coming to rest on the precise spot verbally") or 信 ("Fidelity to the given word. The man here standing by his word"). Gourmont's personal integrity and generosity showed such *sinceritas* to be ethically cognate to *caritas* and *humanitas*—Confucian 仁 ("humanity, in the full sense of the word, 'manhood,' The man and his full contents").[42] Etymologically, "franchement écrire" also pointed back to freedom of speech, which the Enlightenment had enshrined as one of the most basic of man's liberties. In its name Gourmont and Pound fought against literary censorship of any sort; indeed, so literal was Pound's belief in it, that he would later be convinced he was only exercising his constitutionally guaranteed right to free speech in committing those acts for which he was accused of treason.

Gourmont's death in late September 1915 came as a blow to Pound. He wrote home: "His death is a great loss to everybody and a particular loss to me as he had been so interested in the projected magazine."[43] He wrote two long obituaries, the first for the *Fortnightly Review*, the second for *Poetry*. The latter opened:

> Remy de Gourmont is dead and the world's light is darkened. This is another of the crimes of the war, for de Gourmont was only fifty-seven, and if he had not been worrried to death, if he had not been grieved to death by the cessation of all that had been "life" as he understood it, there was no reason why we should not have had more of his work and his company. He is as much "dead of the war" as if he had died in the trenches, and he left with almost the same words on his lips. "Nothing is being done in Paris, nothing can be done, *faute de combattants*" . . . Remy de Gourmont is irreplaceable. I think I do not write for myself alone when I say no other Frenchman could have died leaving so personal a sense of loss in the minds of many young men who had never laid eyes on him. (SP, 420)

Pound was indeed not alone in his sense of loss. Aldington published a solemn obituary in the *Egoist*; back home, Huneker paid fulsome tribute to this "moral hero" and "valient soldier of literature" in his "Remy de Gourmont: His Ideas. The Colour of his Mind" (included in his 1917 *Unicorns*); the young John Cowper Powys opened his thirty-page eulogy of Gourmont's hedonistic humanism with characteristic hyperbole: "The death of Remy de Gourmont is one of the greatest losses that European literature has suffered since the death of Oscar Wilde."[44] In France, Henri de Régnier, Pierre Louys, Camille Mauclair, and André Beaunier supplied prominent homages; but it was Alfred Vallette, director of the *Mercure de France*, who provided the most succinct tribute: "Voilà donc notre *Mercure* découronné. La perte de Gourmont est irréparable."[45]

Pound would have agreed with Vallette, for he later commented on the decline of the *Mercure* after Gourmont's death: "It might be noted that the *Mercure* was founded on decent principles, impersonal franco-centric but with the belief in facts, and in open discussion. Having been *the* great

Introduction

European review of letters for more decades than we can remember, the decline of the *Mercure* is merely the natural fatigue of men who have grown old, and outlasted their strength. It is not voluntary stultification or a refusal of information" (LE, 81). He offered a more melancholy—and more scathing—retrospect in his 1938 *Guide to Kulchur*:

> The young frenchmen of 1920 had NO elders whom they cd. in any way respect. Gourmont was dead. The war had thrown up a few stuffed monkeys, third rate gallic effigies, cranks who hadn't even the excuse of being British to account for their holding the tosh of Manchester they emitted, the bunk of a Romain Rolland, the vacuity of a Gide.
>
> Apart from the unclean daily press of Barrès etc. etc.
>
> The stream of thought that had made the *Mercure* in the beginning, trickled out into the sand. A concept of literary integrity remained among weaker brethren who have finally been gathered into their graves. France rose after 1870 and almost disappeared after 1918. I mean to say that anything that cd. have caused Henry James' outburst of devotion to France, anything that cd. have made Paris the focus of human respect and intelligence and of "respect for intelligence" entered a phase of non-being. (GK, 88)

Gourmont's death in 1915, however, did not diminish Pound's involvement with his oeuvre—if anything, it increased. Throughout the war, Pound continued to adduce Gourmontian dissociations in his strongly Francophile, prointerventionist propaganda for the *New Age;* the Frenchman's literary criticism in turn suffused both Pound's and Eliot's prose contributions to the *Egoist* and the *Little Review* of the middle and late teens. In February 1918 Pound published in the *Little Review* his influential critical anthology, "A Study in French Poets," returning once again to the *Litanies de la Rose.* In March of the following year, he edited a special Gourmont number of the same magazine: it included Aldington's "De Gourmont, After the Interim," T. T. Clayton's "Le Latin mystique," Frederic Manning's "M. de Gourmont and the Problem of Beauty," and John Rodker's "De Gourmont—Yank." Pound's own twenty-page essay, "De Gourmont: A Distinction," provided an overview of the master's work, contrasting it, significantly, with the work of Henry James—as John Espey has shown, this distinction informs the basic thematic structure of *Hugh Selwyn Mauberley*, Pound's most sustained poetic homage to the "complicated sensuous wisdom" of Gourmont (LE, 340).

Mauberley, Pound observed, was also "distinctly a farewell to London" (P, 185)—having spent the spring and summer of 1919 in southern France and June and July of 1920 in Paris dabbling in Dada, Pound officially installed himself on the Left Bank in the spring of 1921. It was around this time that Pound came to know Jean de Gourmont who, after his brother's death, had established the *Imprimerie gourmontienne* with the help of the printer François Bernouard. Jean probably introduced Pound to Gourmont's posthumous *Pensées inédites* in 1920, for he subsequently translated them for the *Dial* under the title "Dust for Sparrows."[46] Pound also completed his translation of Gourmont's *Physique de l'amour* for Liveright in the early summer of 1921—a French version of his "Translator's Postscript" to *The Natural Philosophy of Love* appeared in the *Mercure* in September of the same year.

In terms of its impact on the Pound of both *Mauberley* and the *Cantos*, the *Physique de l'amour* proved to be one of Gourmont's most seminal instigations. Whereas Aldington was repelled by the book ("he ought to have called it 'A Physic for Love' ") and Havelock Ellis dismissed it as the work of a "heroic amateur,"[47] Pound approached it as a textbook of biology, the necessary scientific complement to Gourmont's study of amor and aesthetics among the medieval Latin poets, the troubadours, and Dante (LE, 343).

More the work of a moralist than of a scientist, *Physique de l'amour* provided a further critique of those puritanical Christian prohibitions— Pound refers to them as "Xtn taboos" (L, 141)—that still permeated contemporary attitudes towards sex. By situating man's sexual behavior within the larger context of animal instinct, Gourmont demonstrated the artificial and arbitrary nature of bourgeois morality, most evident in its censure of homosexuality, its cult of the maidenhead, and its hypocritical condemnation of adultery. Against Darwin, whose diachronic account of evolution had obscured man's synchronic relation to the rest of the animal world, Gourmont sought to "situate the sexual life of man within the unique context of universal sexuality,"[48] thus providing Pound with a non-Freudian theory of the role of sexuality in both animal and human society. Gourmont's meditations on the relation of instinct to intelligence, of individual to species, of male to female, in turn proposed a biological vision of culture that Pound would later synthesize with Frobenius's anthropological notion of *paideuma*, "the tangle or complex of the inrooted ideas of any period . . . the gristly roots of ideas that are in action" (GK, 57-58). Most importantly, however, the *Physique de l'amour* opened the world of natural sciences to Pound: the very act of translating the work taught him not only a new attention to organic (and specifically, entomological) processes and designs but also a technique of precise taxonomic description which supplemented the lesson of Flaubert and prepared for his later veneration for Agassiz.

The publication of *The Natural Phiosophy of Love* in 1922 closed Pound's Gourmontian decade. He would thereafter return to the master's works less and less frequently; nonetheless, Pound reserved him a permanent niche in his pantheon of culture heroes—re-bound in half-vellum,

Gourmont's works took their canonical place in Pound's personal library.[49] In the Autumn 1927 issue of Pound's magazine *Exile*, Gourmont appeared in an ideogram of quotations entitled "Modern Thought." By juxtaposing a citation from *Physique de l'Amour* with obiter dicta by Mussolini, Lenin, and (somewhat Dadaistically) Robert McAlmon, Pound attempted to correlate Gourmont's biological defense of individualism with revolutionary political and economic axioms whose purport he believed to be the common good.

> "We are tired of government in which there is no responsible person having a hind-name, a front name and an address." (Mussolini)

> "The banking business is declared a state monopoly. The interests of the small depositors will be safeguarded." (Lenin)

> "The duty of being is to persevere in its being and even to augment the characteristics which specialize it." (Gourmont)

> "People are not charming *enough.*" (McAlmon)[50]

Reviewing Aldington's two-volume translated *Selections* from Gourmont two years later, Pound commented that the anthology "wd. form one of those ensembles which make any country in which they are read a more inhabitable country." Gourmont, he reaffirmed, was "a definite and actual force still operative. We cannot afford to lose sight of his value, of his significance as a type, a man standing for freedom and honesty of thought."[51] During the thirties, Pound again returned to Gourmont in *Jefferson and/or Mussolini* (1935) and *Guide to Kulchur* (1938), and in his Italian journalism of the period he repeatedly insisted on the necessity of an Italian translation of his works.[52]

Pound's involvement in the Italian literary and political life of the thirties and forties entailed a radical revision of his earlier Francophilia—it had already begun to wane considerably during his residence in Paris from 1921 to 1924. The intellectual and artistic preeminence of France, he was now convinced, was a thing of the past. If he accused the "wop litterati" of being "mere pseudofrogs" (GK, 134), it was because they still snobbishly insisted on seeing Paris as *the* cultural vortex instead of looking towards the achievements of Anglo-American modernism or towards their own Italian heritage. The death of Gourmont, Pound observed in the early forties, "dovrebbe significare mettere un termine alla dominazione intellettuale francese"[53]—what was now needed was a "new synthesis," a "new Paideuma" based on the ethical and economic precepts of Confucian China, Jeffersonian America, and Mussolinian Italy. In one of the more coherent of his wartime radio broadcasts Pound reflected nostalgically:

I had already said that after R. de Gourmont's death there was no froggie whom I cd. trust to send in a monthly letter about french contemporary authors for the Lit/ Rev/ or the Dial/

The French were biologically fixed and they were losin the sense of *Responsibility/* intellectual responsibility.

Only a few elderly blokes like A. Mockel and Vallette still felt it/ I mean they didn't have to think that it was yr/ duty to the State to boost a REAL book, and leave the fakes in the discard/ and Vallette was tired; so tired/

offered me the American rubric: at a time when I had no time to read 40 American dud books and make little notes on 'em/ printed the first criticism of Ulysses that was published in France (mine) in the Mercure/ Jean de Gourmont lived in a world in which it was inconceivable that a man wd. CHANGE his thought or withdraw a line of his writing for ulterior motives/ that was a vanishing world/ that was olde France/   one of Gourmont's friends La Marquise de Pierre had never before seen an american/   she looked on me as the representative of Benj/   Franklin/   the U. S. was still the land that Lafayette went to/

I went up her stairs, and was received as if I had been a flamingo or some other rare exotic/

That olde France is NO longer with us. [54]

The same elegiac note informs many of the finest sections of the Pisan Cantos. Although never named, Gourmont is an indirect presence throughout the sequence, associated not only with early memories of Paris ("before the world was given over to wars") but also with that vigilant reverence toward the natural world, which Pound had discovered in the *Physique de l'amour* and to which he now returned from the wreckage:

> When the mind swings by a grass-blade
> an ant's forefoot shall save you   (LXXXIII/553;568)

From Saint Elizabeths he wrote to Cummings in 1947, complaining of his need for "ventilation," for "communication to open wiff the outer air —take me back to 3 or 4 of Remy's more lucid remarks that hev got lorst in the hinterim." [55] Pound's increased affection for Remy during this precarious period no doubt reflected his own fears of being unjustly forgotten by readers and disciples—he wondered, for example, why after his conversion Eliot had so completely neglected their early mentor: "re Rev. Possum missing *the* point that Remy not engaged in 'superior fads' whose racket consists in avoiding dangerous subjects." [56] He wrote Natalie Barney at her old address on the rue Jacob, asking for news about survivors.

He reiterated his belief that "Remy's death" constituted "the end of epoch, so far as France is concerned (when looked AT from outside)." Hearing that Gourmont's old friend André Rouveyre was still alive and writing, Pound wrote back to the "Amazone": "I suppose Rouve[y]re writes in ignorance. One never expects these dilletanti to know of anything outside their own arrondissement. The only chance of his saying something of interest might hv/ been in asking why Eliot has not given due credit to De Gourmont for his real work."[57]

If the following pages begin to give "due credit" to Gourmont for what Pound considered his "real work," they will have achieved their purpose. In relating Gourmont to Pound the intention has been to elicit affinities rather than stress debts, for Gourmont did not influence Pound in the usual sense of the term: he provided, both by his personal example and his works, something far more important—a range of instigations, a series of incitements to experiment and discovery. And it is herein that their respective achievements most rhyme: Remy, Pound wrote Cummings from Saint Elizabeths, definitely ranked among the rare "open writers."[58]

1

"AMAS UT FACIAS PULCHRAM"

Remy de Gourmont was a poet "more by possessing a certain quality of mind than by virtue of having written fine poems," Pound observed in 1919 (LE, 340). Indeed, Gourmont's verse remains the least durable aspect of his oeuvre, marred by many of those "funny symboliste trappings, 'sin,' satanism, rosy cross, heavy lilies" (LE, 340) that Pound would later reprove. When Pound first read Gourmont's verse in 1912, however, he was far less critical of the Symbolist aesthetic: still at a relatively fluid, formative stage, his own poetics could accommodate both the Celtic Twilight of Yeats and the more stringent modernism advocated by Ford Madox Ford. "I made my life in London," Pound said in a 1962 interview, "by going to see Ford in the afternoons and Yeats in the evenings."[1] This visiting schedule is reflected in much of Pound's verse of the period, ambivalently pitched between the respective styles of his two masters.

Pound most clearly expressed the tension in "Status Rerum": "Mr. Yeats has been subjective: believes in the glamour and associations which hang near the words. 'Works of art beget works of art.' He has much in common with the French symbolists. Mr. Hueffer believes in an exact rendering of things. He would strip words of all 'association' for the sake of getting a precise meaning. He professes to prefer prose to verse. You would find his origins in Gautier or Flaubert. He is objective. This school tends to lapse into description. The other tends to lapse into sentiment."[2] Yeats's method, he went on, was "very dangerous," and as for Hueffer, his poems had "rarely 'come off' "—Imagism, Pound implied, would supersede the "diametric opposition" between these two schools of verse. But even though Pound was by this time (the article appeared in January

1913) already engaged in the conscious modernization of his own poetics, he had not fully abandoned his earlier fin-de-siècle proclivities toward a poetry of "indefinite, impalpable" things (SP, 33). His first piece on Gourmont's poetry, published in September of this same year—that is, subsequent to the initial Imagist manifestoes—praised precisely those qualities of his verse that were most characteristic of Yeats and the French Symbolists, namely, "shadowy suggestion" and "indirectness."[3]

Pound's 1913 article on Gourmont was his first sustained essay on a French poet (he had previously written only brief reviews of Romains and Jouve for *Poetry* earlier that year). He introduced him to his *New Age* readers in the second installment of "The Approach to Paris" series:

> M. Remy de Gourmont (b. 1858, etc.) is the author of "Le Latin mystique" and many other works—among them "Le Livre des Litanies" now part of "Le Pèlerin du Silence." I suppose M. De Gourmont knows more about verse-rhythm than any man now living; at least he has made a most valuable contribution to the development of the strophe. It seems to me, the most valuable since those made by Arnaut Daniel, but perhaps I exaggerate.

> Fleur hypocrite,
> Fleur du silence.

he begins, setting the beat of his measure.

> Rose couleur de cuivre, plus frauduleuse que nos joies,
> rose couleur de cuivre, embaume-nous dans tes mensonges,
> fleur hypocrite, fleur du silence.
> Rose au visage peint comme une fille d'amour, rose au
> coeur prostitué, rose au visage peint, fais semblant d'etre
> pitoyable, fleur hypocrite, fleur du silence.
> Rose à la joue puérile, ô vierge des futurs trahisons,
> rose à la joue puérile, innocente et rouge, ouvre les rets de
> tes yeux clairs, fleur hypocrite, fleur du silence.
> Rose aux yeux noirs, miroir de ton néant, rose aux yeux
> noirs, fais-nous croire au mystère, fleur hypocrite, fleur
> du silence.

One can perhaps ascribe Pound's hyperbole to the first flush of enthusiasm; no doubt the desire to astound his British audience had something to do with his superlatives. Nevertheless, it would be wrong to utterly dismiss the impact of Gourmont's verse on Pound as Donald Davie has done in his influential study.[4] True, the *Litanies de la Rose* quoted at length by Pound contain many of those "funny symboliste trappings" that he later disparaged, but he obviously saw through the period flavor of Gourmont's verse to something far more permanent.[5]

He observed in this same *New Age* article: "There are two ways of being influenced by a notable work of art: the work may be drawn into oneself, its mastery may beget a peculiar hunger for new sorts of mastery and perfection; or the sight of the work may beget simply a counterfeiting of its superficial qualities. This last influence is without value, a dodge of the arriviste and of the mere searcher for novelty. The first influence means a new keenness of the ear, or a new flair for wording, or a deeper desire for common sense if the work is what is properly called classic."[6] This "new keenness of ear" is undoubtedly what Gourmont's verse stimulated in Pound. Its musical crafting should be evident just from the few strophes of the *Litanies de la Rose* quoted by Pound (it continues for some fifty more). The basic rhythmic motif ("fleur hypocrite, fleur du silence") is stated at the outset of the poem and subsequently recurs at the close of each strophe, thus zoning off one "rhythm-unit" or "bar" (the terms are Pound's) from the next.

A device common to much French Symbolist verse (and in Baudelaire's case probably derived from Poe), Gourmont's refrain here functions very much like the "constant rythmique" defined by Duhamel and Vildrac in their 1911 treatise on vers libre, *Notes sur la technique poétique*, a work much admired by Pound and his fellow Imagists.[7] Always composed of the same number of syllables, this rhythmic constant would, by its regular recurrence, give the poem the repetitive effect necessary to a unified pattern; the relation between this fixed element and its variables, the interplay of paradigm and deviation, would in turn provide a kind of contrapuntal rhythm more intricate and more musical than conventional metrical schemes. Gourmont's *Litanies* make use of a variety of similar techniques: each strophe, for example, opens with "Rose" modified by either a single word or an adjectival clause, which is subsequently repeated within the body of the strophe, generally as the third of its five constitutive phrases. The refrain, "fleur hypocrite, fleur du silence," composed of two groups of four syllables each (five, if one counts the *e muet* or terminal unpronounced "e" as a syllable) in turn functions as the rhythmic constant.[8] Although not identifiable with any conventional metric, Gourmont's anaphoric pattern is rigorous in its regularity and symmetry: through parallelism and repetition he achieves what Pound in another context called a "residue of sound which remains in the ear of the hearer and acts more or less as an organ-base" (LE, 7). Having established this "base" and having articulated its dominant beat, Gourmont then introduces nuances into his measure through melodic variations that explore "every resolution of sound and repetition subtler than rhyme."[9]

Gourmont's musical procedures may seem somewhat elementary today, but to Pound and his fellow experimentalists in free verse they must have exemplified an exhilarating alternative to traditional metrical norms. Furthermore, they demonstrated that a break with conventional prosody (be it the French alexandrine or the English iambic pentameter) did not necessarily entail abandoning audible form altogether but rather might refine the possibilities of rhythm, composed "in the sequence of the musical phrase, not in the sequence of a metronome" (LE, 3). The very fact that Gourmont was writing in a foreign language perhaps made it easier for them to isolate the purely musical dimensions of his verse. In fact, Pound had recommended the reading of foreign verse precisely for this reason: "Let the candidate fill his mind with the finest cadences he can discover, preferably in a foreign language, so that the meaning of the words may be less likely to divert his attention from the movement" (LE, 5). His fellow Imagists obviously took his exhortation to heart; Taupin observes that the strong cadences of Gourmont's *Litanies* reappear in much of the free verse of the period, especially in the works of Amy Lowell and John Gould Fletcher. Indeed, such was the vogue for the author of the *Litanies* (the French Symbolists, after all, had overvalued Poe for similar musical reasons) that Witter Bynner's contemporary American parody of modernist verse, *Spectra*, was dedicated to Gourmont.[10]

By the time Pound was reading Gourmont's *Litanies* in 1912, he was, as his 1910 *Provença* and 1911 *Canzoni* evidenced, already well advanced in his study of Provençal *motz el son*: that he should consider Gourmont's strophe the most valuable contribution since Arnaut Daniel's is therefore no slight praise. "Symmetry or strophic forms," he wrote of the troubadours, "naturally HAPPENED in lyric poetry when a man was singing a long poem to a short melody which he had to use over and over" (ABC, 199). The shape and length of the strophe was therefore indissolubly linked to the duration of the musical phrase. Gourmont's *Litanies de la Rose*, Pound pointed out, were similarly bound up with song: "It is not a poem to lie on the page, it must come to life in audition, or in the finer audition which one may have in imagining sound. One must 'hear' it, in one way or another, and out of that intoxication comes beauty."[11]

Indeed, as one reads Gourmont's poem aloud, each strophe seems naturally to constitute a single unit of breath. Its length, therefore, derives not from any arbitrary notion of symmetry, but rather from the very physiology of the author: the rise and fall and duration of breath vary with the shade of emotion; rhythms are rooted in the body. Pound compared the "wave-length" of the Gourmontian strophe to "the development of the Greek verse-art [that] came with the lengthening of the foot or bar"[12] and suggested that a combination of syllabic and accentual prosody, of duration and stress, might enrich the rhythmic and melodic possibilities of contemporary free verse, just as a keener ear for consonance and assonance might lead to finer melodic shading: "The art of music which still remains to the poet is that of rhythm, and of a sort of melody dependent on the order and arrangement of varied vowel and consonantal sounds. The rhythm is a matter of duration and individual sounds and of stress, and the matter of the 'word melody' depends largely on the fitness of this duration and stress to the sounds wherewith it is connected."[13]

Pound had recommended Gourmont's *Litanies* and *Fleurs de jadis* for precisely these reasons in an early 1913 review of Tagore's *Gitanjali*: "This metre is . . . not quantitative as the Greek or Sanscrit measures, but the length of the syllables is considered, and the musical time of the bars is even. The measures are more interesting than any now being used in Europe, except those of certain of the most advanced French writers, as, for instance, the arrangements of sound in Remy de Gourmont's *Fleurs de Jadis* or his *Litanies de la Rose*."[14] But though Pound admired Gourmont's assonantal melodic variations as well as his play with syllable and bar length, Davie is certainly right to point out that "Gourmont, like Claudel and St.-John Perse later, has extended the line so far that it is a line no longer and can afford no model for Pound's efforts 'to break the pentameter.' "[15] French poetry, after the dissolution of the alexandrine, could adjust itself to the verset, the verse paragraph, or the prose poem; a major aspect of Pound's achievement, as Davie suggests, is precisely to have resisted this kind of distention of the line. Only by isolating the line as an autonomous entity, only by reducing enjambment, could Pound begin to disrupt or dismember it rhythmically from within, by throwing weight upon the smaller syllabic units that compose it.[16]

Although Pound would therefore not adopt Gourmont's experiments with line or strophe length (just as he was to reject his early enthusiasm for Tagore's measured prose), the "curious evocational form, the curious repetition, the personal sweeping rhythm" (SP, 418) of Gourmont's *Litanies* nevertheless lodged deep in his ear. Pound's interest in liturgical cadences dated as far back as his "Night Litany," first published in *A Quinzaine for this Yule* in late 1908:

> O God of silence,
>> Purifiez nos coeurs,
>> Purifiez nos coeurs,
> O God of waters,
>> make clean our hearts within us,
>> For I have seen the
> Shadow of this thy Venice
> Floating upon the waters,
>> And thy stars
>
> Have seen this thing, out of their far courses
> Have seen this thing,
>> O God of waters,

"Amas ut facias pulchram"

Even as are thy stars
Silent unto us in their far-coursing,
Even so is mine heart
　　　　　　become silent within me.

　　　　Purifiez nos coeurs
　　O God of the silence,
　　　　Purifiez nos coeurs
　O God of waters.　　　　　　　　　　　　(P, 27)

Pound's reading of Gourmont's verse in early 1912 no doubt reinvigo-
rated his sense of the possibilities inherent in the form. The supplicatory
pulse of "The Alchemist, Chant for the Transmutation of Metals," written that same year, bears the unmistakable imprint of Gourmont's use of
rhythm units in both his *Litanies* and *Fleurs de jadis*:[17]

　　Midonz, with the gold of the sun, the leaf of the
　　　　　poplar, by the light of the amber,
　　Midonz, daughter of the sun, shaft of the tree,
　　　　　silver of the leaf, light of the yellow of the
　　　　　amber,
　　Midonz, gift of the God, gift of the light, gift of
　　　　　the amber of the sun,
　　　　　　　　　Give light to the metal.　(P, 75)

　More celebrated, but perhaps no less indebted to the hieratic cadences
of the *Litanies* is Pound's Canto XLV:

　With *Usura*

he begins, setting the beat of his measure. Just as Gourmont had excori-
ated the feminine *fleur du mal* through a reiterative rhythmic figure, so
Pound here deploys anaphora to exorcize a more drastic form of evil:

　　With usura hath no man a house of good stone
　　each block cut smooth and well fitting
　　that design might cover their face,
　　with usura
　　hath no man a painted paradise on his church wall
　　harpes et luz
　　. . . . .
　　with usura, sin against nature,
　　is thy bread ever more of stale rags,
　　is thy bread dry as paper,
　　with no mountain wheat, no strong flour

33

```
        with usura the line grows thick
        with usura is no clear demarcation
        and no man can find site for his dwelling.
        Stonecutter is kept from his stone
        weaver is kept from his loom
        WITH USURA                              (XLV/229;239)
```

This kind of incantatory pattern would become a rhythmic signature of sorts for Pound; variations on it course through the *Cantos*, often surfacing at moments of highest emotional tension:

```
            from under the rubble heap
                            m'elevasti
            from the dulled edge beyond pain,
                            m'elevasti
            out of Erebus, the deep-lying
                from the wind under the earth,
                            m'elevasti
            from the dulled air and the dust,
                            m'elevasti
            by the great flight,
                    m'elevasti,
                            Isis Kuanon
            from the cusp of the moon,
                    m'elevasti                  (XC/606;640)
```

Although this passage has its origins in "The Alchemist" of 1912 ("Out of Erebus, the flat-lying breadth / . . . Bring the imperceptible cool"), such antiphonal suppleness of line and rhythm goes far beyond Gourmont's relatively limited manipulation of the form. If not precisely that of litany, the cadence here nevertheless retains a liturgical resonance appropriate to the ecstatic (and Dantesque) affirmation of rebirth.

As late as 1918 Pound was still praising Gourmont's *Litanies de la Rose* as the exemplary Symbolist poem: "It was one of the great gifts of 'symbolisme,' of the doctrine that one should 'suggest' not 'present'; it is, in his hands, an effective indirectness."[18] Pound's praise, coming when it does—after Imagism, after Vorticism—is curious: was not "direct treatment of the 'thing' whether subjective or objective" one of the central tenets of his poetics (LE, 3)? Although the *Litanies* are constructed around a central image, the image is not presented in any direct visual fashion. Instead, the poem is built on a paratactic series of juxtapositions that accumulate adjectively one upon the other and in the end submerge the perceptual presence of the female rose altogether in favor of a purely conceptual (or musical) pattern of associations. It is a classic Symbolist strategy: the poem is not a statement about something beyond or outside itself but an autonomous lexical and aural event, based not on the referential but on the contextual function of words. The rose is not a natural object concretely perceived but, as in Yeats's Rosicrucian poetry of the nineties or his "Rosa Alchemica," a symbol rhythmically felt or evoked. Although the relationship of Eliot's *Ash-Wednesday* to Gourmont's *Litanies de la Rose* is perhaps tenuous, it provides a modern (and more traditional) instance of this Symbolist procedure:[19]

> Lady of silences
> Calm and distressed
> Torn and most whole
> Rose of memory
> Rose of forgetfulness
> Exhausted and life-giving
> Worried reposeful
> The single Rose
> Is now in the Garden
> Where all loves end

In contrast to Yeats and Eliot, Pound's later treatment of the same Dantesque rose (ocular, like Gourmont's "rose aux yeux noirs" or "rose iridine") concentrates on the physical immediacy of the flower, for "the natural object is always the adequate symbol" (LE, 5). Only through the concrete, only through the particular could the universals of symbolic implication be achieved:

> So slow is the rose to open
> A match flares in the eye's hearth
> then darkness   (CVI/752;777)

Despite what might seem to be his divergent poetics, Pound was not insensitive to the "glamour and associations which hang near the words" of Gourmont's *Litanies de la Rose*. He wrote in the *New Age*: "if you are not too drunk with the sheer naming over of beauty you will wake at the end of the reading and know that the procession of all women that ever were has passed before you."[20] Here is perhaps another clue to Pound's sustained admiration for Gourmont's poem; the sheer naming that characterized the *Litanies* and *Fleurs de jadis*, the catalogs of flowers and gems, the artful blend of common and arcane diction, no doubt appealed to Pound's fascination with the various lexical textures of le mot juste. Although Gourmont was undoubtedly less interested in the scientific exactness of his botanic designations than in their musical sonorities, Pound carefully noted the English equivalents for the French terms in the margins of his own copy of *Le Pèlerin du Silence*: for example, *fraxinelle*-"dittany," *nielle*-"rose-campion," *nigelle*-"fennel," *martagon*-"Turk's cap."[21] His most overtly Gourmontian poem, "The Alchemist," makes skillful use of a similar botanic vocabulary. At once "a procession of all women that ever were" (such as Odysseus saw in Hades) and a Swinburnian invocation of the rebirth of Persephone, the poem fuses American flora with an incantary catalog of exotic Provençal and classical names:[22]

> As your voices, under the larches of Paradise
> Make a clear sound,
> Saîl of Claustra, Aelis, Azalais,
> Raimona, Tibors, Berangèrë,
> 'Neath the dark gleam of the sky;
> Under night, the peacock-throated,
> Bring the saffron-coloured shell,
> Bring the red gold of the maple,
> Bring the light of the birch tree in autumn
> Mirals, Cembelins, Audiarda,
>   Remember this fire.   (P, 75)

Pound's quasi-mystical belief in exact nomenclature, his almost ritual sense of the power of sheer naming is clearly set forth in his essay "Psychology and Troubadours," written shortly after he first read Gourmont:

> Richard St. Victor has left us one very beautiful passage on the splendors of paradise.
> They are ineffable and innumerable and no man having beheld them can fittingly narrate them or even remember them exactly. Nevertheless by naming over all the most beautiful things we know we may draw back upon the mind some vestige of the heavenly splendor.
> I suggest that the troubadour, either more indolent or more logical, progresses from correlating all these details for purpose of comparison, and lumps the matter. The Lady contains the catalogue, is more complete. She serves as a sort of mantram.   (SOR, 96)

The affinity of the troubadour's composite portrait of the Lady (compare "Near Perigord") to Gourmont's "procession of all women that ever were" should be evident: the *Litanies de la Rose* can be seen, in this perspective, as a mantram, a ritual evocation, a conjuring of the goddess who is at once all women and all roses. In this same essay on the love cult of the troubadours, Pound significantly went on to quote several poems from Gourmont's *Le Latin mystique du moyen âge: Les Poètes de l'antiphonaire et la symbolique au moyen âge.* This work was the scholarly source behind Gourmont's own experiments with archaic liturgical verse forms. Originally published with great pomp in 1892 (it was the first book to appear under the Mercure de France imprint), *Le Latin mystique* was more than just an erudite anthology of forgotten poets: it was a defense of the contemporary Symbolist movement. Gourmont declared in his introduction: "Many characteristic features of the Christian Latin poets are shared by contemporary French poetry." Both, he continued, constituted a literary elite opposed to the official ideology of the times, both possessed "a great disdain for prosodic norms."[23] Although Baudelaire's silver Latin and Des Esseintes' hothouse philology tend to permeate the collection (appropriately prefaced by Huysmans), the Decadent blend of exquisite blasphemy and morbid sensuality did not obscure the more important aspects of the work for Pound.

As Symbolist propaganda, *Le Latin mystique* admirably demonstrated how tradition might be pressed into the service of experiment, how innovation might be inscribed within historic precedent. This polemical appropriation of the past may have further confirmed Pound's intuition that his early work on the music of Provençal poetry was not merely antiquarianism, but might potentially serve as the basis of a modernist poetics. Gourmont, he noted, had laid before his readers "a great amount of forgotten beauty, the beauty of a period slighted by philological scholars" (SP, 414). The tradition Gourmont invoked was thus doubly valuable because it was in a sense underground, outside the purlieu of the official custodians of the classics and hence inaccessible to the uninitiated. Aldington, Pound's fellow Gourmontian, was to pass severe sentence on their master's taste for the arcane:

> He wasted far too many years in mere fumbling, far too many years in the acquisition of abstruse learning while neglecting more important studies, and far too many years in the pursuit of a factitious and affected originality. I attribute this unlucky state of affairs to a genuine spirit of contradiction in Gourmont himself.
>
> . . . He affected to prefer the Latin poets of the middle ages to the classics, not because he had made a profound study of Latin literature and gradually come to make this startling reversal of judgment, but because it was a minority opinion, a fad of his friend J. K. Huysmans.[24]

Written in 1928, after the relations between the two ex-Imagists had become strained, Aldington's comments are probably something of a sideswipe at Pound as well. But while the latter no doubt shared Gourmont's fin-de-siècle cultivation of the abstruse and esoteric, deriving from a similar spirit of contradiction, Pound's iconoclasm in matters of literary tradition is in the end fully justified by the sheer amount of "forgotten beauty" he managed to unearth in the course of his various archaeological raids upon the neglected sites of the past.

Gourmont's *Latin mystique* mapped out one such crucial domain, namely, the postclassical Latinity of the Middle Ages and the Renaissance. Gourmont considered this the true international tradition of the West: unlike vernacular literature (which had been the focus of Pound's 1910 *Spirit of Romance*, though he did devote a final chapter to "Poeti Latini"), Latin provided the dominant medium of intellectual exchange among the European elite well into the eighteenth century. Like the later Pound, Gourmont was convinced that cosmopolitan culture had suffered incalculably from the extinction of Latin as the lingua franca of free spirits. Moreover, as an amateur philologist Gourmont was fascinated with the rich morphologies of medieval and Renaissance Latin: here, he claimed, the French tongue had its purest and most vital roots. A similar delight in the various shades of late Latin colors the entire spectrum of Pound's work, from Divus's Renaissance Latin translation of the *Odyssey* in Canto I through Lacharme's eighteenth-century Latin versions of the Confucian *Odes*. Late in the *Cantos*, rummaging for the components of an ideal *paideuma*, Pound would return to the same terrain surveyed by Gourmont in his *Latin mystique*. To cite but two examples: Gourmant's sixth chapter, on the Carolingian Renaissance, resurfaces (via Migne's *Patrologia*) with Deacon Paul's "De Gestis Langobardorum" in Canto XCVI; Gourmont's praise for the acute if misogynistic psychology of St. Anselm's Hymns to the Virgin—"Si quis habet sponsam turpem, fastidit et odit: / Si pulchram moechos anxius ipse timet"—reappears (again via Migne and Remusat) in Canto CV as

> Ugly? a bore,
>> Pretty, a whore!
>>> brother Anselm is pessimistic
>>>> (CV/750;775)

For the Pound of 1912-1913, however, the most important disclosure of Gourmont's *Latin mystique* was its chapter on the development of the medieval sequence[25] in the compositions of the monk Notker Balbulus, also known as Goddeschalk. Gourmont's comments on Goddeschalk's prosodic innovations undoubtedly confirmed Pound's convictions as to the necessity of conjoining words and music: "Notker was a musician and composed his verbal and vocal phrases together."[26] Indeed, Hugh Kenner suggests that Pound may have taken his notion of absolute rhythm from Gourmont's work:

> *Le Latin mystique* makes it plain that the phrase "absolute rhythm" was used by the Gregorian musicians to refer to the relation of the anterior and posterior morphologies of words and syllables. As a structural relation, not an abstractable quantity, and rooted in basic human gestures . . . "absolute rhythm" provides at once a psycho-

logical and objective correlative of emotions and shades of emotion transcending both exegesis and vocabulary. The structural principle of a Gregorian chant, the exact and indissoluble union of the music phrase by phrase and rhythm by rhythm with the sacred text is obviously related to *vers libre* as the opposite conception of a tune to which words are fitted is related to the stanza form.[27]

Although the precise expression "absolute rhythm" appears nowhere in Gourmont's book, his comments on the birth of the medieval sequence in the liturgical compositions of Goddeschalk may have corroborated Pound's own researches into the antecedents of vers libre: "Less out of ignorance of metrics than out of musical refinement, the poets began to number syllables instead of measuring them: there are no longer any absolute shorts or longs; there are only shorts and longs according to position; quantity is no longer determined by the morphology of the syllable, but rather by rhythmic necessity."[28]

Gourmont's portrait of Goddeschalk as "a man of imagination, an inveterate visionary who recounts, after gradual, the divine dreams that have visited his meditations"[29] no doubt further served to stimulate Pound's interest in the eleventh-century monk. It was, however, above all a single visionary sequence of Goddeschalk's, addressed to Christ and sensually evoking his love for Mary Magdalen, that Pound singled out as a masterpiece. He translated it in the essay "Psychology and Troubadours" and later included this version in his anthology of world poetry, *Confucius to Cummings*:

> The Pharisee murmurs when the woman weeps, conscious
> of guilt.
>   Sinner, he despises a fellow-in-sin. Thou, unacquainted
> with sin, hast regard for the penitent, cleansest the
> soiled one, loved her to make her most fair.   (SOR, 98)

Pound probably used Gourmont's French version as a crib:

> Chez Simon le lepreux, au repas figuratif, le Pharisien
> murmure et, consciente de ses fautes, la Femme pleure.
>   —Le pécheur méprise sa soeur en péché: Toi qui es sans
> péché, tu exauces la pénitente, tu purifies la souillée,
> tu l'aimes, afin qu'elle soit belle.[30]

And he certainly read Gourmont's commentary with care, for in his gloss on the poem, Gourmont had quoted the last phrase above in its original Latin, "Amas ut pulchram facias," adding "ô noble cervelle si avancée en idéalisme." This phrase, singled out by Gourmont as the kernel of Goddeschalk's sequence, would become, as we shall see, a permanent touchstone for Pound. Gourmont's characterization of the medieval poet as an idealist, however, needs some explanation, for it is central to his vision of both Dante and contemporary Symbolist verse.

Reacting to what he considered the crassly deterministic materialist aesthetic of Zola's Naturalism, in his early criticism of the 1880s Gourmont had adduced the terms "idéal" and "idéalisme" to define, on the contrary, a more Baudelairean, more Platonic notion of art and beauty based on what he would later call "l'imagination créatrice." One of the first essays in which he explored this concept was published in 1883 and dealt, significantly, with "Béatrice, Dante et Platon." Attempting to locate Dante's ideal vision of Beatrice in a tradition that he claimed stretched back to Plato through Boethius, Augustine, and the Shepherd of Hermas, Gourmont observed: "According to the Christian notion, the only pathway to the knowledge and possession of God is saintliness; according to scholastic philosophy, it is science as summed up in that science of sciences, theology; according to Plato, it is the contemplation of beauty. In taking Beatrice as a guide through his life and through his work, Dante combines in her the three natural and supernatural means which are offered to man that he might attain the presence of 'la divina potestate, la somma sapienza e'l primo amore' " (*Inferno*, III, 5).[31]

Gourmont's interest in the *Divine Comedy* was, as Karl Uitti points out, rather unusual for the period in France, since Dante had on the whole been neglected by the Romantics and nineteenth-century critics (with the notable exceptions of Chateaubriand, Joseph de Maistre, and Gérard de Nerval). His interpretation of Dante's ideal love for Beatrice as a metaphor for the contemplation of beauty (and hence of the eternal and of the divine) is, however, in many respects quite close to Pound's Pre-Raphaelite Platonic reading of Dante in the *Spirit of Romance*.[32] Like Pound, Gourmont came to see the Florentine very nearly as a contemporary: Dante's striving after the ideal, his exercise of love as a radiant act of the mind, "casting his gods back into the *nous*" (XXV/119;124), seemed to Gourmont a basic impulse of modern French Symbolist verse as well. As he observed in the preface to the first *Livre de Masques* (1896):

> A new truth has recently appeared in literature and art, an entirely metaphysical truth, *a priori* (in appearance) and quite new, since it is only a century old and has not yet been pressed into the service of aesthetics. This truth . . . is what Schopenhauer popularized in that clear and simple formula: the world is my representation. I do not see what is; what is, is what I see. This doctrine . . . is so beautiful and so supple that it can be transposed into practice without jostling the liberal logic of the theory.[33]

Although Gourmont's slant here is far more explicitly philosophic (he had finally discovered German Idealism in the late eighties through, among other works, Ribot's 1874 *Philosophie de Schopenhauer*), his idealist defense of Symbolist subjectivism and relativism clearly hearkens back to his earlier essays on Dante. At the core of this philosophy, he explained in such popularizing essays as *L'Idéalisme* (1893), lay the notion of the mind as active, apperceptive creator of forms of beauty out of flux. He quoted Hegel in corroboration: "Beauty in nature only appears as the reflection of the beauty of the mind."[34]

Gourmont's version of Idealism is thus akin to that esemplastic, projective power of the mind which Pound attempted to define in such early essays as "Psychology and Troubadours." Speaking of the "universe of fluid force," "the germinal universe of wood alive, of stone alive" that characterized the animistic, mythic worldview of the Greeks, Pound distinguished sharply between mere passive reflection of the universe ("what the Greek psychologists called the *phantastikon*") and a more active, literally more germinal consciousness: "The thoughts are in them as the thought of the tree is in the seed, or in the grass, or the grain, or the blossom. And these minds are the more poetic, and they affect mind about them, and transmute it as the seed the earth. And this latter sort of mind is close on the vital universe; and the strength of the Greek beauty rests in this, that it is ever at the interpretation of this vital universe, by its signs of gods and godly attendents and oreads" (SOR, 92).

For both these students of Dante, then, Amor was the highest and most intense form of this germinal force of the mind. Love, to Gourmont, was the seed of all beauty, indeed, of all art: "Whatever leads to love seems beautiful; whatever seems beautiful leads to love. There is undeniable interlacing. One loves a woman because she is beautiful; and one thinks her beautiful because one loves her . . . Take love away, and there is no more art. Take art away, and love is scarcely anything but a physiological need."[35] These observations can be read as an expanded commentary on what Gourmont terms the idealism of Goddeschalk's "amas ut pulchram facias." They may also explain why this Latin phrase would become a permanent touchstone for Pound. In his 1919 essay on Gourmont, he juxtaposed it with Propertius's "Ingenium nobis ipsa puella fecit" and with the King of Navarre's "De fine amor vient science et beauté," underscoring the persistence throughout Western tradition of the seminal power of love as art and knowledge (LE, 343). Late in the *Cantos*, he would again rhyme Goddeschalk's phrase with Dante, this time with the *Convivio*:

> l'amor che ti fa bella
> ("ut facias"—Goddeschalk—"pulchram")
> That love is the "form" of philosophy
> (XCIII/626;659)

He returned to it for the final time in Canto XCVIII:

"Ut facias pulchram"
there is no sight without fire.   (XCVIII/684;714)

Pound's "Psychology and Troubadours," conceived in early 1912 under the influence of the esoteric doctrines of G. R. S. Mead,[36] casts further light on the extraordinary importance he accorded to Goddeschalk's sequence. This essay investigated the various pagan and Christian prototypes of chivalric love. In the sensuous devotional verse collected in Gourmont's *Latin mystique*, and particularly in Goddeschalk's ecstatic visions, Pound thought he discerned "a new refinement, an enrichment, I think, of paganism. The god has at last succeeded in becoming human, and it is not the beauty of the god but the personality which is the goal of the love and invocation" (SOR, 98). Goddeschalk's erotically charged cadencing of Christ's love for Mary thus not only proved the survival of (Ovidian) pagan tradition (the god as fertility symbol, descending to earth in metamorphosis to seek union with mortals) but also provided a significant prefiguration of the "mediumistic function or cult of Amor" among the troubadours (SOR, 97). Sex, Pound noted in this same essay, has "a double function and purpose, reproductive and educational; or, as we see in the realm of fluid force, one sort of vibration produces at different intensities, heat and light" (SOR, 94). It was the latter intensity that the troubadours cultivated: in their rites of Amor, Pound suggested, they made disciplined use of the "charged poles" of sexual opposites in order to create within themselves an almost magnetic susceptibility to gradations of emotion. The tensions thus evoked in their personality would sensitize them to—and ultimately merge them with—the "universe of fluid force" or Platonic mind (*nous*) about them.

Though their chivalric code was, according to Pound, as rigorous as Christian asceticism, the troubadour cult aimed not at the mortification of desire but rather at its fullest expansion: it was an energy to be sensed and shaped, the vital material of their art. In this respect their approach to love was almost scientifically experimental: their own emotions, their own personalities were the medium in which they observed the patterns and vortices elicited by the force of Amor. As Pound later realized, a remarkable affinity exists between these medieval investigations into the various modalities of mind induced by love and the researches of the Symbolists and Surrealists into uncharted states of consciousness.[37] The goal of the troubadours, however, was not a Rimbaldian "derangement of the all the senses" but rather the attainment of that "place where the ecstasy is not a whirl or a madness of the senses, but a glow arising from the exact nature of the perception" (SOR, 91). An "aristocracy of emotion," a "cult for the purgation of the soul by refinement of, and lordship over the senses," troubadour religion was therefore centered on the "sheer love of beauty and a delight in the perception of it" (SOR, 90). Only by transmuting "all heavier emotion" into Amor (or art) could the

initiate create the beauty of the beloved as "a function of the intellect"—
"amas ut pulchram facias" (SOR, 91).

Pound would again and again emphasize this ecstatic precision of perception, this cultivation of "the fine thing held in the mind," as the essential donation of Provence to medieval Italian poetry (LE, 151). Gourmont explored this same filiation in his *Dante, Béatrice et la poésie
amoureuse, Essai sur l'idéal féminin en Italie à la fin du XIIIe siècle.*
Though as a Symbolist he insisted on the Platonic nature of the ideal
embodied by the *donna angelicata*, Gourmont nevertheless praised the
sensual (and decidedly un-Mallarméan) exactness with which the thir-
teenth-century poets of the *dolce stil novo* presented their visions of perfection:

> The *donna angelicata* inspires the new Florentine school with lines
> of verse which one would say were dictated by a singular intensity
> of objectification. The less reality the idea possesses, the more their
> poetry grows precise in its expression; the lines are impalpable, but
> sharply drawn.[38]

Pound had made very nearly the same point in his early essay, "Dante":

> Anyone who has in any degree the faculty of vision will know that
> the so-called personifications are real and not artificial. Dante's pre-
> cision both in the *Vita Nuova* and in the *Commedia* comes from the
> attempt to reproduce exactly the thing which has been clearly seen.
> (SOR, 126)

This is that same "radiant world where one thought cuts through another
with clean edge, a world of moving energies . . . magnetisms that take
form, that are seen, or border on the visible" which Pound located in the
"clear lines and proportions" of Cavalcanti's verse (LE, 154). Gourmont,
too, was fascinated with the author of *Donna mi pregha*; he observed of
Cavalcanti's meticulous analyses of love: "it is quite curious, and quite
human, and at the same time quite Platonic, that this ideal love should
always enter the heart through the eyes; it is material beauty which ig-
nites his spiritual flame."[39] Or as Pound repeatedly phrases it in his late
Cantos: "Ubi amor ibi oculus est" (XC/609;643).

Like Pound, Gourmont considered the eye the privileged organ of perception, the true locus of love and revelation: the entire theoretical structure of his influential *Problème du style* was based on the primacy of
vision—its impact on the Imagist Pound was, as we shall see, considerable. "J'ai plus aimé les yeux que toutes les autres manifestations cor-
porelles de la beauté," Gourmont confessed in the "Sonnets en Prose"
included in his 1914 *Lettres à l'Amazone.* In his 1915 obituary of Gour-

mont, Pound praised these sonnets as "among the few successful endeavours to write poetry *of our own time."* "I know there is much superficial modernity, but in these prose sonnets Remy de Gourmont has solved the two thorniest questions. The first difficulty in a modern poem is to give a feeling of the reality of the speaker, the second, given the reality of the speaker, to gain any degree of poignancy in one's utterance" (SP, 418). Gourmont's sonnets, Pound continued, "begin in the metropolis" and their speaker ("past middle age") "has worn off the trivialities of the day, he has conquered the fret of contemporaneousness by exhausting it in his pages of dry discussion" and in "the conversational, ironic, natural tone of the writing, the scientific dryness, even." In his study of the development of Pound's narrative voice in the early stages of the *Cantos*, Ronald Bush calls attention to the importance of these formulations: here, for the first time, Pound defines the particular dramatic tone and texture toward which his own long poem had, with varying success, been striving.[40]

Although Pound's comments here are perhaps far more applicable to Eliot's "Prufrock" (or to certain of his own *Lustra*) than to Gourmont's sonnets, they nevertheless capture something of the urbane flavor of these poems; despite certain similarities in cadence, their inflection is more modern and more scientific than the Symbolist *Litanies*—unlike many of his generation, Gourmont's ears had remained open to the new voice of the times. But as the various quotations Pound culled from these sonnets indicate, it was above all the passages devoted to eyes that seized his attention:

> I have loved eyes far more than all other physical manifestations of beauty. Eyes partake of light
> And partake of water. They partake of mind and partake of love. They tell the pressure of the cerebellum, and how the sacred nerves are stretched.
> They tell the state of blood, the level of the river, the sudden surges against its dikes and valves, or, on the other hand, they tell its peace.
> Eyes are the manometer of the animal machine.[41]

Gourmont's elaborate blazon of the beloved's eyes continuous for some six more pages—"I would speak of eyes, I would sing of eyes all my life. I know their every color, their every wish, their fate" (SP, 419). John Espey has demonstrated the relationship of the eyes that dominate these sonnets to the ocular imagery of Pound's *Mauberley*.[42] Indeed, this characteristically nineteenth-century configuration of eyes, light, and liquidity (it was a favorite metaphor of Gautier's; one of Gourmont's short stories was entitled "Yeux d'eau") pervades Pound's entire oeuvre. As John Peck observes, eyes are everywhere in the *Cantos*:

"Amas ut facias pulchram"

They are the eyes of that muse which hypnotized a century, shifting momentarily, as De Quincey says of his Mater Lachrymarum, between "soft and subtle, wild and sleepy"—the eyes that gaze from nearly every page of the fourth chapter in Mario Praz's *The Romantic Agony*. It may seem inevitable, then, that Pound would limn, with delicate satire, the pre-Raphaelite Stunner in *Mauberley*, with the aid of Gautier's attention to the eyes of such women: long-staring, pale and sea-green, les yeux glauques . . . But when Pound infused the Helens and Aphrodites of the *Cantos* with eyes of the same character, he committed himself to a deeper study of their power.[43]

As Peck goes on to note, though the eyes of the *Cantos* owe much to the nineteenth century's obsession with the gaze of the femme fatale, Odysseus-Pound would leave these Sirens and Circes behind to voyage into the "full Εἰδώς"(LXXXI/520;555) at once reflected and cast by Aphrodite's eyes. Far more visionary than the "yeux glauques" of *Mauberley* ("Thin like brookwater, / With a vacant gaze"), the eyes of the goddesses of the later *Cantos* nevertheless retain a family resemblance to those of Gourmont's sonnets, their power derived from the fusion of dark and light, water and fire, sea and sky:

> Such light is in sea-caves
> e la bella Ciprigna
> where copper throws back the flame
> from pinned eyes, the flames rise to fade
> in green air.   (XCIII/631;663)

The eyes that launched Gourmont's "Sonnets en Prose" belonged to Natalie Barney, the wealthy American expatriate who would later become a lifelong friend of Pound's. Gourmont's passion for the Amazone was impossible by definition—he was disfigured with lupus and she was lesbian—and in this impossibility he discovered his keenest emotions. The most revealing commentary on these *Lettres à l'Amazone* remains Gourmont's essay on the love of the aging Guillaume de Machaut for the youthful Peronne d'Armentières.[44] Gourmont's letters explore the same sensations of late love with a mixture of tenderness and despair that clearly moved Pound, for he equated the poignancy of Gourmont's tone with the directness of Anacreon's:

> Λέγουσιν αἱ γυναῖχες
> Ανακρέων γέρων εἶ

> Women say to me
> Anacreon, you're an old man   (SP, 420)

45

Comparing himself to Dante and addressing Miss Barney as one of those "Donne, ch'avete intelleto d'amore" ("women who have knowledge of love"), Gourmont ranges over many of the topics that so fascinated the Provençal courts of love. Like the Cavalcanti of *Donna mi pregha* or the Stendhal of *De l'Amour* (to whom he also compares himself), Gourmont is simultaneously passionate and analytic, inspecting his own emotions "through windowpanes, almost in the way in which, with astronomic coolness, one observes an eclipse through smoked glass."

> Love, in short is like radium, known to us only by the union it forms with its composites. One supposes its existence. One has never seen it.
> . . . . .
> Love has served as the model for all mystic religions . . . it is their prototype. Religion is its plagiary and its substitute.
> . . . . .
> Love lives on representations as much as on realities, and more on beliefs than on certainties . . . Which means one always loves the same being under different masks, because representations are always merely the projection of self into the field of the imagination.
> . . . . .
> To breathe the soul is to breathe the body in its purest and most assimilable form.
> . . . . .
> We only truly exist in the eyes that love us.
> . . . . .
> To cease desiring would be to cease living.[45]

Gourmont's *Lettres à l'Amazone* were one of his most popular works among the young Anglo-American authors of the mid-teens: Aldington would later translate them into English and a number of their remarks resurface in T. S. Eliot's early criticism—indeed, the Tiresias to whom Gourmont devoted a chapter might conceivably be one of the many sources behind the seer of Eliot's great poem on the failure of sexual love.

For Pound the central message of Gourmont's *Lettres à l'Amazone* (as it had been of his *Latin mystique*) was "the conception of love, passion emotion as an intellectual instigation" (LE, 343). Pound related this, in turn, to the "profound psychological knowledge in medieval Provence" which "was carried into early Italian poetry" (LE, 344). Reasserting the essentially pagan nature of these sophisticated notions of love, Pound equated Gourmont's insights with "the wisdom which those ignorant of Latin may, if the gods favor their understanding, derive from Golding's *Metamorphoses*" (LE, 344). Gourmont, he continued, "arouses the senses of the imagination, preparing the mind for receptivities. His wisdom, if not of the senses, is at any rate via the senses" (LE, 345). This "Epicurean receptivity" to sensation, this manner of embedding "his philosophy in a luxurious mist of the senses" (SP, 414) Pound located in, above all, Gourmont's short stories and novels. While admitting that "you could scarcely contend he was a novelist," he compared Gourmont's fiction favorably with Henry James's:

> [Gourmont] was intensely aware of the differences of emotional timbre; and as a man's message is precisely his *façon de voir*, his modality of apperception, this particular awareness was his "message."
>
> Where James is concerned with the social tone of his subjects, with their entourage, with their *superstes* of dogmatized "form," ethic, etc., Gourmont is concerned with their modality and resonance in emotion.
>
> Mauve, Fanette, Néobelle, La Vierge au Plâtres, are all studies in different *permanent* kinds of people; they are not the results of environments or of "social causes," their circumstance is an accident and is on the whole scarcely alluded to. Gourmont differentiates his characters by the modes of their sensibility, not by sub-degrees of their state of civilization. (LE, 340)

However permanent Gourmont's variations on the eternal feminine may have seemed to Pound, in the end his stories and novels remain mere period pieces, episodes of that particular erotic sensibility which Praz has chronicled in *The Romantic Agony.*[46] Despite their overwrought and somewhat cerebral sensuality, these short stories and novels nonetheless exerted a considerable attraction for Pound—John Espey has explored their impact on the themes and imagery of *Mauberley.* Indeed, the Pound of 1919 who praises the exquisite hyperesthesia of these works still sounds very much like a child of the nineties: "One reads *Les Chevaux de Diomède* (1897) as one would have listened to incense in the old Imperial court. There are many spirits incapable. Gourmont calls it 'a romance of possible adventures'; it might be called equally an aroma, the fragrance of roses and poplars, the savour of wisdoms, not part of the canon of literature, a book like *Daphnis and Chloe* or like Marcel Schwob's *Livre de Monelle;* not a solidity like Flaubert; but a pervasion" (LE, 342). The sense of beauty that Pound the avowed modernist so prized in Gourmont's fiction is closer to the synesthetic palette of Whistler's *japonaiseries* than to Wyndham Lewis's austere Vorticism. "The mist clings to the lacquer," commented Pound of *Diomède,* adding that Gourmont's "spirit was the spirt of Omakitsu [that is, Wang Wei]; his *pays natal* was near to the peach-blossom-fountain of the untranslatable poem" (LE, 343).

In the unhurried hedonism of Gourmont's fiction Pound discerned an alternative both to the misogyny that characterized what he called "Strindberg's sexual stupidity" and to the prurience that marked Anglo-Saxon puritanism. Gourmont, in short, was "an artist of the nude"—the pastoral tableaux of a novel like *Songe d'une femme*, the glimpses of nymphs bathing in pellucid streams, the erotic play of light and shade, the subtle delineations of desire, blended the delicate coloring of Impressionism with the contours of Puvis de Chavannes' neoclassical paganism:

> Leda is admirable; I had never before seen a nude with a shape of such splendor and with nuances of such liveliness, such excitement. I wish a single word could capture the blended tones which coursed through her flesh, the pinkish ivory of her skin, quickened by the blue reflection of the willow, the small violet shadows that rolled along her muscles, the sun falling about her shoulders like great golden medals which seem to splash like ruby water onto her arms, onto her knees, showering sparks up towards her belly where a dark crescent seemed to drink them in; under this web of light, the breasts seemed more alive, more free; changing their shape with every movement of the body, their form was always pure, large flowers with hearts of amber and purple, spurs stained with the blood of murders.[47]

A similar, if less sanguinary eroticism suffuses the original version of Canto I, first published in 1917:

> Gods float in the azure air,
> Bright gods, and Tuscan, back before dew was shed,
> It is a world like Puvis'?
>   Never so pale, my friend,
> 'Tis the first light—not half light—Panisks
> And oak-girls and the Maenads
> Have all the wood.
> . . . . .
>
> And the water is full of silvery almond-white swimmers,
> The silvery water glazes the up-turned nipple.[48]

Though Pound here dissociates his own pagan sensuality from Puvis's more etiolated version, the artistry of the nude in the *Cantos* perhaps owes more than has been realized to that late nineteenth-century "blend of perception and association" which Pound defined as "Listening to Incense" (GK, 80) and which obviously attracted him to the "luxurious mist" of Gourmont's prose. Gourmont did "not grant the duality of body and soul," but rather experienced "an interpenetration, an osmosis" of the two. The "exquisite treatment of all emotion" in Gourmont's fiction had shown that "sex, in so far as it is not a purely physiological reproductive mechanism, lies in the domain of aesthetics, the junction of tactile and magnetic senses; as some people have accurate ears both for rhythm and for pitch, and as some are tone deaf, some impervious to rhythmic subtlety and variety, so in this other field of the senses some desire the trivial, some the processional, the stately, the master-work" (LE, 341).

These last phrases again tend to recall the studied eroticism of the fin de siècle, but sex in this light ceases to be "a monstrosity or an exclusively German study" (for example, Sacher Masoch or Freud?), but instead aspires to the condition of music: based in love and ritual, it leads, like any art or religion, to "union with the absolute" (SOR, 99). Love as an "intellectual instigation"—the Amor of Goddeschalk, of the troubadours, of Cavalcanti and Dante—is one pole of Gourmont's art: one might call it his 'Mystique de l'amour." His "complicated sensuous wisdom" would be incomplete, however, the magnetisms could not take form, without an opposite pole. This would be the subject of Gourmont's *Physique de l'amour, Essai sur l'instinct sexuel,* translated by Pound in 1922.

2

THE PROBLEM OF STYLE

The *Litanies* and *Le Latin mystique* were the first of Gourmont's works that Pound discussed in print; these same years, 1912-1913, also saw his initial reading of the Frenchman's literary criticism and theory. This aspect of Gourmont's work is perhaps still best known through its impact on Eliot's *Sacred Wood*—indeed, Eliot's influential collection of essays can be read as a sustained homage to the man whom he called "the critical consciousness of a generation."[1] Quotations from Gourmont appear as chapter epigraphs, and axioms and insights are freely borrowed from the master's prose: the very blend of "sensitiveness, erudition, sense of fact and sense of history, and generalizing power"[2] that Eliot so praised in Gourmont was to become a distinguishing characteristic of his own renovation of the English critical stance and idiom. Although he was later to reject the validity of much of Gourmont's work, Eliot handsomely acknowledged his early debt in the preface to the 1928 edition of *The Sacred Wood*. Eliot's transfusion of Gourmont into English criticism has become an official episode in the history of Franco-American (and Franco-British) literary relations, yet Pound's part in this influence has sometimes been underemphasized. When Eliot writes of Pound "My own critical debt to him is as great as my debt in versification,"[3] we may assume that at least a portion of this debt involved Pound's introduction of Eliot to Gourmont's work in late 1914 or 1915. An examination of Pound's early reading of Gourmont's criticism might therefore not only cast additional light on his own complex development during this period but provide a background for Eliot's later critical formulations.

Gourmont's initial critical reputation was founded on his two-volume

Livre des masques. First published in 1896, this collection of essays by the "Sainte-Beuve of Symbolism"[4] introduced the newer authors to the wider French public. Three years later Arthur Symons would provide the same service for English readers with *The Symbolist Movement in Literature*—its impact on the undergraduate Eliot is too well known to require more than a passing indication. Pound too may have read Symons's survey (though he never mentions it, despite his admiration for certain of Symons's poems and translations),[5] but it seems more likely that his knowledge of French Symbolism derived at least in part from Gourmont's collections. Although he commented in 1919 that *Le Livre des masques* was "not particularly important" in the context of Gourmont's total oeuvre, that it was "a book of the nineties, of temporary interest, judgement in mid-career," he added that the work provided a "necessary scaffolding." This sort of criticism, he continued, was "a duty imposed on a man by his intelligence" and "the debt to Gourmont, because of it, is ethical rather than artistic" (LE, 49-50). Not "a carving of statues, but only holding a torch for the public," Gourmont's book, as Pound elsewhere observed, nevertheless put "a new generation on the map."[6] The same phrase might well be applied to Pound's own tireless campaigns on behalf of his contemporaries and those younger writers he referred to as *les jeunes.*

Gourmont's map of his generation was characteristically generous and characteristically eclectic. Symbolism, as defined in the preface to the first *Livre des masques*, was not a tightly knit avant-garde but rather a confrerie of kindred spirits; it was not an ideology or school but a collection of individuals:

> What does *Symbolism* mean? Taken in its strict etymological sense, almost nothing. But if one goes beyond this, it can mean: individualism in literature, freedom in art, abandonment of learned formulas, a tendency towards the new, the strange, and even the bizarre. It can also mean idealism, disdain for social anecdote, anti-naturalism, the tendency to take from life only the characteristic detail . . . finally, for poets, symbolism seems linked to free verse . . . The only excuse a man has for writing is to write himself . . . his only excuse is to be original; he must say things that have never been said before and he must say them in a form that has not yet been formulated. He must invent his own aesthetic.[7]

Much of this was to be requoted in the preface to *Some Imagist Poets* (1916), although by this point Pound was no longer associated with the movement, convinced as he was that Amy Lowell had diluted it into "Amygism." Gourmont himself was to emphasize the Symbolist ancestry of the Imagist writers; Amy Lowell cited him in *Poetry* in 1915: "The English Imagists obviously derive from the French Symbolists. One sees this primarily in their horror of the cliché, their horror of the rhetorical and the grandiose, of the oratorical, a facile genre which the imitators of Victor Hugo have rendered permanently disgusting; the precision of language, clarity of vision, concentration of thought which they love to synthesize in a dominant image."[8] Although Pound no doubt considered Gourmont's wide definition of Symbolism a valuable incitement to innovation, the terms in which it was couched were too vague to provide a coherent basis for the specifically technical renovations he considered crucial to Imagism. Symbolism for Gourmont was a cast of mind; for Pound, Imagism was instead a discipline, poetics rooted in praxis.

The two volumes of *Le Livre des Masques* nonetheless may have introduced (or at least further exposed) Pound to some of the French authors he in turn would popularize in "The Approach to Paris" (*New Age*, 1913) and the "Study of French Poets" (*Little Review*, 1918): Verhaeren, Régnier, Tailhade, Jammes, Fort, and, most significantly, Laforgue and Corbière. In addition, Gourmont's "important" essay on the Goncourts, in which he compared their stature to Flaubert's, may have fueled Pound's enthusiasm for their theory of the novel. Despite divergences in taste and aim (Gourmont was merely compiling a broad survey of the newer writing; Pound's anthologies of modern French verse had the more specific critical purpose of selecting models for comparison and importation), one of the things Pound most admired in Gourmont the popularizer was his magnanimity towards a wide spectrum of experiment. This "absolute fairness," Pound wrote, derived from the fact that Gourmont "was absolutely independent, that he was not tied to any institution, that his position was based on his intelligence alone and not on his 'connections' " (SP, 415). You could "have said to Gourmont anything that came into your head; you could have sent him anything you had written with a reasonable assurance that he would have known what you were driving at" (LE, 339).

Though his affiliations with the *Mercure de France* grouped Gourmont with the generation of the nineties, this "perfect and gracious placidity" accounted for the extraordinary respect which the younger writers of prewar Paris, Apollinaire and Cendrars among others, accorded to the doyen of Sybolism. Here was an elder who, Pound acknowledged, had "never lost touch with the men born ten or twenty years after he was," who could provide a "final and kindly tribunal where all work would stand on its merits" (SP, 422)—not only French work, one might add, but also the experiments of such young Hispanic modernists as Rubén Darío or those of the Anglo-American Imagists. As late as 1960 Pound would still remember Gourmont's unfailing generosity towards *les jeunes*. He was thinking in particular of Gourmont's recognition of the work of an unknown sculptor who had died—"Quick eyes gone under earth's lid" (P, 191)—in the trenches of Neuville St. Vaast: "Remy de Gourmont wrote the first French acknowledgement of Gaudier's existence, a brief obit labelled 'Maçon,' which had been Gaudier's answer on the army form re his profession" (G-B, 146).[9]

Apart from the sheer ethical dimension of Gourmont's critical activity, it was specifically *Le Problème du style* (1902) that in early 1912 provided Pound with what Eliot would call "the conscious formulas of a sensibility in the process of formation."[10] Like most of Gourmont's criticism, it is a heterogeneous work; originally conceived as an attack on a current writer's manual, *Le Problème du style* ranges from experimental psychology to applied stylistics, from the function of physiology to the function of metaphor, from Homer to Flaubert. Indeed, the very diversity of the terrain Gourmont seemed so effortlessly to cover no doubt contributed to Pound's interest in the book: just as Gourmont attempted to incorporate modern scientific discoveries of Ribot and Rabier into literary criticism, so Pound would adduce theories of "the newer psychologists, such as Hart" for his definition of the Image.[11] Although the theoretical influence of *Le Problème du style* on Pound is more elusive than, say, Eliot's debt to it in *The Sacred Wood,* Gourmont's work is nevertheless essential to a full understanding of the development of Pound's poetics in the early and middle teens. Pound did not swallow the book whole (he called it "profound, but not categorical or necessarily correct")[12]—his disagreements with certain of its facets are as important as his assent to others, for both equally involved a refinement of his own poetic and critical vision.

Perhaps more important than any of the specific theories enunciated in *Le Problème du style* was the very nature of Gourmont's critical activity itself—here Pound could observe in action what Ford Madox Ford had called the critical attitude, a quality of mind fundamental to the health of the republic of letters (and, for that matter, of the body politic). Like Ford, Pound looked above all to France for this attitude: Gourmont became for him, as he later would for Eliot, the exemplar of those "perfect critics" who "cause an amelioration in the art which they criticize." As Pound insisted in 1913: "Criticism being a far more civilised form of conscious activity than is artistic creation, it is natural that American criticism should be in a more deplorable state than American creative art. Indiscriminating energy may produce a work, but it has never yet brought forth a critique."[13] Fusing the creative with the critical temperament, the intuitive with the analytical method, Gourmont could therefore provide a lucid antidote—and a conscious direction—to the "indiscriminating energy" of American or the stultification of British letters.

The primary critical target of *Le Problème du style* was Antoine Albalat, author of *De la formation du style par l'assimilation des auteurs* and other successful manuals. At first glance this attack on Albalat's manual of style seems quite ironic, given Pound's later penchant for textbooks (Davie notes his "How to Read" might equally well be titled "How to Write");[14] yet Pound's pedagogic works were never the mere inventories of stylistic tricks and rhetorical devices that Albalat peddled to aspiring writers as time-tested formulas (for example, the recipe for amplification: "Out of a single idea, make two.—Divide up points of view.—Add striking features.").[15] Albalat (whom Gourmont wittily compared to Bouvard and Pécuchet's immortal professor of rhetoric, Dumouchel) proposed the slavish imitation of earlier models as a guarantee of success: "One should always keep the great classical models before one's eyes, one should devote incessant attention to their thought, their form, their style."[16] To which Gourmont quite sensibly countered that it was more important for a writer to keep his eyes simply on what he had in front of him: "When writing, a writer should think neither of his masters nor of his style. If he is seeing and feeling, he will say something; it will be interesting or dull, beautiful or mediocre, depending on luck. But to try to bamboozle ignoramuses and imbeciles by skillfully transposing some famous passage is vile craftsmanship and an idiotic attitude. Style involves feeling, seeing, thinking, and nothing more" (p. 31).

Pound, in such early essays as "The Serious Artist" (1913), was no less uncompromising: he considered it the business of the poet, as of the scientist, to focus solely on his data, be it objective or subjective, and to present it economically, honestly, directly. Though Pound might propose imitation (or translation) as a mask, as a calisthenic, as a mode of criticism, or as an exploration of the possible resources of the medium, such imitation was a much more complex affair than the mere copywork Albalat propounded: "Neither is surface imitation of much avail, for imitation is, indeed, of use only in so far as it connotes a closer observation, or an attempt closely to study certain forces through their effects" (LE, 93).

One of the most obvious questions that Albalat's doctrine of imitation raised was the very nature of influence or, more broadly, the relation of tradition to the individual talent. The answers Pound and Eliot formulated to this question would be basic to their particular versions of modernism, and no doubt Gourmont's own complex attitude towards tradition in part shaped theirs. Gourmont had written in the second *Livre des masques*, "Du nouveau, encore du nouveau, toujours du nouveau: voilà le premier principe de l'art"—the formula echoes Baudelaire and announces Pound's later motto, "Make It New" (itself initially derived from Pauthier's version of the *Ta Hio*: "Renouvelle-toi complètement chaque jour; faise-le de *nouveau*, encore de *nouveau*, et toujours de *nouveau*"[17]). In a specially commissioned 1914 article on the subject of tradition, published in Aldington's translation in both *Poetry* and *The Egoist*, Gourmont expressed the intolerable burden of the French literary past: "It is a chaos, a bog in the forest. We can no longer see the sky." Tradition, he added, "is a great power opposing the originality of writers."[18] Yet in this same essay he posited an important distinction between "the continuous tradition" and "the renewed tradition." In the former case tradition was merely a fact, a "mass of contradictory tendencies"; in the latter, it became a choice, an act of criticism, and hence an imposition of order upon what Eliot would call the "indiscriminate bolus" of the past.[19] The Romantics' rediscovery of the Middle Ages, Gourmont observed, was one example of renewed tradition—just as his own exhumation of the poets of *Le Latin mystique* had been.

It was this active concept of tradition that Gourmont opposed to Albalat's dreary procession of imitation upon imitation. On the one hand, one could not simply disown the past ("What is the past," he wrote elsewhere, "if not the very matter of which we are shaped"[20]); on the other hand the past had to be constantly reinvented in light of the present. History, for the idealist Gourmont, was an a priori construction like any other: "no works are definitive," he maintained, "every century must reshape them in order to be able to read them."[21] This dynamic interplay of present and past tended in certain respects to collapse the distinctions between the two. "All ages are contemporaneous," Pound had written in his 1910 introduction to the *Spirit of Romance*—it is perhaps the intuition most fundamental to his entire oeuvre. A similar perception of "not only the pastness of the past, but of its presence"[22] had enabled Gourmont to read the medieval Latin poets and Dante as contemporaries, and in 1908 he more explicitly articulated this synchronic vision of tradition in "Une Loi de constance intellectuelle."

That essay built on the zoologist Quinton's theory that animals tend to conserve the body temperature given them at the time of their first appearance on earth. As against Darwin's evolutionism, Quinton proposed permanence: only forms (that is, anatomies) change; physiology remains constant.[23] Gourmont applied this notion to the human intelligence itself; like physiology, it too was fixed, fixed at the moment of man's first invented tools: "Successive races have presented themselves, not with superior aptitudes or a vaster intelligence, but each with a fresh intelligence, each with a curiosity more naive and more resolute."[24] The steam engine may be beautiful, but is it at all superior, Gourmont asked, to the burin that carved "that beautiful reindeer in the [Dordogne] caverns?"[25] We need only juxtapose Eliot: "The poet must be quite aware of the obvious fact that art never improves, but that the material of art is never quite the same. He must be aware that the mind of Europe—the mind of his own country—a mind which he learns in time to be much more important than his own private mind—is a mind which changes, and that this change is a development which abandons nothing *en route*, which does not superannuate either Shakespeare, or Homer, or the rock drawing of the Magdalenian draughtsmen.[26]

Eliot may well have been thinking of another of Gourmont's remarks published in the *Egoist:* "My tradition is not only French; it is European."[27] That Albalat confused these two traditions was another accusation Gourmont leveled at him: Albalat, he said, systematically confounded "imitation within the same literature and imitation between two different literatures" (p. 20) and in so doing seemed to ignore the complex dynamics (and, one might add, anxieties) of influence. "Discontinuous traditions," he observed in the *Egoist*, "are most fertile when the period renewed is distant and unknown."[28] Similarly, although most young writers inevitably begin by imitating their immediate predecessors, the influence of the accepted classics of one's own literature is almost wholly unproductive of originality, unless the works imitated are considerably removed in time. Influence, then, involves not passive assimilation but, rather, a vital renovation of the past and hence of the present. For this to happen the author or period recovered must be sufficiently remote, sufficiently forgotten—in a word, sufficiently new:

> One can now easily understand that for a French poet to imitate Euripides—which, given genius, results in a Racine—is not the same thing as imitating Racine—which, also given a little genius, results in a Voltaire. Today, the influence of Euripides could, in an original mind, determine interesting works; whereas the imitator of Racine would barely transcend unintentional comedy. The study of Racine will only become profitable several centuries from now and then only on the condition that, completely forgotten, he seem entirely new, entirely foreign, the way Adenès li Rois or Jean de Meung have become for today's public. (p. 24)

Pound quoted this passage in his 1919 essay on Gourmont: the attitude towards tradition here expressed could equally well characterize his own particular anatomy of influence. "Be influenced by as many great artists as you can," he wrote in 1913 (LE, 5), but in practice Pound tended increasingly to abandon the imitation of his immediate harbingers (the Pre-Raphaelites, Browning, Yeats, and the poets of the nineties) in favor of the more selective influence of such forgotten figures as the "Seafarer" poet or, to the extent that even they had in some way been lost, the Greek lyricists, Propertius, the troubadours, Cavalcanti, among others. Pound's decision to open the *Cantos* not with Browning but with Homer (and more specifically with the most distant episode of the *Odyssey*, the *Nekuia*) is emblematic of this evolution.

One mode of renewal, then, was founded on strategic archaeology (Gourmont himself, always attracted to the pariahs of literary history, was to rehabilitate such seventeenth-century libertines as Cyrano de Bergerac, Théophile de Viau, and Saint-Amant).[29] An important corollary to this renovation of tradition involved the introduction of foreign components, distance in time here converting into distance in space. Gourmont wrote in *Le Problème du style*: "An innovation in literature, in art, in politics, in manners, can never arise from within the same ethnic group. Every group, once formed, once individualized, is constrained to a uniform production, or at least to a production systematized into fixed varieties; race, soil, climate determine the particular nature of its acts and works and limit their diversity. Man has the capacity for change, but he cannot change spontaneously: some leaven exterior to the dough is always necessary" (p. 20).

Gourmont's comments on the United States seized Pound's attention (he would quote them in his 1919 essay on Gourmont): "If closed to immigration, the United States would grow listless, without the European travels of their aristocracy, without the extreme diversity of the climates, of the soils, and consequently of the races evolving in that vast empire" (p. 21). Pound equally marked[30] Gourmont's application of these scientific analogies (derived from Quinton's mutationist theories) to the fertilization of French literature by foreign influences: "Exchanges between peoples are as necessary to the invigoration of each people as social intercourse is to the heightening of individual energy. Those who speak regretfully of the influence of foreign literatures on our own have not taken this necessity into account. Since the eleventh century, there has not been a single age in which French thought has not been revived by a fresh ferment. Its strength has lain in its ability to undergo all these successive commotions and to emerge fresher and livelier from each crisis" (p. 22). Written at the height of literary nationalism in France, this was an unpopular position for Gourmont to take; against Barrès' denunciations of "les Déracinés," he would acclaim "les Transplantés."

This campaign for a more genuinely international tradition was carried on not only in the *Mercure de France*'s regular articles on contemporary developments in foreign literatures (Pound's *Personae* and *Exultations*, for example, were reviewed in Davray's "Lettres anglaises" in December 1909) but also in Gourmont's own *Promenades littéraires*. He was one of the few in France in the 1880s to write on Washington Irving, Longfellow, Emerson, Hawthorne, and Bret Harte; later articles included "La littérature anglaise en France" (an excellent overview of literary crosscurrents between the two nations) and "Le livre français en Amérique" (in which he praised his American colleague and imitator, James Huneker).[31] Throughout his career Pound would aspire to the same role of cultural intermediary. He wrote in "Provincialism the Enemy" (1917): "At present the centre of the world is somewhere on an imaginary line between London and Paris, the sooner that line is shortened, the better for all of us, the richer the life of the world. I mean this both 'intellectually' and 'politically.' France and England have always been at their best when knit closest. Our literature is always in full bloom after contact with France. Chaucer, the Elizabethans, both built on French stock" (SP, 200).

Translation, Gourmont observed in the *Promenades littéraires*, was an integral aspect of that renewal through assimilation which determined the basic rhythms of French literary history. If translators were not inventors they were at least crucial consolidators.

> The truth is that French literature, whose liveliness is due to its constant self-renewal, has always found fresh life in the breezes that blow from abroad, often from very far away. This has been the case from earliest to most recent times, from the twelfth century, with the "matière de France" giving way to the "matière de Bretagne," to the nineteenth century, when the "matière romantique" superseded the "matière classique," the latter merely being the quickly faded flowering of the work of the sixteenth-century translators who had suddenly cast the "matière de l'antiquité" into the French imagination . . . Antiquity seemed dead or travestied for good when the group of sixteenth-century translators resuscitated it and awarded it such powerful influence that for three centuries it supplanted French civilization.[32]

In his 1913 essay "The Tradition" Pound similarly analyzed the international dynamics of literary renaissance:

> The Italians of that century had renewed the art, they had written in Latin, and some little even in Greek, and had used the Hellenic meters. DuBellay translated Navgherius [sic] into French, and Spenser translated DuBellay's adaptations into English, and then as in Chaucer's time and times since then, *the English cribbed their technique from over the channel.* The Elizabethans "made" to music, and they copied the experiments of Paris. Thus as always one wave of one of these traditions has caught and overflowed an earlier wave receding. (LE, 92)

A year later, writing of the possibilities of an American risorgimento, he said "the first step of a renaissance, or awakening, is the importation of models for painting, sculpture or writing" and went on to outline the foreign artistic capital America might profitably invest at home (LE, 214).

Pound's own interest in translation of course antedated his reading of Gourmont, but it may be that the French critic encouraged him to generalize its larger literary historical function: "A great age of literature is perhaps always a great age of translation, or follows it," he observed in his "Notes on Elizabethan Classicists" (LE, 232). Gourmont had underlined the French debt to foreign literatures; Pound in turn would emphasize that "the history of English poetic glory is a history of successful steals from the French." The great periods of English verse, he added, "have been the periods when the poets showed greatest powers of assimilation."[33] Conversely, and despite the translations of Villon that "revived our poetry in the midst of the mid-Victorian desiccation," the major "disease of both England and America during the last century is due precisely to a stoppage of circulation" between France and England which coincided with the Napoleonic wars (SP, 200). Quoting Kipling's "Transportation is civilisation," Pound warned: "whatever interferes with the 'traffic and all that implies' is evil. A tunnel is worth more than a dynasty" (SP, 119). This conviction governs not only Pound's early crusades against American book tariff regulations (impeding as they did the free international flow of knowledge) but also his later obsession with usury as a malevolent clotting of the circulation of purchasing power: for Pound, wealth—be it literary, cultural, or economic—was always based on exchange.

Apart from these larger questions of tradition and influence, Gourmont's basic quarrel with Albalat (and the school of criticism he represented) involved the very nature and definition of style. For Albalat style was nothing more than a repertoire of rhetorical devices that one might studiously assimilate from the classics and then more or less ornamentally drape over one's subject matter.

Gourmont's notion of style was instead radically organic and, he thought, scientific—he had by 1902 revised his earlier idealism to include, somewhat contradictorily, a more materialistic, more physiological account of the workings of the mind. Style, he maintained, was the "specialization of the sensibility"; the art of writing was "the art of seeing, the art of feeling with every organ, with every nerve-ending, and nothing more" (p. 32). Irreducibly individual, style could no more be learned, consciously imitated, or changed than life or personality itself: "Style can tire, like the man; it can age, just like the intelligence and sensibility of which it is the sign; but it can no more change personality than the individual can, barring some psychological cataclysm. Diet, a sojourn in the country or in Paris, affairs of the heart and their consequences, illnesses—all these have far more influence on true style than do bad books. Style is a physiological product and one of the most constant, albeit dependent on a variety of vital functions" (p. 19). Gourmont's entire concept of style could be inscribed under Buffon's celebrated maxim: " 'Le style est l'homme même' ('Style is the man') is the remark of a naturalist who knows that the song of birds is determined by the shape of their beak, the joining of their tongue, the diameter of their throat, the capacity of their lungs" (p. 33). Underscoring the "interpenetration," the "osmosis of body and soul" that characterized Gourmont's "complex sensuous wisdom," Pound singled out exactly this profoundly psychosomatic vision of language: "My words are the unspoken words of my body" (LE, 341).

Hulme echoed Gourmont's physiology of style: "all our analogies spiritual and intellectual are derived from physical acts . . . All poetry is an affair of the body." And Eliot observed, "all thought and all language is based ultimately upon a few simple movements."[34] Although Pound never explicitly referred to Gourmont's theories in this connection, it is just possible to relate his "physique du style" to his notion of absolute rhythm. If style for Gourmont was the articulation of a man's total sensibility (physical, emotive, intellectual, etc.), so for Pound rhythm was absolute because it was intimately (and physically) rooted in the poet's wholly individual mode of experience; as in the case of le mot juste, no other rhythm could be substituted without falsifying accuracy or authenticity. Moreover, if "le style est l'homme même," it followed for the Imagist Pound that "technique is the test of a man's sincerity" or, as he would later affirm from a more Confucian perspective, that "a man's character is apparent in every one of his brush strokes" (GK, 91). Style was so sensitive an ethical seismograph, he maintained, that any given age's tolerance of usury could be discerned in the very quality of line manifested by its painting (SP, 323). "With usura, the line grows thick."

Having posited what he called the "psycho-physiological" (as opposed to merely rhetorical) foundations of style, Gourmont proceeded to a more general typology: "There are two kinds of style; they correspond to these two great classes of men—the visual ("les visuels") and the emotive ("les émotifs"). The visual will retain the memory of a scene in the form of an image, more or less sharp, more or less complex; the emotive will only remember the emotion to which this scene gave rise in him" (p. 33). Later in the work Gourmont would further define these two types of style as "sensoriel" versus "idéo-émotif," or "plastique" versus "sentimental." These broad distinctions, based on the psychologist Ribot's differentiation between visual and verbal memory,[35] are no doubt overly reductionist and remain the weakest aspects of Gourmet's theory of style.

Pound's early 1912 speculations on the same subject were far less schematic:

> Making a rough and incomplete category from personal experience I can say that certain people think with words, certain with, or in, objects; others realise nothing until they have pictured it; others progress by diagrams like those of the geometricians; some think, or construct, in rhythm, or by rhythms and sound; others, the unfortunate, move by words disconnected from the objects to which they might correspond, or more unfortunate still, in blocks and *clichés* of words; some, favoured of Apollo, in words that hover above and cling close to the things they mean. And all these different sorts of people have most appalling difficulty in understanding each other. It is the artist's business to find his own *virtù*. (SP, 28-29)

Pound obviously considered Gourmont's distinction between "visuels" and "émotifs" incomplete, as either a psychological or a stylistic model, for beside the above quotation from *Le Problème du style* he noted in the margin, "+ auditifs" with a page reference to the following passage:

> I intentionally omit the auditory source because of its ambiguity, but I do not disregard it. I know just how much musical poets and fine prose writers owe to their ears. The ear is the portal through which rhythmic impressions enter; through this gateway all sorts of ideas also penetrate us, and even images in a state of reflection, that is, already transposed into words. In short, over and beyond its actual role of perceiving sounds, the ear, like the eye, possesses the ability to receive a representation of the exterior world in the form of signs. (p. 41)

Pound's marginal comment is quite suggestive, for in a way it announces his later division of poetry into three rough classes: melopoeia ("auditif"), phanopoeia ("visuel"), logopoeia ("idéo-émotif").

Although these three categories are implicit in much of his earlier criticism, Pound first assembled them in his 1927 "How to Read."[36] There is therefore probably no *direct* correlation between Gourmont's typology and Pound's. Even so, a juxtaposition of their respective schemata might illuminate Gourmont's theories in relation to Pound's own developing poetics. One major difference between the two is, of course, that Gourmont's categories deal with qualities of mind (more specifically, of memory) whereas Pound's describe modes of verse—though since both men considered mind (or experience, sensation and so on) as literally embodied (Gourmont's word was "incorporé") in style, the discrepancy is perhaps not so great as it seems.

Melopoeia ("wherein the words are charged, over and above their plain meaning, with some musical property, which directs the bearing or trend of that meaning": LE, 25) had been a constant concern of Pound's poetics from the very outset, as we have seen in the context of Gourmont's *Litanies*. "In short, behave as a musician, a good musician, when dealing with that phase of your art which has exact parallels in music," he wrote in 1913 (LE, 6). Pound's own investigations of melopoeia would lead him from the Greek lyric to Provençal *motz el son*, from the Elizabethan song writers to the Confucian *Odes*. It is obvious, then, why he felt that Gourmont's merely parenthetical mention of the auditory dimension of style was woefully inadequate. Ironically, though his own Symbolist verse was almost sheer melopoeia, Gourmont the theoretician of style, constrained to Ribotian theories of memory and a Lockean analysis of the transformation of sensation into idea or representation, was almost wholly deaf to this crucial mode of charging words with meaning.

Pound's phanopoeia ("a casting of images upon the visual imagination") is a more complex stylistic category to define. Pound remarked in his *ABC of Reading:* "I have taken to using the term phanopoeia to get away from irrelevant particular connotations tangled with a particular group of young people who were writing in 1912" (ABC, 52). Adopting the term was therefore an attempt to disassociate himself from the Imagist label: nevertheless, it isolates in a specialized manner one of the dominant concerns of his early poetics, a concern, it would seem, for which Pound is at least partially indebted to Gourmont's focus on the visual dimensions of style—prior to his reading of *Le Problème du style* Pound's criticism shows no especial emphasis on the (visual) image, as de Nagy points out.[37] A full analysis of the origins and developments of Pound's Imagist poetics is of course beyond our scope here—as is the entire debate concerning the influence of T. E. Hulme's aesthetic theories on Pound's Imagist doctrines. Many of Hulme's earlier speculations were directly plundered from *Le Problème du style* (as well as from Bergson) and in certain theoretical respects he remained a far more literal disciple of Gourmont than Pound ever was. This, however, is largely irrelevant, for whatever the impact of Hulme's conversation and scattered writings in 1910-11, Pound's own Imagist program only began to crystallize in the spring of 1912, that is, after he had himself read *Le Problème du style* for the first time.

At its most basic, Gourmont's problem of style can be reduced to the relation of the world of sensations to the world of words or ideas: "*Nihil in intellectu quod non prius fuerit in sensu:* the senses are the unique gateway of everything that enters and lives in the mind, they are the very notion of consciousness, the very feel of personality. An idea is only a stale sensation, an effaced image. To reason with ideas is to assemble and combine into a labored mosaic faded cubes that have become almost indistinguishable" (p. 69). This passage, heavily marked in Pound's own copy of the work, captures the crux of Gourmont's theory. If, as Locke had proposed, all thought derived from sensations, it was the business of style to embody those sensations or impressions (and not merely the ideas or emotions they evoked) as immediately, as directly, as possible. " 'Ideas' as the term is current are poor two-dimensional stuff, a scant, scratch covering," wrote Pound in 1918, " 'Damn ideas, anyhow.' An idea is only an imperfect induction from fact."[38]

Although the Gourmontian imprint is evident here, Pound had by this time acquired Fenollosa's essay, *The Chinese Written Character as a Medium for Poetry.* To Gourmont's "labored mosaic" of "faded, almost indistinguishable cubes" one might juxtapose Fenollosa's analogy for the "tyranny of medieval logic": "According to this European logic thought is a kind of brickyard. It is baked into little hard units or concepts. These are piled in rows according to size and then labeled with words for future use. This use consists in picking out a few bricks, each by its convenient label, and sticking them together into a sort of wall called a sentence, by the use either of white mortar for the positive copula 'is,' or of black mortar for the negative copula 'is not.' In this way we produce such admirable propositions as 'A ring-tailed baboon is not a constitutional assembly.' "[39] This process of Western abstraction, Fenollosa continued, involved "for ever building pyramids of attenuated concept until we reach the apex 'being' . . . At the base of the pyramid lie *things*, but stunned, as it were."[40] Furthermore, "the whole delicate substance of speech," he emphasized, "is built upon substrata of metaphor. Abstract terms, pressed by etymology, reveal their ancient roots still embedded in direct action."[41] Gourmont similarly observed: "Language is full of clichés which were originally bold images, happy discoveries of the power of metaphor. All abstract words are the figuration of a material act: to ponder is to weigh" (p. 36). It followed that one of the fundamental tenets of Pound's Imagism was "Go in fear of abstractions" (LE, 5).

Gourmont considered vision (or more specifically "la mémoire visuelle") the crucial means of reaching back to the stunned particulars behind concepts; only by seeing (and, like Conrad, by making his reader see) was the writer able to reachieve immediacy, to "metamorphose the abstract into the concrete, to make even stone breathe, to achieve 'the palpitation of stars' (Chateaubriand)." "Without the visual memory, without that reservoir of images from which the imagination draws new and infinite combinations, there is no style, no artistic creation. It alone allows us not only to paint the various movements of life by means of verbal figures, but to immediately transform into vision every association of words, every second-hand metaphor, even every isolated word— in short, to give life to death" (p. 35).

Although Pound shared Gourmont's convictions about the regenerative power of the eye, he no doubt paid little attention to the epistemology underlying the theory. Nor would he limit the imagination to a mere combinatory faculty: this resembled Coleridgian fancy far more than the esemplastic act of creation (as Schneidau points out, a similar underestimation of the power of the imagination was one of the major weaknesses of Hulmean theory).[42] Gourmont noted further on in *Le Problème du style* in what would seem a substantial reversal of his earlier idealism: "To imagine is to associate images and fragments of images; it is never to create. Man cannot create an atom of matter nor an atom of idea. All imaginative literature, like all positive literature and like science itself, is therefore based in reality" (p. 125). Pound commented in the margin: "it is quite possible, nevertheless, that the imagination does create. I can not remember metal[l]ic architecture—i.e. interior decoration - bronze - from life, etc."

Pound's comment, though only alluding to the formal designs of architecture, goes to the core of the question—Gourmont's theory could not provide for abstract or nonrepresentational styles. Reducing the field of the imagination to the domain of immediate perceptual data, Gourmont could account for the importance of vision but not for the visionary.

Blake had railed against the determinism implicit in such Lockean sensationism, proposing instead "to see through the eye and not with it" while at the same time retaining a reverence for the minute particulars that passed through the gates of enlarged perception. Pound wrote in late 1914: "There are two opposed ways of thinking of a man: firstly, you may think of him as that toward which perception moves; as the toy of circumstance, as the plastic substance *receiving* impressions; secondly, you may think of him as directing a certain fluid force against circumstance, as *conceiving* instead of merely reflecting and observing" (G-B, 89). Pound's post-Imagist evolution involved the latter, more explicit affirmation of active perception; that is, the eye not only registered and reflected light but might also cast it; the imagination not only selected and combined images but could create pure, abstract forms—the "planes in relation" of Gaudier-Brzeska's sculpture, of Lewis's canvases, and of the *Cantos.*

Related to the Lockean epistemology of *Le Problème du style* was Gourmont's tendency to speak of the visual style as descriptive. Whereas much of Imagist verse aspired to render "this series of sharp, almost luminous pictures" (p. 67) which Gourmont so praised in the styles of Taine and Flaubert, Pound specifically cautioned against being "viewy." "Don't be descriptive; remember that the painter can describe a landscape much better than you can, and that he has to know a deal more about it. When Shakespeare talks of the 'Dawn in russet mantle clad' he presents something which the painter does not present. There is in this line of his nothing that one can call description; he presents" (LE, 6).

Although the Imagist emphasis on "direct treatment of the 'thing' whether subjective or objective" (and the corollary that "the natural object is always the *adequate* symbol") no doubt owed much to the Gourmontian focus on the thing (visually) perceived rather than on the emotion thereby induced, Pound's divergence from the underlying theoretical assumptions of *Le Problème du style* should be clear. It was not mere *ut pictura poesis* that he sought in Imagism. "Presentation not Representation," as May Sinclair remarked, was the watchword of the school[43]— and by presentation Pound intended not the Gourmontian transformation or translation of the "thing" (object, sensation) into words, but instead a direct rendering of the "thing" in and as itself. The Image (or for that matter language) was not to describe reality but to coalesce with it, to be in Charles Olson's phrase, "equal, that is, to the real itself."[44]

Pound's third class of verse, logopoeia ("the dance of the intellect among words"), was "the latest come, and perhaps the most tricky and undependable mode" (LE, 25). Its relation to the *Problème du style* is perhaps tenuous, though Gourmont's description of the idéo-émotif personality can be correlated with the complex attitude of mind that logopoeia expresses: "It employs words not only for their direct meaning, but it takes count in a special way of habits of usage, of the context we *expect* to find with the word, its usual concomitants, of its known acceptances, and of ironical play. It holds the aesthetic content which is peculiarly the domain of verbal manifestation, and cannot possibly be contained in plastic or in music . . . Logopoeia does not translate; though the attitude of mind it expresses may pass through a paraphrase" (LE, 25).

The memory of Gourmont's émotif, as we have seen, retains not the (visual) sensations or impressions of any given experience, but only the emotions it evoked in him. This distinction becomes clearer within the framework of Gourmont's tripartite model of mental and linguistic activity: first, sensations are transformed into images ("mots-images"); second, images are transformed into ideas ("mots-idées"); third, ideas become emotions ("mots-sentiments").[45] The émotif thus finds himself at a double remove from experience; the words he employs will necessarily be abstract, having lost what Gourmont in *Le Problème du style* (p. 149) calls their "symbolic connexity" with original sensations, which—in Fenollosa's analogy—lie stunned at the base of the pyramid. What has happened, then, is that "the world of things has been supplanted by a world of signs which does not appear to the eye in any perceptible shape whatsoever" (p. 37). Severed from their origins in and their reference to physical reality, drained of their flesh and blood, words assume an autonomous spectral existence. Blind to the concrete world of things, the émotif wanders through a solipsistic, hallucinatory realm in which "little by little, life is filled with spectral beings who, incapable of feeling the moment in which they breathe, build with sounds and signs a city of the future which they people with notions of archangels and oratory" (p. 56). The émotif, in short, loses himself "in pure verbalism, in the ideal region of signs."[46]

Now "verbalism" was precisely Pound's original term for logopoeia. He wrote in 1917: "I do not think one can too carefully discriminate between Laforgue's tone and that of his contemporary French satirists. He is the finest wrought; he is most "verbalist." Bad verbalism is rhetoric, or the use of cliché unconsciously, or a mere playing with phrases. But there is good verbalism, distinct from lyricism or imagism, and in this Laforgue is a master" (LE, 283). One should perhaps not make too much of this coincidence in terminology (though Pound at this point was still reading and rereading Gourmont), but it is not altogether impossible that Gourmont's particular definition of "verbalism," together with Eliot's Laforguian experiments, exposed Pound to a poetry more complexly rhetorical than the musical or presentative modes.

Imagism tended to concentrate on the referential function of the verbal sign in order to convey the "thing" as directly and as transparently as possible. Words were accordingly to be stripped of their associative or suggestive "glamour" so that they might present with greater immediacy "an intellectual and emotional complex in an instant of time" (LE, 4).

"Verbalism," or logopoeia, on the other hand, focuses on the ambiguous process of signification itself. It is, as Pound defined it elsewhere, a "poetry that is akin to nothing but language";[47] that is, it employs words not only for their direct meaning" but for the sundry (and often contradictory) connotations they have acquired through various habits of usage and context (LE, 25). Logopoeia thus subordinates the referential function of language to the metalingual: it is language commenting upon its own possibilities and limitations as language; in short, to use Gourmont's terms, it deals rather with the ambivalences of the world of signs than with the world of things. In Laforgue's or Eliot's hands, logopoeia becomes a strategy of irony, enabling them simultaneously to expose and attempt to heal the irrevocable cleavage (or "dissociation of sensibility") that has come between these two worlds:

> Words strain,
> Crack and sometimes break, under the burden,
> Under the tension, slip, slide, perish,
> Decay with imprecision, will not stay in place,
> Will not stay still.[48]

Although Pound would make frequent use of such logopoetic techniques as "exact imprecisions, carefully designed indefinitions, just slightly inappropriate usages,"[49] his verse, at least superficially, seems far less dominated than Eliot's by the dilemma of the word. In this sense he resembles Schiller's naive artist (of whom Homer is the paragon) or Gourmont's visuel far more than the alienated modern émotif who painfully experiences the dissociation of word and thing, signifier and signified, idea and sensation, ideal and real. This view of Pound tends, however, to reduce him to a simple nominalist, impervious to the linguistic crisis that has so profoundly shaped the course of modern poetry. Despite his having proclaimed with Aquinas (via Dante) that "nomina sunt consequentia rerum" ("names are the consequence of things"), his *Cantos* show him no less haunted than Gourmont by the chasms that can come to cut the world of signs from the world of things.

Gourmont had warned at the conclusion of *Le Problème du style* that to separate form from content was equivalent to the artificial division of the total human organism into body and soul. He insisted instead with the naturalists that "content engenders form as the tortoise or oyster engender carapaces or husks of shell or mother-of-pearl" (p. 152). Pound was struck by the image, for he returned to it, in a somewhat different context, in his first editorial for the *Little Review*: "The shell-fish grows its own shell, the genius creates its own milieu."[50] The latter half of his statement derives equally from the *Problème du style*: "A superior man is recognizable by the fact that he creates his own milieu; he does not succumb to it, but inevitably creates it out of the very materials that compose this milieu" (p. 66). The image could be strikingly reversed, how-ever: "most men," Pound noted with Gourmont, "think only husks and shells of the thoughts that have already been lived over by others" (LE, 371). In Canto VII he presented precisely such a ghostly world, peopled by hollow men and their exoskeletal words, "shells given out by shells."

> Thin husks I had known as men,
> Dry casques of departed locusts
>   speaking a shell of speech...
> Propped between chairs and table...
> Words like the locust-shells, moved by no inner being;
>   A dryness calling for death;   (VII/26;30)

Canto VII is in a certain sense a Hell Canto, and Pound's vocation would increasingly involve descents into such semiotic infernos: as in the *Nekuia* of Canto I, spectral words must be given (the poet's) sacrificial blood to drink so that, reviving, taking on body, they might reveal their accumulated wisdom. Pound's earliest formulation of this vocation appeared in "The Wisdom of Poetry" (April 1912): "Thought is perhaps important to the race, and language, the medium of thought's preservation, is constantly wearing out. It has been the function of poets to new-mint the speech, to supply the vigorous terms for prose. Thus Tacitus is full of Vergilian half lines and poets may be 'kept on' as conservators of the public speech" (SP, 361). Pound probably drew his monetary metaphor from a passage in *Le Problème du style* in which Gourmont (in turn borrowing the analogy from Mallarmé) compared clichés and abstractions to worn coins—"médailles usées"—whose original images had been completely effaced:

> Speech is all images; even the smoothest conversation is a fabric of metaphors coarser than any page of Goncourt or Saint-Pol-Roux. These metaphors have been called worn coins, and this is almost true. But whether worn or mint, they are coins whose meaning on departure is "heads" and whose meaning on arrival is "tails." There are "heads" and "tails" that have been so obliterated that even the most tyrannical imagination can no longer animate them. (p. 36)

Eliot would pursue the analogy in "Eeldrop and Appleplex": "The majority of mankind live on paper currency: they use terms which are merely good for so much reality, they never see actual coinage."[51] Eliot's phrase at once admirably condenses the entire thrust of *Le Problème du style* and at the same time curiously portends Pound's later economic vision.

3

DISSOCIATIONS

Pound considered Gourmont's occasional prose (the *Promenades*, the *Epilogues*, and similar works) "perhaps the best introduction to the ideas of our time" that any "raw graduate . . . contemplating a burst into intellectual company" could desire. Just as Montaigne had "condensed Renaissance awareness," so Gourmont's essays together constituted "a portrait of the civilized mind. I incline to think them the best portrait available, the best record that is, of the civilized mind from 1885-1915" (LE, 344). Several salient traits of Gourmont's "portrait" can be discerned in Pound's political and cultural persona of the mid and late teens—especially as expressed in his various articles for the *New Age*, the *Egoist*, and the *Little Review*.

It was a critical period for Pound. In the social, political, and artistic turmoil that immediately preceded the First World War, the ascetic decorum and exclusively literary concerns of Imagism had necessarily given way to a more militant assertion of the irrevocable and salutary collapse confronting modern civilization. For Pound the Vorticist, the artist could no longer be content to remain a mere artisan or observer but, as he wrote in early 1914, had to adopt the "craft and violence" of a "savage" who would "sweep out the past century as surely as Attila swept across Europe."[1] But while one persona of Pound enacted the drunken helot, another preferred the aristocratic lucidity of Remy de Gourmont, a man independent of ideological polemics, a "Confucian, Epicurean, a considerer and entertainer of ideas" (LE, 340) who "walked gently through the field of his mind" (SP, 418). As late as 1929 Pound, already considerably politicized, could still praise this aspect of Gourmont "as a definite and actual force still operative. We cannot afford to lose sight of his value, of his significance as a type, a man standing for freedom and honesty of thought." As a defense of "liberty of expression, liberty of morals, liberty of action," Gourmont's works formed "one of those ensembles which make any country in which they are read a more inhabitable country."[2] To fight against tyranny, be it political, religious, social or linguistic, was, in short, Gourmont's most durable message to Pound. Associating this adamant libertarianism with "the light of the eighteenth century" (LE, 340), Pound, like Gide, considered Gourmont the last of the philosophes, a modern Voltaire.[3]

Gourmont himself came to Voltaire fairly late in his career. His early Idealist-Symbolist leanings were obviously incompatible with an admiration for the culture-hero of M. Homais. In the 1902 *Problème du style* he still referred to Voltaire as "le type banal de l'écrivain abstrait" (p. 46), though his books of this period (*La Culture des idées, Le Chemin de velours, Epilogues*) clearly show him to be a philosophe malgré lui. A few years later, however, conscious of his evolution towards a more scientific, empiricist outlook, Gourmont came to admit this obvious affinity openly. "I like versatile minds, and this is what makes me so admire Voltaire, whose greatness I have finally come to understand." Elsewhere he wrote:

> After having detested almost everything of Voltaire's, I now love almost all of him, for in reading him I have become aware, quite simply, that this man is not only a great writer, but also the very embodiment of a sage. Everything that he praised deserved praise, everything that he jeered at deserved disdain. His mind is perhaps the steadiest I know of, and the least superficial as well, despite what fools say. If he talked of everything, it is because he knew everything. Read him, Voltaire is an astonishment.[4]

Indeed, he explicitly invited his readers to compare his own work with that of the philosophe: "It is with the dead, I admit, that I most enjoy struggling and quarreling. I hope people read Voltaire so that there will still be those capable of judging whether I have occasionally drawn near to him. It would flatter me a great deal."[5] One of his English disciples, Aldington, would reply to the invitation with a 1925 critical biography of Voltaire.

It is less clear whether Pound initially discovered Voltaire through Gourmont. His biographer notes that in late 1909 Pound vacationed in Lincolnshire at the home of a certain Arthur Galton, a Church of England minister who read Voltaire. Galton subsequently left his set of Voltaire (the celebrated 1785-1789 Kehl edition, seventy volumes, in octavo) to Olivia Shakespear on condition that it eventually go to Pound's wife Dorothy.[6] Dorothy, who became as ardent an admirer of the great sceptic as the donor could have wished, probably came into the set around

1913 or 1914, for it is at this point that the philosophe's name begins to crop up increasingly in Pound's letters and criticism. The acquisition of the Kehl edition (the irony of its provenance certainly did not go unnoticed) was, like the bequest of the Fenollosa papers, one of those almost providential conjunctions of circumstance that Pound (*polumetis*, like Odysseus) learned to exploit to the full advantage of his own work. Voltaire would become a lifelong admiration, shaping several crucial aspects of the *Cantos*, most notably the Enlightenment vision of China.[7] In 1914, however, Pound's perspective on Voltaire was undoubtedly more Gourmontian than Confucian; it is therefore his adaptation of the views of both philosophes to his immediate polemical needs of this period that concerns us here.

One of the most pervasive, and thereby most elusive results of Pound's combined reading of Gourmont and Voltaire was the cultivation in his journalism of an aggressive tone of ironic superiority vis-à-vis the philistine. "Voltaire called in a certain glitter to assist him," Pound noted in one of his essays on Gourmont (SP, 418), perhaps intending to call attention to a similar brilliance in the latter's style. The implied comparison as Davie suggests,[8] can be misleading, for Gourmont's prose is far less honed, his irony far less barbed than Voltaire's. Whereas the white heat of Voltairean wit is stoked by savage indignation, Gourmont's cooler style instead affects the bemused disdain of the aristocrat who takes a prophylactic distance from the fray. Voltaire undertakes swift sorties against the enemy; Gourmont's Symbolist tactic is rather one of strategic retreat: "If one happens to wish for a derailment, one must speak, one must write, one must smile, one must abstain—this is crucial—from all civic life . . . One must poison Authority, slowly, playfully . . . One must remain perfectly indifferent; irony in one's eyes, one must make one's way through the tangle of anti-liberal laws.[9] Though the target of Gourmont's irony may be the same as Voltaire's (that is, authority in all its guises), his pose on the whole rather recalls the nineteenth-century dandy's more apolitical mode of subversion. All dandies, Baudelaire had recognized,

> share the same disposition to opposition and revolt; all are representative of what is finest in human pride, this need, all too rare today, to fight and destroy triviality. Among dandies, this is what gives birth to that haughty attitude which, even in its coldness, bespeaks a caste of provocateurs. Dandyism surfaces especially during transitional periods, when democracy is not yet all-powerful and the aristocracy is only partially tottering and debased. In the turmoil of these periods, a handful of men—disinherited, disgusted, idle, but with a wealth of native energy—can conceive the project of founding a new kind of aristocracy, one which will be all the more difficult

to smash because based on the most precious and most indestructible of abilities, on those heavenly gifts which neither work nor money can confer. Dandyism is the last burst of heroism in decadences.[10]

Gourmont of course did not have to found his aristocracy; he had it by birth—a fact that Pound perhaps unconsciously emphasized by almost invariably citing his surname with a capitalized particule. Pound, on the other hand, like Baudelaire (and like Eliot), had to invent for himself a "literary and reserved camouflage," a "classic and impeccable exterior" to fend off the vulgarians (L, 112). To the "digestive" bourgeois ("the gross stomach and gross intestines of the body political and social")[11] he opposed the artist's "nostrils" and "invisible antennae" and agreed with Baudelaire that "the aristocracy of entail and of title has decayed, the aristocracy of commerce is decaying, the aristocracy of the arts is ready again for its service."[12]

Like Eliot's mentor Irving Babbitt, and like Gourmont, Pound laid the blame for the rising tide of mediocrity on Rousseauistic conceptions of equality:

The "Confessions" having done their work have left a field for Bergson and for a democracy of commentators who believe not only that every man is created free and equal, with a divine right to become an insignificant part of a social system, but that all books are created equal and that all minds are created equal and that any distinguishing faculty should be curtailed and restricted. Carlyle idealized the hero. The Victorian age went in for great figures and the world was overrun with people pretending to be great figures. Our decade has reacted against great figures and the scholiast has become ashamed. The publicist has become apologist. They are pretending that there never were any great figures and they are trying to prevent the possibility of recurrence. The mediocre have set up a cult of mediocrity and deal in disparagement . . . There is no truce between art and the vulgo. There is a constant and irrefutable alliance between art and the oppressed. The people have never objected to obscurity in ballads. The bitterest and most poignant songs have often been written in cypher—of necessity.[13]

Pound's animus against Rousseau and Bergson was no doubt sharpened by Wyndham Lewis's Vorticist blasts against the "floaty" democratic Zeitgeist he saw embodied in these two authors (later intensified in his 1927 *Time and Western Man*); Eliot would come to a similar stance through Benda and Maurras. The complex nostalgia for Carlyle's vitalist hero worship seems, on the other hand, more Nietzschean (here again Lewis's impact can be felt): Pound's permanent fascination with great figures would not only inform the *Cantos* but also his later admiration for Mussolini. The "constant and irrefutable alliance between art and the oppressed" would seem to derive from an equally Romantic political perspective (say, Ruskin's) and the allusion to ballads recalls Yeats's vision of the aristocracy and the people as reservoirs of tradition, atavistically united against the bourgeoisie.

Pound's notion of the artist as an aristocrat without class (Baudelaire's word was "déclassé") did not derive, however, from an underlying authoritarian temper but, rather, like Gourmont's, from a deeper anarchistic libertarianism that he would never fully abandon. Given Pound's later political evolution, it is interesting to note to what extent he could dissociate his concern for civilization from any political engagement: "Fundamentally, I do not care 'politically,' I care for civilization, and I do not care who collects the taxes, or who polices the thoroughfares. Humanity is a collection of individuals, not a *whole* divided into segments or units. The only things that matter are the things which make individual life more interesting" (SP, 199-200). "Bales are written on the false assumption that you can treat the arts as if they were governed by civic analogies. The two things are not alike, and there is an end to the matter" (PD, 57).

These passages, written in 1917 and 1918 respectively, date from the very years during which Pound was discovering Douglas's Social Credit theories through Orage—a discovery that would eventually lead him to explore precisely those civic (and economic) analogies that he here dismisses. Much of Pound's journalism of this period manifests the conflict he felt. Increasingly conscious of the political and economic causes of the current war, Pound realized that his earlier aestheticism was no longer an adequate stance. Yet at the same time, although aware that Gourmont "leaned towards the symbolistic error of detachment,"[14] Pound was unwilling to abandon the prerogatives of the latter's individualism and was hesitant to allow his lucidity to be clouded by any ideological commitment. *Mauberley* was, in a sense, an attempt to come to terms with this tension, to resolve it through intricate irony—though the clash between the aesthete and the politically engaged artist, between the mandarin and the revolutionary, would continue to characterize the contradictions of his later social and political criticism as well.

If Gourmont blended the philosophe with the Baudelairean dandy, Pound found a more immediate sartorial and stylistic model in his fellow expatriate James McNeill Whistler, at whose "Gentle Art of Making Enemies" he apparently succeeded all too well during these London years. The original frontispiece of *Pavannes and Divisions* showed Pound in profile, seated, cloak draped over his shoulders, a visual quotation of Whistler's portrait of Carlyle.[15] Contemporary reviewers were quick to pounce on the dandified affectations of the collection. Untermeyer, critical of its "mannered prose and ostentatious finalities," commented: "The nimble arrogance of Whistler has been a bad example for him. For where Whistler carried off his impertinences with a light and dazzling dexterity, Pound, a far heavier-handed controversialist, begins by being truculent and ends by being tiresome."[16]

Aiken similarly chided Pound's "naive delight in booing at the stately," his "need for espousing the out-of-the way and remote and exceptional, so as to add a sort of impact and emphasis to personality by solitariness of opinion." Pound, he commented, had become "so fetishistic in his adoration of literary nugae that he has gradually come to think of style and filigree as if the terms were synonymous."[17] Carnevali, writing in *Poetry*, compared Pound to such "délicats" as Wilde and Gourmont and accused him of lacking roots, like these other "select selectors and elite-makers and aristocrats."[18] Though all these critics, hinting at the exhaustion of Pound's creative vein, were only too willing to write his artistic obituary, they nevertheless called salutary attention to his dandyish need to astound, confound, and *épater* in a style uneasily borrowed from Whistler and the French. Rapier wit and dazzling paradox were never Pound's forte and he would soon purge his prose of its Gallic pretenses, abandoning the persona of the dandy in favor of its more American inversion—what would eventually become the folksy cracker-barrel populism of Uncle Ez.

A hangover from the nineties, the aristocratic, dandified pose of both Pound and Gourmont partakes of a certain period style and as such should not obscure their underlying outlooks as philosophes. Gourmont's scepticism was not merely a facile posture of disaffiliation but rather, as one of his critics has suggested, his master tool.[19] In the preface to the *Problème du style*, he cited Bayle's "my business is to sow doubts," remarking that this motto contained "an entire method and entire ethics." Only through doubt could what Renan called humanity's "horrible manie de la certitude" and its attendant tyrannies be dismantled: "The major point is not to believe, not to have a single principle, or rather to have one so encompassing that all contradictions can move about in it with ease."[20] In an early essay Pound similarly included poets as "friends of this religion of doubt." "As the poet was, in ages of faith, the founder and emendor of all religions, so, in ages of doubt, is he the final agnostic; that which the philosopher presents as truth, the poet presents as that which appears as truth to a certain sort of mind under certain conditions . . . The poet is consistently agnostic in this; that he does not postulate his ignorance as a positive thing. Thus his observations rest as the enduring data of philosophy. He grinds an axe for no dogma" (SP, 361).[21]

In Gourmont's case, scepticism and relativism resulted not from an eschewal of commitment but rather from an Odyssean openness to experience, as he made clear in *Les Chevaux de Diomède*, Pound's favorite among his novels: "Besides, I have to experience every emotion as well as every sensation. Nothing must surprise me, but nothing should leave me indifferent. To hoist sail and await the caprice of the breeze; even if it lead to reefs or shipwreck, I shall still be superior to those who have only sailed the sad waters of canals choked with dead leaves."[22] The poet, the philosophe, the scientist must have no principle other than "the permanent examination of each thing," for "only one thing counts, fact. Theory must bow humbly before fact."[23] Pound again and again emphasized this aspect of Gourmont's intellectual temper: "De Gourmont, with his perfect and gracious placidity, had implied—yes, implied, made apparent rather than stated—that no formula can stand between man and life; or rather that no creed, no dogma, can protect the thinking man from looking at life directly, forming his own thought from his own sensuous contact and from his contact with thoughts" (SP, 421).

Eliot no doubt sensed a similar quality in Henry James when he praised his "mind so fine that no idea could violate it." Comparing James to the "best French critics" whose point of view was "untouched by a parasite idea," Eliot went on to observe that "in France, ideas are very severely looked after; not allowed to stray, but preserved for the civic pride in a Jardin des Plantes, and frugally dispatched on occasions of public necessity"—whereas England was infested with ideas as Australia was overrun with rabbits.[24] Pound in like fashion defined Paris as "the laboratory of ideas . . . it is there that poisons can be tested, and new modes of sanity be discovered. It is there that the antiseptic conditions of the laboratory exist. That is the function of Paris" (SP, 415).

Pound contrasted Gourmont's lucid savoring of ideas with the German gluttony for Kultur: "Ideas came to him as a series of fine wines to a delicate palate, and he was never inebriated. He never ran *amok*. And this is the whole difference between the French and Tedescan systems: a German never knows when a thought is 'only to be thought'—to be thought out in all its complexity and its beauty—and when it is to be made a basis of action" (SP, 415). Nietzsche, he observed, did "no harm in France because France has understood that thought can exist apart from action" (SP, 421). Practical implementation tended to dull the edges of ideas; as mere vehicles of action, they lost their contours and quickly slid into nebulous—and dangerous—abstractions. Because Gourmont dealt with them in their "pure" form, his thoughts on the contrary "had the property of life . . . they were immersed in the manifest universe while he thought them, they were not cut out, put on shelves and in bottles" (SP, 418)—the image once again recalls Fenollosa's "brickyard" and Gourmont's "labored mosaic." Like Dante, then, Gourmont was "able to consider two thoughts as blending and giving off music" (SP, 421); he had, in short, not lost that "radiant world where one thought cuts through another with clean edge, a world of moving energies," which Pound discovered in the verse of Cavalcanti (LE, 154).

Gourmont's almost scholastic play with ideas for ideas' sake would

seem diametrically opposed to Pound's later (and more Voltairean) pro-
mulgation of ideas into action. In *Guide to Kulchur* (1938) Pound returned to the distinctions he had drawn in his Gourmont essays more
than twenty years earlier: "At this point we must make a clean cut between two kinds of 'ideas.' Ideas which exist and/or are discussed in a
species of vacuum, which are as it were toys of the intellect, and ideas
which are intended to 'go into action,' or to guide action and serve us as
rules (and/or) measures of conduct. Note that the bloke who said: all
flows, was using one kind, and the chap who said: nothing in excess, offered a different sort" (GK, 34). Pound was here attempting to maintain
the validity of both kinds of ideas, but his impatience with the former
("toys of the intellect") is indicative of his increasing politicization, of his
rejection of speculative metaphysics in favor of praxis. Discriminating
between "studying thought" and "dealing with history (action)" (GK,
43), Pound went so far as to claim: "Not only is the truth of a given idea
measured by the degree and celerity wherewith it goes into action, but a
very distinct component of truth remains ungrasped by the non-partici-
pant in the action" (GK, 182).

Though he immediately added that "this statement is at diametric remove from a gross pragmatism that cheapens ideas or accepts the 'prag-
matic pig of the world,' " Pound's almost complete about-face from his
early Gourmontian stance should not be underemphasized: such rever-
sals are as vital to the metamorphic totality of his work as are its underlying continuities—without contraries is no progression. In an early
piece, which appeared under the pseudonym of Bastien v. Helmholtz,
Pound provided a valuable insight into the contradictions that traverse
and energize his work: "My life is a series of contradictions, because I
find myself incapable of putting hate into action. Hate can be for a mass,
but one's actions are always against some individual. I melt before the individual. I give away to pity. The swine say that I 'have a good heart.' "[25]
This passage goes far to illuminate not only the "Compleynt against Pity"
of Canto XXX, but also the permanent tension between Pound the poet's
deep reverence for the individual and his equally profound need as a
polemicist to put his genuine outrage against social injustice into action.

The coexistence of conviction and contradiction is perhaps the root affinity between Pound and Gourmont. The latter wrote: "Contradiction
coincides within an intelligence with the ability to associate and dissociate ideas rapidly. No conviction is stable in a brain thus organized, always on the move, always in revolution. Ideas mingle together like the
colors of a palette, producing every nuance of thought and of doubt . . .
Contradiction, however, can coexist with conviction; one might even say
that true contradiction is based on conviction."[26]

"The ability to associate and dissociate ideas rapidly" was precisely the
method and the ethics to which Gourmont alluded in connection with

Bayle's "my business is to sow doubts," and it is here that he most tangibly rejoins the tradition of the philosophes. He first formulated this method in his widely acclaimed essay, "La Dissociation des Idées" (1899):

> There are two ways of thinking. Either you accept current ideas and associations or, what is more rare, undertake original dissociations of ideas. An intelligence capable of this last effort is more or less, depending on the degree, the abundance, and the variety of its other gifts, a creative intelligence. It is a matter of either imagining new relationships among old ideas and images, or of separating old ideas, old images united by tradition, and considering them one by one, even if this entails juggling them and arranging an infinite number of new couplings which a new operation will again disunite until new bonds, always fragile and equivocal, are formed.[27]

Typically it was Gourmont's interest in the experimental psychology of Ribot and Rabier that had originally drawn him to apply scientific method to the purely intellectual domain. The relevance of "La Dissociation des Idées" to the questions raised by *Le Problème du style* should be evident, for at the crux of both works lies the problematic relation between the world of signs and the world of things. If in the latter work Gourmont demonstrated how the rift between these two inevitably led to an abstract, ornamental style lacking in visual immediacy, so here he analyzed how ideas, on a more purely intellectual plane, detached themselves from live fact to congeal into inert abstractions and clichés blindly accepted as immutable truths.

The tendency of the human mind to flee the complexities and contradictions of immediate experience for the pseudocomfort and pseudocoherence of ready-made abstractions was, in Gourmont's eyes, the source of all tyranny, social, religious, political, or linguistic. He noted of political rhetoric in the *Epilogues:* "Abstract ideas, which represent nothing more than their own syllables, are extraordinarily useful as passkeys, false keys, substitutes for the image. Mere labial movement replaces brainwork."[28] Pound would echo him: "The disease of the last century and a half has been abstraction. This has spread like tuberculosis" (LE, 39). Yet if the mind was capable of forging its own manacles, so it equally possessed the means to cast them off. It was not enough to sow doubts, Gourmont observed, "one must go further, one must destroy, one must set fires. Intelligence is an excellent instrument of negation."[29] If Flaubert believed that the immense prison house of received ideas could be demolished simply by quoting it verbatim in an encyclopedic *sottisier,* Gourmont's attack rather resembled the analysis and synthesis of a chemical operation or the Nietzschean stratagem of the transvaluation of values, "Umwertung aller Werte." As a method dissociation could be applied either to words or to ideas, either to clichés or to platitudes.

It was a question, then, of investigating how various associations had come to crystallize around certain words, so encysting them that their original meanings were lost (which entailed, as Kenneth Burke has shown, the obverse application of the Symbolist aesthetic of evocation[30]). It could be done by etymologically or philologically tracing the progressive distensions and disintegrations of the meaning of individual words; or entire nuclear clusters of stock phrases could be broken apart into their component words for examination. Similarly, a study of the history of ideas could illuminate the progressive blurring or degradation of certain concepts into accepted commonplaces, or else demonstrate the arbitrary nature of what the uncritical mind took to be eternal verities. Gourmont's sensitivity to the individual shapes of thoughts enabled him to split these supposed truths into nothing more than prejudiced—and Pavlovian—associations of ideas (for example, the automatic apposition of Byzantium and Decadence, of sexuality and procreation, of death and necessity, of glory and immortality). Cemented together by generations of sloppy thinking and terminology, gradually these inert bricks of thought completely walled the mind off from experience. Gourmont's "dissociation des idées" was a means of attacking the mortar directly— precisely the strategy of those earlier demolition experts, the philosophes, updated by the scientific methods of modern linguistics and experimental psychology.

Gourmont's specific applications of the dissociation of ideas often seem less successful than his theory; nevertheless, he had posited a valuable method. Pound made use of it in his early journalism; he observed, for example, in 1918:

> For the "normal" American mind the word *Democracy* and the word *Civilization* are interchangeable. The European intellectual, fed upon Remy de Gourmont and his contemporaries, prefers to keep the two concepts separate; at least, it scarcely occurs to him to think of the two words as synonyms . . . The term Democracy means nothing more than government by the people; it is described also, by certain optimists, as *for* the people. The term Civilization implies some care for, and proficiency in, the arts, sciences and amenities.[31]

"We advance by discriminations," Pound had declared in December 1911, "by discerning that things hitherto deemed identical or similar are dissimilar; that things hitherto deemed dissimilar, mutually foreign, antagonistic, are similar and harmonic" (SP, 25). It is unclear whether Pound had already read Gourmont by this point, but the parallels with the latter's "dissociation des idées" are striking: Gourmont (and Fenollosa) would only further sharpen these tools. Such discriminations provided the basis not only of Pound's poetics (image cutting through image with clean edge, vowels clearly bounded by consonants, each syllable separately shaped[32]) but also of his literary criticism. The study of letters, he insisted, demanded "a complete revision of contrasts" (SP, 285); and if Pound has changed the dimensions of our tradition it is largely because of these new demarcations and more exact definitions which he felt to be the function of the serious critic (GK, 169).

The same method would underlie his social and political thought: the early dissociations between civilization and democracy would give way to, for example, dissociations between usury and sane banking, between share and fixed charge, between Marx's theory of value and that of Douglas—indeed, as Pound saw it, "you can study economics almost entirely as dissociation of ideas" (SP, 281). Conversely, he would attempt such new associations as fiscal and political sovereignty, Jefferson and Mussolini, Confucianism and Neo-Platonism—Pound was no less driven than the Symbolist Gourmont by the demon of analogy: his ultimate heuristic device, as Kenner observes, was always the subject-rhyme.[33]

Behind Pound's dissociations lies the vulnerable status of language itself. Gourmont had analyzed how words clotted into clichés, into "infrangible blocks which can be manipulated *ad infinitum.*"[34] Pound in early 1912 echoed him with a more mesmeric metaphor: "As far as the 'living art goes,' I should like to break up clichés, to disintegrate these magnetised groups that stand between the reader of poetry and the drive of it . . . For it is not until poetry lives again 'close to the thing' that it will be a vital part of contemporary life" (SP, 41). Although he here restricted cliché to a purely literary context, Pound would progressively come to realize the larger implications of the divorce between word and thing, signifier and signified:

> It is the curse of our contemporary "mentality" that its general concepts have so little anchor in particular and known objects; that, for example, in a legislative body (read House of Commons) trying to make laws about coal, there is only one man who knows how coal lies in the rock . . . As the philologist or student of manuscripts knows, an unfamiliar word always tends to be confounded with and replaced by the familiar. Asparagus becomes in rural speech "sparrow grass." Ideas suffer a like battering into the mould of current cliché.[35]

Like Gourmont, Pound therefore saw his duty as a philosophe as "an endeavour to improve the contemporary condition of thought in the faint hope that it will diminish infinitesimally the imbecilities of future action. One criticizes, one rectifies or even attempts to enrich the ideas or tones of ideas in circulation."[36] This entailed exposing "the type and types of mentality which cause the obstructions to peace, to sane economics, to sane 'customs'; and which make possible the prolongation of 'superstitions,' superstes, left-overs." Following Gourmont's dissociative method, Pound went on to assert:

> Some of these clots of *superstes* coagulate about metaphorical clichés like "the blood of the lamb." Translate these clichés into some other equivalent linguistic form, such as "lamb's blood," or call the dove a pigeon and a large part of the narcotic falls out of them. Some of the clots are gathered about phrases having genuine entity, such as "La Patrie." In these cases the *superstes* are irrelevant elements, never necessary, or obsolete elements no longer necessary to the true entity, but still entangled with it in the popular mind.[37]

"When words cease to cling close to things," Pound wrote in 1915, "kingdoms fall, empires wane and diminish." Rome decayed "because it was no longer the fashion to hit the nail on the head. They desired orators." Renaissance Italy "went to rot, destroyed by rhetoric, destroyed by the periodic sentence and by the flowing paragraph" (G-B, 113-114). Contemporary America remained provincial because it "tolerated and sipped and guzzled the pink-tea of the 'Century' and the wide and wallowing whoop."[38] And the "hell of contemporary Europe" was largely due to the "befoozlement of Kultur" as embodied in the "mush of the German sentence, the straddling of the verb out to the end" (P/J, 90). The measure of individual or national civilization was, in short, its "respect for accurate statement" and the Flaubertian mot juste.[39] Pound would later correlate this notion with the Confucian doctrine of *chêng ming* ("the rectification of names") and in *Guide to Kulchur* he explicitly related the latter to Gourmont: "The art of not being exploited begins with 'Ch'ing Ming'! and persists invictis, uncrushable on into Gourmont's *Dissociation d'idées* [sic]" (GK, 244). Increasingly, Pound came to associate the perverters of language with the malevolent forces behind usury, for if the former were engaged in clouding the meanings of words, the latter attempted to obfuscate the meaning of money: both encouraged the individual to sacrifice his trust in immediate perceptions for a world of ready-made abstractions: "Usury is contra naturam. It is not merely in opposition to nature's increase, it is antithetic to discrimination by the senses. Discrimination by the senses is dangerous to avarice. It is dangerous because any perception or any high development of the perceptive faculties may lead to knowledge. The money-changer only thrives on ignorance" (GK, 281).

"In the beginning was the word, and the word has been betrayed," Pound wrote in 1942 (SP, 306). The Biblical allusion underscores his almost theological obsession with the "black myth" of the usurers who by their "Black Mass of money" had "created this satanic transubstantiation" of nature's increase (the true basis of wealth) into inert gold (SP,

307). Money in their hands had ceased to be a medium of exchange, but had been transformed into a commodity that might be cornered, hoarded, and manipulated in value according to the market demand. Usury falsified the "monetary *representation* of extant goods" (or their "money picture") by constantly altering the value of gold (SP, 277). Money, this "false representation," was thereby endowed "with properties of a quasi-religious nature. There was even the concept of energy being 'concentrated in money' as if one were speaking of the divine quality of consecrated bread" (SP, 347).

The sign, in short, had usurped the thing(s) it originally served to signify. Severed from any human or natural referent, it acquired an autonomous, spectral and arbitrary existence of its own far ghostlier, far deadlier than any of the shades of Hades.

If Gourmont's "dissociation des idées" contributed to Pound's later insistence on *chêng ming* and (through Fenollosa) to his elaboration of the ideogrammic method, Pound's journalism of the middle and late teens also shows the impact of Gourmont's specifically social and political writings: most of these appeared as monthly columns for the *Mercure de France* and were subsequently collected in the *Epilogues*. Pound called the first volume of these (the 1895-1898 series) "a book of accumulations. Full of meat as a good walnut" (SP, 345) and prescribed it to William Carlos Williams as a medicine against what he considered his friend's provincialism (L, 123). Indeed, "provincialism the enemy" was as pervasive a theme of Gourmont's *Epilogues* as it was of Pound's articles of this period: both considered its most pernicious form the nationalism they saw burgeoning around them.

At the very outset of his career, while the emotions raised by the 1870 defeat were still high, Gourmont had been fired from his post at the Bibliothèque Nationale for a satirical piece entitled "Le Joujou patriotisme" —this official disgrace, however, did nothing to dampen Gourmont's continued attacks on the shibboleth of "La Patrie." To nationalism he opposed individualism, insisting that "at this hour, such a thing as the Latin spirit exists no more than does the Russian spirit or the Scandinavian spirit; what exists is a European spirit and, here and there, individuals who assert themselves as unique, special, and complete." Like the philosophes, Gourmont proclaimed himself a citizen of the world: "There is no glory in being either British, French or German . . . we find the miserable condition of citizen repugnant, all we want to be is men."[40] Just as Pound had observed that the American people had sold out their liberties "for a mess of soda water and walnut sundaes,"[41] so Gourmont maintained that the French citizen had allowed himself to be degraded to the subhuman state of "devotion, resignation, and stupidity; he primarily exercizes these qualities via three physiological functions—as a reproductive animal, as an electoral animal, as a tax-paying animal" ("comme ani-

mal reproducteur, comme animal electoral, comme animal contribu-
able").[42] Pound would return to this passage in *Guide to Kulchur* and,
more eliptically and more compassionately, in one of his late Cantos:

> "Not political", Dante says, a
>> "compagnevole animale"
> Even if some do coagulate into cities
>> πόλις, πολιτιχή
> reproducteur,
>> contribuable. Paradis peint   (XCV/643;676)

The "paradis peint" here is Villon's, from "Ballade Pour Prier Notre
Dame."

> Femme je suis pauvrette et ancienne
> Qui rien ne sais; oncques lettres ne lus.
> Au moutier vois, dont suis paroissienne,
> Paradis peint où sont harpes et luths,
> Et un enfer ou damnés sont boullus

The penultimate line first occurs in Canto XLV as an indication of the decline of medieval artisanship in the face of the forces of Usura:

> With usura
> hath no man a painted paradise on his church wall
> *harpes et luz*   (XLV/229;239)

In the Pisan Cantos, however, the context of Villon's "Ballade" is more
disconsolate:

> pouvrette et ancienne oncques lettre ne lus
> I don't know how humanity stands it
>> with a painted paradise at the end of it
>> without a painted paradise at the end of it
>>> (LXXIV/436;463)

To define both the nature and possibility of paradise was one of
Pound's major quests. It was a consistent concern of Gourmont's as well:
he wrote in "Les Paradis" (included in the volume of *Promenades philosophiques* in Pound's possession): "The characteristic of modern paradises is that they are terrestrial. They exist in opposition both to the conception of heavenly bliss and to the idea of a golden age. Christianity, a
very complete religion, at once possesses a terrestrial paradise situated in
the world's earliest times and a celestial paradise, an indefinite region
where God lives and where his elect will go to join him. Philosophical

Utopians have only held on to the first of these paradises, and have situated it in the future instead of the past."[43] In his 1917 series, "Studies in Contemporary Mentality," an exploration of the degraded religion and mythology to be found in the fantasies of popular pulp literature, Pound commented similarly on the nature of modern paradises: "In this series we have noted the tendency to make otherworlds, paradisaical retreats from reality: the unattainable, or with difficulty attainable Ritz glitters as a new Jerusalem before the truly spiritual mind which will have no earthly content in the Regent's Palace."[44]

Pound presented variants on these "paradisaical retreats from reality" in Cantos XX (the Lotophagoi) and XXVIII (the drug addict). Although he, like Baudelaire, reproved these artificial paradises, he was nevertheless driven to build his own New Jerusalem—not in the afterworld, not in some Eden, but in the present tense, here on earth, in the polis: a *paradiso terrestre*. "Le paradis n'est pas artificiel," he maintained in the Pisan Cantos, though his errors and wrecks lay about him: if Mussolini's Rome had collapsed, the archetypal city of Dioce "whose terraces are the colors of stars" nonetheless remained "now in the heart indestructible" (LXXIV/425;451). Paradise was terrestrial, yes,

> but spezzato apparently
> it exists only in fragments unexpected excellent sausage,
> the smell of mint, for example
> (LXXIV/438;465)

or else "dove sta memoria" in the light of the eye, heart, mind.

According to Gourmont, it was not only the promise of some painted paradise—be it socialist, Catholic, or of whatever religious form—that had narcotized the modern citizen into animal docility. Patriotism, he contended, was equally effective as an ideological opium of the people. Champion of "le cosmopolitanisme littéraire," Gourmont commented ironically on the retrograde influence of nationalism on the evolution of poetic forms: "Traditional versification is patriotic and national; the new verse is anarchistic, a citizen of no country. It would seem that rich rhymes were indeed part of the National Trust: one is stealing from the State when one softens the sonority of the drone. 'La France, Messieurs, manque de consonnes d'appui!' On the other hand, the use of assonance has something positively retrograde to it which offends true democrats."[45]

Nowhere did Gourmont see nationalism and culture so militaristically intertwined as in the nascent German ideology of Kultur—and with the outbreak of World War I he put his pen at the service of the Allied cause. To many disciples this final act of political engagement seemed like a betrayal of their master's intransigent individualism: he had abandoned his world citizenship for the very patriotism he had so consistently combatted. Pound's evolution was similar: in his prointerventionist propaganda for the *New Age*, he applauded Gourmont's wartime polemics just as he praised Henry James's adoption of British citizenship as a protest against American neutrality. Although after the war Pound would return to his campaign for anarchistic "denationalism," his later admiration for Mussolini's colonialistic Italy showed him all too vulnerable to nationalistic ideologies.

One could correlate the political vantage point of Gourmont's *Epilogues* and occasional prose with the recurrent themes of Pound's journalism of this period: Pound's prose seems to echo Gourmont's attack on literary censorship ("tomorrow they will go shooting ideas"[46]) and the capitalist structure of the book trade; his animus against ideological zealots, be they revolutionaries, pacifists, suffragettes, socialists, prohibitionists, or missionaries; and, more ominously, his denunciation of the "money tyranny" exercized by the "odious economic oligarchy" of "Jewish high finance."[47] Gourmont commented on what he considered to be the financial manipulations of public opinion during the Dreyfus Affair: "Gold has gotten a hold over souls; one has seen or will see martyrs on the installment plan. Gold has determined certain convictions and the absence of gold has in turn determined diametrically opposed (and hence identical) convictions. *This transmutation of metal into idea-forms is to be noted"*.[48]

For Gourmont and Pound, as for Voltaire, the underlying cause of all these tyrannies was intolerance, superstition—in short, fanaticism. As such, these despotisms were merely secular manifestations of an essentially religious phenomenon. Gourmont observed, "what constitutes the religious phenomenon is not the belief in a religion, but rather the belief in any truth whatsoever."[49] The corollary of this was perfectly clear: "all faith implies persecution; where there is persecution, there is religious belief, there is faith."[50] But whereas Gourmont made use of this basic insight to analyze modern beliefs in science, progress, reason, revolution, fatherland, and so on, as basically religious phenomena, Pound, like Voltaire, focused his rage more specifically on the institutions and doctrines of the Church. The vehemence of Pound's anticlericalism is one of the most striking aspects of his polemics of the teens—no less than Voltaire, he might have taken "écraser l'infâme" ("crush infamy") as his motto. He admonished his *New Age* readers: "Nor would I have anyone forget for half an hour that the inquisition was re-established in 1824; and that burning for heresy occurred so late as 1751. The degradation of the French intellect at the hands and pens of the Claudel-catholico present movement is but a re-irritation to brandish these facts with new vigor".[51] Chesterton came in for a sneer for similar reasons: "all his slop—it is really modern catholicism to a great extent, the never taking a hedge straight, the mumbo-jumbo of superstition dodging behind clumsy fun and paradox" (L, 116). Even the editors of *Poetry* were accused, after censoring several of Pound's poems, of making an "idiotic fuss over christianizing all poems they print" and of capitulating to "local pudibundery" (L, 107).

Pound's objections to Christianity went far beyond its literary manifestations. Like Voltaire, he attacked the papacy as "a political organization exploiting a religious system" and praised England for having resisted it.[52] Nor was the British clergy (especially after Pound had read Trollope) left unscathed: "There are thousands of prim, soaped little Tertullians opposing enlightenment, entrenched in their bigotry, mildly, placidly, contentedly entrenched in small livings and in fat livings, and in miserable degrading curacies, and . . . they are all sterile save perhaps in the production of human offspring, whereof there is already a superabundance" (P/J, 70).

One of the most immediate irritants was a set of clangorous church bells immediately adjoining Pound's quarters in Kensington; in such magazines as *Blast* and the *Little Review* he poured out his righteous wrath against this "campanolatry" that polluted the peace of the vicinage with its "filthy racket" (GK, 300). But the object of Pound's vituperations was, as he noted, "purely allegorical"—"the act of bell-ringing is symbolical of all proselytizing religions."

"All religions are evil because all religions try to enforce a certain number of fairly sound or fairly accurate or 'beneficial' propositions by other propositions which are sheer bluff, unsoundness, will-to-power, or personal or type predilection, regardless of the temperament or nature of others. Every religion is a 'kultur'; an attempt to enforce a type or cliché; an attempt to impose a thought-mould upon others."[53] Organized religion, then, was merely "a state graft or a priest graft";[54] it arose, like any tyranny or provincialism, from the desire to "coerce others into uniformity" (SP, 189). The "vendors of taboos, and practitioners of sacerdotal monopolies" were nothing more than "bigots who will pretend to a right, a sort of droit de seigneur, to interfere in other men's lifes."[55] Though the analysis is Gourmontian, the vehemence is clearly Voltairean. Pound wrote to fellow-philosophe H. L. Mencken in 1916:

> Seriously I think what is wrong is simply that neither England nor America have had an Eighteenth Century deist. I don't believe superficial work is any good.

> A society for the publication of selections of Voltaire, in five and ten cent editions, translated, of course, into English, PLUS a general campaign of education would be the best beginning.

> Christianity has become a sort of Prussianism, and will have to go. All the bloody moral attacks are based on superstition, religion, or

whatever it is to be called. It has its uses and is disarming, but it is too dangerous. Religion is the root of all evil, or damn near all.

(L, 97)

It was characteristic of Pound's fundamentalist temperament that he should attempt to uncover the "root of all evil," and during this period he came to locate it less in the institutions of Christianity per se than in the underlying belief in monotheism. Pound's isolation of monotheism as the *radix malorum* is a curious synthesis of Gourmontian and Voltairean points of view. Pound quoted Gourmont's *Epilogues*:

> Neither the belief in a single God nor morality is the true foundation of religion. No religion, even Christianity, has ever exercised more than a mere check on manners and morals; its influence has been that of a raised hand. Religion must begin its preaching anew with every generation, not only with every human generation but with every phase of an individual's life. Since it does not provide any self-evident truths, and since its teachings are soon forgotten, all it leaves in souls is the dread of uncertainty and the shame of being subject to a terror or a hope whose phantom charms hobble not only our acts but our desires.[56]

Elsewhere Gourmont had written, "If believing in and praying to a single God is a pious act, it is far more pious and far more beautiful to believe in all the gods of the Pantheon and to offer fruits and lambs to each of them. Why only Jupiter or only Jehovah? Where have they ever demonstrated their objective existence more convincingly than heroes or saints?[57]

Gourmont's position was typically contradictory, for despite his Voltairean anticlericalism, he remained profoundly attracted to the paganism he saw perpetuated in popular Catholicism: "Once one knows its theology, the only important thing in any religion is its folklore: its traditional superstitions, the surprises of its liturgy, its religious tales, the legendary lives of its saints and martyrs, the entire popular dimension of religion, everything that makes a religion alive and durable."[58] In such essays as "Le Paganisme Eternel" Gourmont drew up lists that correlated the sites of classic temples and the beliefs surrounding classic gods with those of Christian shrines and popular saints: he hoped thereby to demonstrate to what extent the people had conserved the older traditions of paganism in their religious practices and beliefs. With such anthropologists as Frazer and such folklorists as Van Gennep, Gourmont affirmed "there has always been but one religion, the religion of the people, as eternal and immutable as human feeling itself."[59]

Gourmont distinguished sharply, however, between the intrinsic paganism of Catholicism and what he described as the "glacial Christianity" of Protestantism: "One accepts an idol enclosed in a golden shrine because of its shine, but one refuses the ugly naked Christ of St. Paul and its morality, so destructive of all civilization, so inimical to all beauty, all freedom of the flesh, all grace of intellect."[60] Gourmont intimated that at bottom every Protestant was a proselytizer, and nowhere did he see "evangelical fanaticism" more clearly embodied than in Luther, that "crafty, credulous peasant," or in the aridity of Calvin.[61] Antisensuous, anti-intellectual, antitraditional, sectarian, destroyer of graven images, Protestantism had, in Gourmont's opinion, "slowed down the development of civilization by roughly three centuries."[62] Even Rome, "which sculpted beauty into eternal marble," had been reduced by the Reformation to "what it is today, a hierarchical kind of Protestantism, just as frigid, just as inimical to all art and sensual beauty."[63] The greatest casualties of the Reformation had been the indigenous polytheistic traditions of Europe: "In removing the cult of saints from Christianity, the Protestants took away everything that made it humanly valid. True gods have to have existed at one point; they will be chosen by a people according to its conception of the divine, that is, according to its notion of the heroic. One can deal more harmoniously with gods who were men or who at least have the appearance of men by their bodies, perfected though these be by their passions, by their loves."[64]

Protestantism, then, had replaced the sensuous, human immediacy of the gods with a single God no less abstract, no less vengeful than an ideological principle: "Abstract ideas are unhealthy for common minds: they suffocate on them. What despots principles are! With the ancient gods one at least had something human in common, one argued, one arrived at agreements; whereas principles are inflexible."[65] The Protestant belief in monotheism and Providence contained the seed, Gourmont thought, of all subsequent modern fanatic ideologies, for "the belief in a single cause is certainly the most dangerous superstition humanity can fall prey to."[66] But perhaps the seed lay further back yet: Protestantism, he claimed, was really only a later form of what he termed "Jehovism." To Gourmont, the real conflict of the Reformation involved nothing less than the perennial battle between Hebrew and Hellene, between Roman paganism and Semitic monotheism.[67]

Although one could draw parallels between almost any of Gourmont's remarks on paganism and Pound's later writings on religion,[68] during the teens Pound had not yet fully dissociated Catholicism from Protestantism: his early attacks were rather leveled at Christianity per se and he accordingly raided the Voltairean arsenal for weapons to *écraser l'infâme*. Perhaps the most explosive of these involved discrediting Christianity as a humane and enlightened religion through its very Hebrew paternity. If Bossuet made the annals of the Old Testament the basis of his Universal History, Voltaire subverted this Christian historiography by exposing the factual and moral incoherence of these same scriptures. Similarly, the roots of Christian fanaticism and intolerance could be explicitly traced to the Jews—and Voltaire made use of nascent comparative mythology to prove that they were not the chosen people but rather just another Arab horde who had borrowed what he considered its fierce, abhorrent customs and beliefs from other primitive Near Eastern peoples. The foundations of the Church could thus be shown to rest on nothing more solid than the half-savage superstitions of a small desert tribe whose records happened to survive. The strategy obviously appealed to Pound's intense anticlericalism, for he submitted a translation of Voltaire's "Genèse" to the *Little Review*:

> It is not wildly exciting, and it is not news, but it is a small scrap of Voltaire's *Dictionnaire Philosophique*, which considering its date might serve to show how far far far etc., how long long long etc., it takes for a light to travel across the darkness of Anglo-American literature . . . Frazer has of course done the whole job monumentally, BUT good god how slowly, in how many volumes. No reader of the *Golden Bough* is likely to relapse into bigotry, but it takes such a constitution to read it. A reminder that "There once was a man called Voltaire" can do no harm. The measure in which he is unread, can I think be found by printing the fragments as "translated from an Eighteenth Century author" and see how many people place it. (L, 134)

Few people did in fact place it: one reviewer complained of Pound's "digging up the Baron Holbach" (PD, 185).

Pound's translation was only in part mystification. The allusion to Frazer indicates how seriously he took Voltaire as a comparative mythographer: "As Voltaire was a needed light in the eighteenth century, so in our time . . . *The Golden Bough* has supplied the data which Voltaire's indecisions had shown to be lacking. It has been a positive succeeding his negative" (LE, 343). Both dissolved theology into mythology—Voltaire in order to attack the validity of the former, Frazer in order to assert the universality of the latter. Pound's own evolution would stretch between these two poles. In "Genesis," however, he still remained more Voltairean in his disgust for the Old Testament strain of Christianity: "People say: What sort of a book is this? The book of a reprobate people, a book where right, reason and decent custom are outraged on every page, and which we have presented us as irrefutable, holy, dictated by God himself? Is it not an impiety to believe it? Is it not the dementia of cannibals to persecute sensible, modest men who do not believe it?" (PD, 183-4).

Voltaire had gleefully culled the contradictions from the Book of Genesis, noting that they merely derived from savage superstition. One of the most interesting of Voltaire's passages deals with the Biblical account of the creation of light:

The Jewish author lumps in the light with the other subjects of creation; he uses the same turn of phrase, "saw that it was good." The sublime should lift itself above the average. Light is not better treated than anything else in this passage. It was another respected opinion that light did not come from the sun. Men saw it spread through the air before sunrise and sunset; they thought the sun served merely to reinforce it. The author of Genesis conforms to popular error: he has the sun and moon made four days after the light. It is unlikely that there was a morning and evening before the sun came into being, but the inspired author bows to the vague and stupid prejudice of his nation. It seems that God was not attempting to educate Jews in philosophy or cosmogony. (PD, 169)

Since both Voltaire and Pound considered light the prime revelation of the divine, the Biblical degradation of it to the status of any other object of creation seemed proof not only of the Jews' "continuous ignorance of Nature" ("they did not know that the moonlight is merely reflection") but also of their gross materialism. The latter was corroborated by their primitive belief in a corporeal god whose cruelty and fickleness Voltaire found only too human: far from transcendent, he lived with his chosen people in a "torrid intimacy of passions."[69] Pound would refer to him as "the intemperate and sensuous J'h'v" (P/J, 70) or as "that narsty old maniac JHV" (L, 339).

Voltaire did not object to monotheism per se; indeed, he saw the belief in a Supreme Being as a definite advance on barbaric paganism. It was specifically the parochial nature of the Old Testament God, guardian of his own people but intolerant of all others, that enraged him—here was a theological justification for bigotry. Pound saw it rather as a scare tactic or mode of coercion: "There is no greater curse than an idea propagated by violence. The African savage invokes his 'Ju' when he wants to bash the next tribe successfully; his god is an assistant to his worst instincts; the Jew, however, received a sort of roving commission from his 'Jhv' to bash all and sundry . . . The curse of this monotheism and intolerance descends into both the offspring of Judaism, Mohametanism, and Christianity."[70] Although Pound jeered that "the lions of the Tribe of Judah" had metaphorically given up the sword for the pawn-shop, he added that "inasmuch as the Jew has conducted no holy war for nearly two millennia, he is preferable to the Christian and the Mahomedan."[71]

One of the most illuminating insights into Pound's condemnation of monotheism is provided by his autobiographical account of how a deity can become a weapon in the hands of bullies:

At the age of ten or eleven we—that is, the son of the Presbyterian minister and myself—invented, not a god, but a djinn, possessed of nearly all the divine attributes—i.e., infinite expansibility, infinite compressibility, infinite metamorphosability, a capacity for incarnation, now in one, now in the other of us. We used this djinn solely for the annoyance and mystification of a third and younger small boy who bored us and who persisted in lending us his company. I take it that until mankind arrives at a certain maturity, a certain freedom from personal malice and a desire to impose on, or to be avenged on, surrounding persons, mankind will continue to found or to continue religions. I don't claim that our friend Leidy was ever a whole-souled convert, but he spent at least a year in the state of a man who sends for the priest on his death-bed. He couldn't "make out what it was," but he, on the other hand, "couldn't be sure that it wasn't." The enjoyment of this sort of hoax lasts into mature states of society; apart from the maniac and the fanatic, one has the newsgetter and the fake-litterateur, who preserve these savage or puerile tendencies.[72]

Elsewhere Pound commented that "the first clever Semite who went out for monotheism made a corner in giantness. He got a giant 'really' bigger than all other possible giants."[73] Pound's economic metaphor is no accident, for just as giantness or God could be cornered to the advantage of a particular religion or group, so, for example, goods or money (witness Baldy Bacon in Canto XII) could be cornered by private interests to their own financial profit and to the economic exploitation of others. Monotheism and monopoly capitalism were, in this respect, cognate—and Pound's early attacks on the former would, during the thirties, give way to an equally fierce campaign against the latter. "The orthodox church of Economics" (SP, 207), founded on Usura, with a Rothschild as its Pope and an international clergy of bankers, supplanted Christianity as the root of all evil. Though the focus of Pound's wrath had changed, the underlying motive of what Eliot perceptively labeled his "Theology of Economics" remained the same.[74]

Pound's condemnation of monotheistic Christianity and its Judaic roots is thus a curious synthesis of Gourmontian and Voltairean arguments. Following Voltaire's ploy, he would scoff at the Bible as a compendium of incoherent, barbaric rites and cite it as a *sottisier*:

> We turn to the work in question: "Then Zipporah took a sharp stone, and cut off the foreskin of her son, and cast *it* at his feet, and said, Surely a bloody husband *art* thou to me.
> So he let him go: then she said, A bloody husband *thou art*, because of the circumcision." —Exodus IV, 25-26.
> Really this work is more entertaining than one remembered it to be, more comic; but that twentieth century man should be influenced by this antique abracadabra is a degradation, an ignominy past all bounds of the comic. The Roman Church defended her posi-

tion with great ingenuity in opposing the translation and popularisa-
tion of the Scriptures; or, indeed, any examination of title-deeds;
but whatever cerebration Luther and Co. may have incited in their
time, five centuries stand witness to very little result. There are still
hordes excited by a buncombe prophecy of the approaching end of
the world; there are still hordes capable of reading and writing who
continue to "rejoice" at Nature's gift of stupidity.[75]

He bemoaned the deleterious effect of King James diction on Victorian
translations of Homer: "For, having, despite the exclusion of the *Dictionnaire Philosophique* from the island, finally found that the Bible couldn't
be retained either as history or as private Reuter from J'hvh's Hebrew
Press Bureau, the Victorians tried to boom it, and even its wilfully bowd-
lerized translations as literature. 'So spake he, and roused Athene that already was set thereon . . . Even as the son of . . . even in such guise....' "
(LE, 250). By 1940 Pound's animus against the "god-blithering tosh, low
moral tone, black superstition and general filth" of the "old testy-munk"
had grown more virulent:

> All the Jew part of the Bible is black evil. Question is mainly how
> soon can one get rid of it without killing the patient. Some kind of
> reminder of the divine is desirable. Humanity being what it is, I
> don't see that one can start with a perfectly new and pure religion
> containing only what one really thinks decent. I mean as practical
> politics it may not be advisable.
> Xtianity a poor substitute for the truth, but the best canned goods
> that can be put on the market immediately in sufficient quantity for
> general pubk??? I admit the problem is difficult. Mebbe best line is
> to get rid of worst and rottenest phases first, i.e., the old testy-
> munk, barbarous blood sac, etc., and gradually detach Dantescan
> light. (L, 345)

As this passage indicates, Pound had by this time grown considerably
more tolerant of the Catholic Church. His discovery "that there could be
clean and beneficent Christianity" (GK, 301) first occurred during his
visits to Italy in the early twenties: like Gourmont, he came to assert the
basic continuities between paganism and Catholicism as practiced in
Italy: "A live religion can not be maintained by scripture. It has got to go
into effect repeatedly in the persons of the participants. I wd. set up the
statue of Aphrodite again over Terracina. I doubt, to a reasonable extent,
whether you can attain living catholicism save after a greek pagan re-
vival. That again is why Christianity is tolerable in Italy and an offence
in England, France and most of America" (GK, 191).

In such articles as "Terra Italica" and throughout the *Cantos* he would
similarly affirm the affinities between live Christianity and "the light of

Eleusis," insisting with Gourmont that "the glory of the polytheistic an-
schauung is that it never asserted a single and obligatory path for every-
one" (SP, 56). More specifically, Pound came to admire Catholicism
largely because of the Church's economic doctrines (the strictures on
usury and the theory of the "just price" in canon law) and because of the
neo-Platonic strain (or what he called the "Dantescan light") that he detected in medieval Christianity. Fascinated by the heretics and pariahs of
the Chruch, Pound in a sense had to construct his Catholicism syncreti-
cally:

> Given a free hand with the Saints and Fathers one could construct
> a decent philosophy, not merely a philosophism. This much I be-
> lieve. Given Erigena, given St Ambrose and St Antonio, plus time,
> patience and genius you cd. erect inside the fabric something modern
> man cd. believe.
> The question is: how much more wd. Rome try to load onto you?
> This much I believe to be also true: there is more civilization lying
> around unused in the crannies, zenanas, interstices of that dusty and
> baroque fabric than in all other institutions of the occident. (GK, 76-
> 77)

The about-face from his early Voltairean anticlericalism seems to be
complete.

Though Pound evolved towards an idiosyncratic amalgam of paganism, Confucianism, and neo-Platonism, his distaste for the "Jewish poison" in Christianity remained unchanged (SP, 320). In evaluating
Pound's antisemitism, however, one must measure the extent to which
his reaction against "all this damn near eastern squish" (L, 342) involved
his own Protestant background. He often alluded to his American "sun-
day school," "Y.M.C.A." upbringing, admitting that he "took the stuff
for granted, and at one time with great seriousness" (GK, 300)—in fact,
he was moved to write his most overtly Christian poem, "The Goodly
Fere," because he had "been made angry by a certain sort of cheap irrev-
erance which was new" to him.[76] He wrote to his father in 1919:
"Damned mania for reforming things due to my presbyterian training, I
suppose, otherwise I might not have begun trying to improve America's
???? quantity of brain-substitute."[77] Writing to John Quinn in 1918 about
Maud Gonne's revolutionary fanaticism, he confessed: "Heaven knows, I
may have a touch of it re Xtianity, but I try to control it, and it is really a
development of the belief that most of the tyrannies of modern life, or at
least a lot of stupidities, are based on Xtn taboos" (L, 141). The object of
his indignation in his prose of the thirties and forties is as much the Protestant as the Jew. "Race prejudice," he observed, "is a red herring. The
tool of the man defeated intellectually, and of the cheap politician . . . It

is nonsense for the anglo-saxon to revile the Jew for beating him at his own game" (SP, 299). As "a usury politic" (L, 340), the Protestant ethic was inextricably bound up with the development of modern capitalism: "putting usury on a pedestal, in order to set avarice on high, the protestant centuries twisted all morality out of shape. 'Moral' was narrowed down to application to carnal relations" (GK, 256). "The effect of Protestantism has been semiticly to obliterate values, to efface grades and gradations" (GK, 185).

Pound came to equate the Protestant with the schismatic, and more significantly, with the iconoclast:

> The power of putrefaction aims at the obfuscation of history; it seeks to destroy not one but every religion, by destroying the symbols, by leading off into theoretical argument. Theological disputes take the place of contemplation. Disputation destroys faith, and interest in theology eventually goes out of fashion: not even the theologians themselves take any more interest in it.
> . . . . .
> Suspect anyone who destroys an image, or wants to suppress a page of history.
> Latin is sacred, grain is sacred. Who destroyed the mystery of fecundity, bringing in the cult of sterility? Who set the Church against the Empire? Who destroyed the unity of the Catholic Church with this mud-wallow that serves the Protestants in the place of contemplation? Who decided to destroy the mysteries within the Church so as to be able to destroy the Church itself by schism? Who has wiped the consciousness of the greatest mystery out of the mind of Europe —to arrive at an atheism proclaimed by Bolshevism, in Russia but not of Russia?
> Who has received honours by putting argumentation where before there had been faith? (SP, 317)

This passage is governed by a series of oppositions crucial to the entire thrust of the middle and late Cantos: monism versus schism; the precise terminology of Latin versus the obfuscation of language; an agrarian economy versus mercantilism and usury; tradition versus revolution; historiographical honesty versus the suppression of fact; mystery versus reason; faith versus atheism; contemplation versus disputation; fecundity versus sterility; the organic totality of body and mind versus schizoid dualism; concretion versus abstraction; imagism versus iconoclasm; the union of signifier and signified versus false representation. Though ostensibly aimed at Protestantism, Pound's denunciation obviously involves something far more profound and far-reaching—the infamy he excoriates is, in his eyes, nothing less than the dominant cultural ideology of modern Western civilization. Pound's tone no longer derives from the caustic ironies of a Voltaire nor from the bemused detachment of a Gourmont, but rather from a deep religious fervor—the unmistakable Biblical cadences of this passage (like those of the Usura Canto or the celebrated close of Canto LXXXI) are those of the pulpit. Indeed, one of the most profound insights into his complex relationship with Eliot was Pound's quip that their disagreements could be reduced to "a religious disagreement, each of us accusing the other of Protestantism" (SP, 321). Both were perhaps correct: if Pound scratched the Possum and found a parson, so Eliot might well have discerned the preacher and prophet behind Pound the philosophe.

Ultimately, Pound's polemics all stem from the same religious impulse to *écraser l'infâme*, from the same fundamentalist drive to do battle with the Anti-Christ, to root out evil, whether it take the form of provincialism, nationalism, Protestant or Judaic monotheism, or the "black myth" of the usurers and their "Black Mass of money." Gourmont with his usual perspicacity had observed: "The most religious men of today are perhaps those who wage wars on religions."[78]

4

FLAUBERT AND THE PROSE TRADITION

Summarizing his generation's debt to modern French literature in the *Nouvelle Revue Française* of November 1923, T. S. Eliot acknowledged that it was Gourmont who had been its guide to the work of Flaubert:

> Sur cette partie de ma génération dont je peux parler avec sympathie, je sais combien forte a été l'influence de Remy de Gourmont; et Gourmont est l'un des guides qui nous firent étudier Flaubert, lequel fut un maître à la fois d'art et de pensée.[1]

> I know how strong the influence of Remy de Gourmont was on those members of my generation of whom I can speak with sympathy. Gourmont is one of the guides who led us to study Flaubert, who was himself a master both of art and of thought.

Eliot's comment illumines yet another essential component of Pound's ideogram of Gourmont, for like Mauberley, the French critic might well have claimed Flaubert as "his true Penelope." Though he never was to devote a full-length study to his fellow Norman, Gourmont boasted of faithfully reperusing the master's oeuvre every two years and confessed to his own readers, "You know by my various allusions and scattered references that he has perhaps been my major literary preoccupation."[2]

From late 1912 on, Pound shared something of Gourmont's sustained preoccupation with Flaubert. In an essay published as late as 1941 he still proclaimed himself an orthodox Flaubertian ("it being my nature to stay orthodox always a little too long").[3] In *Guide to Kulchur* he ranked "Papa Flaubert" (the honorific perhaps deriving from Flaubert's own tendency in his *Correspondance* to refer familiarly to the venerable—for example, "le père Hugo") alongside the four Confucian classics as the only prose that could equal what he termed the "totalitarian" reach of poetry (GK, 121). Flaubert, he insisted, "was certainly the grandfather of any verbal renovation of our time" (SP, 455); he was "the archetype" of the "attempt to set down things as they are, to find the word that corresponds to the thing, the statement that portrays, and presents, instead of making a comment" (ABC, 74). In short, no other modern novelist (with the possible exception of Joyce) was so securely and so permanently enshrined in Pound's literary pantheon.

Flaubert was a "donative" author in the fullest sense of Pound's term: at once a classicist and an experimentalist, Flaubert numbered simultaneously among "the inventors" ("men who found a new process, or whose extant work gives us the first known example of a process") and among "the masters" ("men who combined a number of such processes, and who used them as well as or better than the inventors") (ABC, 39). He was, in Eliot's distinction, "un maître à la fois d'art et de pensée," and Pound would revere him not only as a craftsman and thinker, but as the exemplary modern hero and martyr of letters.

Eliot's account of his generation's discovery of Flaubert is characteristically generous towards Gourmont; neverthless, it omits—perhaps not unintentionally—mention of that other equally influential guide to the French novel, Ford Madox Ford.[4] As Pound observed in the thirties, arguing against the Joycean "revolution of the word" propounded by Eugene Jolas' magazine, *transition*: "The revolution of the word began so far as it affected the men who were of my age in London in 1908, with the LONE whimper of Ford Madox Hueffer . . . Hueffer (Ford) read Flaubert and Maupassant in a way that George Moore did not. Impressionism meant for him something it did not to Mr Symons . . . Mr Hueffer was getting himself despised and rejected for preaching the simple gallic doctrine of living language and le mot juste."[5] Or as he had proclaimed in 1913: "Mr Hueffer has preached 'Prose' in this Island ever since I can remember. 'Prose' is his own importation. There is no one else with whom one can discuss it."[6] Though Pound may well have discussed modern French prose with Ford as early as 1908 or 1909, he proved to be, as Schneidau remarks, a curiously recalcitrant pupil: even while he was Ford's secretary in 1911, he wrote home that they disagreed "diametrically" on every question, "art, religion, politics."[7]

Not until 1912 did Pound—like Mauberley, "for three years, out of key with his time"—finally began to incorporate Ford's Flaubertian preaching into the conscious modernization of his own poetics and criticism. This coincided not only with Pound's emergent Imagism but also, as we have seen, with his first reading of Gourmont, notably *Le Problème du style*. In all likelihood, Gourmont's critical essays provided a crucial theoretical confirmation of the "gallic doctrine" to which Pound had previously been exposed by Ford. In any event, Gourmont's contribution to Pound's particular perception of Flaubert and of the nineteenth-century French prose tradition in general should not be overlooked, for both are closely entwined with the literary and ideological concerns analyzed in the preceding chapters.

Pound apparently first began reading Flaubert after his return from a summer walking tour in southern France. He wrote his mother from London in August 1912:

> I'm giving myself a course in modern literature and think it might amuse you to do the same. One is always hearing of Turgeneff [sic] and Flaubert and thinking they'll be dull, and Russians are so disgustingly stupid that one can't mention 'em without a shudder, etc. Anyhow I've taken the plunge. I thought Turgeneff the only sane modern, after I'd read the "Nichée des Gentilshommes" but Flaubert can give him points on how to write. T. is however the more charming mind, comprehension or whatever you want to call it. And F. the absolute master of speech. James and Anatole France infants by comparison.[8]

It was not by accident that Pound read Turgenev in a French translation: Henry James had included "Turgénieff" among his *French Poets and Novelists,* and Ford in such works as *The Critical Attitude* (1911) had habitually grouped the Russian with Flaubertians like Maupassant and the Goncourts. Pound's characterization of Flaubert as "the absolute master of speech" equally bears the imprint of Ford—rightly or wrongly, the latter considered Flaubert the supreme practitioner of contemporary language, the master of modern diction and of the cadences of daily speech. Ford attributed this "living language" to modern French verse as well: "In France, upon the whole, a poet—and even a quite literary poet—can write in a language that, roughly speaking, any hatter can use. In Germany, the poet writes exactly as he speaks."[9] Surprising as these generalizations might sound to the reader of Mallarmé or Stefan George (or for that matter, of Flaubert's *Tentation* or *Salammbô*), Ford's insistence on contemporary diction and spoken language was merely an aspect of his larger ambition "to register my own times in terms of my own time."[10] Linguistically, this involved bringing the idiom of literature up to date with current usage: "tertiary archaisms" such as still characterized Pound's 1911 *Canzoni* (which occasioned Ford's legendary critical roll on the floor) had to be purged in favor of a cleaner, simpler diction that might begin to approach the "real language of men."

Gourmont, like Corbière and Laforgue before him, registered something of the same modernist shift toward a more dynamic, oral conception of language in a passage of the *Epilogues* underscored by Pound:

"Languages develop in the streets, not in the universities: they remain pure only on the condition that they be neither codified nor taught."[11] Gourmont, who shared Pound's admiration for Dante's *De vulgari elo-quio* (sic), applied this intuition in his late prose sonnets: though hardly street language, these texts appealed to Pound precisely because of "the conversational, ironic, natural tone of the writing"—they were, he remarked, "among the few successful endeavours to write poetry *of our own time*" because, among other reasons, they gave "a feeling of the reality of the speaker" (SP, 418). In short, Gourmont's techniques in these sonnets (at least as Pound construed them) were diametrically opposed to that Symbolist mystique of "poésie pure," which demanded not "the reality of the speaker," not the immediacy of voice, but, on the contrary, as Mallarmé phrased it, "the disappearance of the poet-as-speaker, who leaves the initiative over to words."[12] Language itself, freed from the contingencies of personal utterance, was to be the poem's speaker (and subject), transmuting the merely conversational, local, transient textures of words (Mallarmé's "hasard") into the autonomous, nonreferential condition of music—or silence. As an artifice of eternity, the ideal Symbolist poem (such as Gourmont's early *Litanies*) was thus pure in proportion to the amount of prose it excluded. In Valéry's analogy, prose was to poetry as walking was to dancing: though both might use the same medium, they represented two distinctly different modes of activity—Valéry left little doubt as to the aesthetic, autotelic superiority of the latter.[13]

In theory, then, the Symbolist posited an absolute discontinuity between poetry and prose, between the condition of music and the condition of quotidian speech. The poem torqued and dissolved common patterns of syntax in order to recompose them into new hieratic structures; the denotative functions of words were to be abolished so that they might hermetically achieve the formal, nondiscursive purity of the musical sign.

It is against this background that the "revolution of the word" to which Pound alludes must be measured. If the Symbolists insisted on writing poetry as pure as music, Pound on the contrary maintained that "Poetry must be *as well written as prose.* Its language must be a fine language, departing in no way from speech save by a heightened intensity (i.e. simplicity). There must be no book words, no periphrases, no inversions. It must be as simple as De Maupassant's best prose, and as hard as Stendhal's" (L, 48). This was what Pound referred to as the "prose tradition in verse."

In his 1913 "Approach to Paris" series Pound attempted to define and locate that tradition. The context is significant, for it was here, in relation to contemporary French poetry, that Pound for the first time ventured a rough inventory of prose techniques in verse, ranging from the satires of Tailhade to the *unanimisme* of Romains, from the narrative realism of Jammes and Vildrac to the Whitmanesque derivations of Verhaeren and Barzun. In short, all the poets Pound discussed (with the exception of the

Gourmont of the *Litanies*) were counter-Symbolist in tendency. Romains provided, as against the Symbolist lyric, "possibly the nearest approach to true epic that we have had since the middle ages."[14] Vildrac, in turn, had "brought narrative verse into competition with narrative prose" in his "short stories in verse" just as Jammes had written "a novel in verse as a series of scenes with the speaker marked as in a play."[15] Against the hyperesthesia of Symbolism ("that melange of satin and talcum powder which we are apt to believe to be French verse") there was the vigor of Corbière, "as careless of style as a man of swift mordent speech can afford to be."[16] Jammes, too, had broken with the rarefied diction of the aesthetes: "We read his books of verse. It is as if he entered our room. He speaks in a normal tone. He produces conversation. He does not seem to monopolize it."[17] It was this same prose tradition that Pound, again in 1913, praised in Frost and D. H. Lawrence. Frost, who in "natural spoken speech" had put "New England rural life into verse," Pound compared to Jammes. Lawrence, he maintained, "has attempted realism and attained it." Like Vildrac, Lawrence "employed verse successfully for short stories" and "lived up to the exigencies of prose" in both his diction (the daily speech of the coal country) and his "real" characterization (LE, 385-388).

Although Pound's comments in "The Approach to Paris" begin to give a more precise sense of what he intended by the "prose tradition in verse," they take on a fuller meaning in the context of his own concurrent reading of the nineteenth-century French novel. "Poetry must be as well written as prose"—the imperative was borrowed from Ford, though its ancestry can be traced yet further back. Voltaire, for example, had similarly decreed: "Poetry must have the clarity and purity of the most proper prose."[18] His criteria in this case were neoclassical: against the grandiloquence of the Old Testament, the bombast of barbarians, the bric-a-brac of the baroque, Voltaire posited clarity, purity, concision—"le style naturel"—as the highest, and most civilized qualities of letters. Though considered the age's finest poet, Voltaire realized that French verse in his century had decayed into ornament and preciosity: no longer the vigorous vehicle of major ideas or epic themes, poetry in the *siècle des lumières* tended to retreat into the salon, overshadowed by prose. As Pound put it:

> From the beginning of literature up to A.D. 1750 poetry was the superior art, and was so considered to be, and if we read books written before that date we find the number of interesting books in verse at least equal to the number of prose books still readable; and the poetry contains the quintessence. When we want to know what people were like before 1750, when we want to know that they had

blood and bones like ourselves, we go to the poetry of the period. (LE, 31)

It was not with Voltaire, however, but with Stendhal, son of the philosophes, that Pound dated the fundamental recognition that the serious art of writing had gone over to prose:

> And one morning Monsieur Stendhal, not thinking of Homer, or Villon, or Catullus, but having a very keen sense of actuality, noticed that "poetry", *la poésie*, as the term was then understood, the stuff written by his French contemporaries, or sonorously rolled from the French stage, was a damn nuisance. And he remarked that poetry with its bagwigs and its bobwigs, and its padded calves and its periwigs, its "fustian à la Louis XIV," was greatly inferior to prose for conveying a clear idea of the diverse states of our consciousness ("les mouvements du coeur"). (LE, 31)

The passage to which Pound refers occurs in Stendhal's *De l'Amour*, in a fragment devoted to "L'Amour Antique." Contrasting the love poetry of Ovid, Tibullus, and Propertius with that of such moderns as Parny or Colardeau, Stendhal concludes: "Tibullus, Ovid, and Propertius had more taste than our poets; they painted love such as it existed among the proud citizens of Rome."[19] Only modern prose (Rousseau's *Nouvelle Héloïse* or Goethe's *Werther*, for example) could compete with the intense realism of the ancient love poets. Prose, not poetry, had become the vehicle for the analysis of states of consciousness and "les mouvements du coeur." *De l'Amour*, not the contemporary lyric, was the true successor of, say, Cavalcanti's meticulous investigations of love. As for poetry, Stendhal considered it not only artifical and outmoded, but no longer capable of clarity or precision: "Poetry, with its obligatory comparisons, with its mythology which the poet does not believe, with its stylistic fustian à la Louis XIV, with all its apparatus of so-called poetic ornaments, is far inferior to prose when it comes to conveying a clear and precise idea of the movements of the heart—and in these matters, clarity alone can move us ('or, dans ce genre, on n'émeut que par la clarté')."[20] Although Pound located the origins of this decline of poetry vis-à-vis prose as far back as the Renaissance ("with Rabelais, Brantôme, Montaigne, Fielding, Sterne, we begin to find prose recording states of consciousness that their verse-writing contemporaries scamp": LE, 31), Stendhal would remain for him the crucial turning point in the emergence of the modern prose tradition.

It is very likely that Gourmont's writings first introduced Pound to Stendhal (whom Ford had, on the whole, overlooked). *De l'Amour*, in particular, was one of Gourmont's favorite works: "The first books which opened the world to my soul," he confessed in the *Egoist*, "were Stendhal's *De l'Amour* and Flaubert's *Madame Bovary*, found in the cupboard of the house."[21] Stendhal and Flaubert were to be similarly linked in Pound's mind as the dual creators of the new prose (ABC, 97). He observed in a 1916 letter: "Certainly one ought to read the opening of the *Chartreuse de Parme*, and the first half or more than half of the *Rouge et Noir*. Shifting from Stendhal to Flaubert suddenly you will see how much better Flaubert writes. And YET there is a lot in Stendhal, a sort of solidity which Flaubert hasn't. A trust in the thing more than the word. Which is the basis, i.e. the thing is the basis" (L, 89).

Pound's partial recommendation of *Le Rouge et le noir* and *La Chartreuse de Parme* may not be pedagogically sound, but it at least indicates what he considered the most valuable aspect of Stendhal's work—that is, its historical, social, satirical dimension, and in particular the treatment of Fabrice's exploits at Waterloo, which Pound echoed in an unpublished draft of what was apparently to be Canto IV: "Here is your modern world, and I'm no Stendhal / Napoleon lands from Elba in the north / . . . / Fabrice starts, falls upon Waterloo, / Then there's the Parma court, / stupidities."[22] Gourmont, too, called attention to the revolutionary nature of Stendhal's eye-witness historiography in the *Problème du style:* "It is true that the visions of historical actors (like those of other actors) are always fragmentary; Stendhal, with fine irony, incorporated this into his novels."[23] Pound would make extensive use of this insight in the *Cantos*, perhaps nowhere more effectively than in Canto XVI. Although only three months before the outbreak of World War I Pound had lamented, "Our life has not the pageantry of Waterloo to give us a send-off for the beginning of a new *Chartreuse de Parme*,"[24] this Canto, written in the aftermath, employs Stendhalian techniques to register not the comedy but the horror of war as seen through the immediate, incoherent perceptions of battle of a French poilu:

> Les hommes de 34 ans à quatre pattes
>   qui criaient "maman." Mais les costauds,
> La fin, là à Verdun, n'y avait que ces gros bonshommes
>   Et y voyaient extrêmement clair.
>   . . . . .
> Mais les rapaces
>   y avait trois dans notre compagnie, tous tués.
> Y sortaient fouiller un cadavre, pour rien,
>   y n'seraient sortis pour rien que ça.   (XVI/73;77)

The Canto concludes with an analogous, alternatively epic and subjective presentation of the Russian Revolution. The entire Malatesta sequence, juxtaposing the official records and data of history with the elusive states of consciousness of actual participants, is built on similar techniques and insights derived from the French prose tradition.

The solidity Pound sensed in Stendhal was no doubt related to the Enlightenment heritage—cosmopolitan, ironic, analytic—which the latter shared with Gourmont. Though he tended to compose his prose improvisationally, he achieved the spontaneity of speech without sacrificing the concision he had learned from his manual of style, Napoleon's *Code civil* (whose fierce laconism Gourmont cited in *Le Problème du style:* "Tout condamné à mort aura la tête tranchée").[25] T. S. Eliot praised this razor-edged incisiveness in a 1919 article: "Stendhal's scenes, some of them, and some of his phrases, read like cutting one's own throat; they are a terrible humiliation to read, in the understanding of human feeling and human illusions of feeling that they force upon the reader."[26] Whereas Eliot read Stendhal as primarily an acute psychologist, Pound would typically define him as more of a philosophe: he ranked him with Voltaire and Flaubert as part of "the traditional struggle, the struggle of driving the shaft of intelligence into the dull mass of mankind." Stendhal's mind, like Pound's, was "the mind aching for something that it can honour under the name of 'civilization' . . . striking at the host of trivial substitutes presented to it."[27]

Stendhal (again like Pound) may have located his ideal civilization in the Italian (or Napoleonic) past, yet he refused to allow his lucidity or his astute analysis of the present to be clouded by romantic nostalgia. He retained the classic virtues of "clear, hard prose" which, Pound insisted, was "the safeguard of civilization and should be valued as such. The mind accustomed to it will not be cheated or stampeded by national phrases and public emotionalities" (P/J, 91). Prose, in short, was synonymous with the critical attitude or what Pound called "French Clarity." Because of this clarity, he wrote in 1918, "France has held firm, has held as no other nation . . . France has had her gushers, but there has been this solid core in her intellectual life,"[28] a core consisting of the tradition of Montaigne, Brantôme, Voltaire, Stendhal, Flaubert, Maupassant, the Goncourts—and of course Gourmont. As opposed to the provincialism and imperialism of Britain, America, and Germany, France, "built on these solidities of sense . . . has had inner strength and a means of communication with the rest of the world. A means of speaking of people *whom she does not govern,* and in whose commercial affairs she may have little concern."[29] Now the key to these solidities of sense was "a speech and a style where word and fact cling together," that is, language based on the Flaubertian precept of le mot juste.[30]

Pound credited Ford with the importation of this concept into England. Ford was preceded, however, by Pater, equally aware that imaginative prose had become "the special and opportune art of the modern world." Pater had written of Flaubert's mot juste in his seminal essay on "Style" in *Appreciations* (1889): "The one word for the one thing, the one thought, amid the multitude of words, terms, that might just do: the problem of style was there!—the unique word, phrase, sentence, paragraph, essay or song, absolutely proper to the single mental presentation or vision within."[31] Though Pater himself displayed keen insight into the author of *Madame Bovary*, his fin-de-siècle disciples tended to discern only the aesthete in Flaubert; he appeared to them primarily as the author of *Salammbô*, *La Tentation de Saint Antoine*, and "Hérodias," and in their hands le mot juste too often became confused with the rare, sonorous verbal jewel, more opalescent than exact.

Pound, approaching Flaubert as Voltaire's heir, construed le mot juste as an ethical precept instead: since technique was the test of a man's sincerity, "the application of word to thing" accordingly became "the very essence" of the literati's work—should that be "slushy and inexact, or excessive or bloated, the whole machinery of social and individual thought and order goes to pot" (LE, 21). The just word, in short, was merely an aspect of that larger ethic of precise definition which Pound would later define politically as Confucian *chêng ming* or economically as the "just price" of medieval canon law. Stylistically, it entailed "expression coterminous with the matter" (GK, 285). Semiotically, it implied an almost mystical belief in the potential identity of the world of signs and the world of things—le mot juste approached the status of the *logos* (or Word) as revealer of the quiddity or essence of things. In a yet broader sense the just word was synonymous with "the value of realism in literature, . . . the value of writing words that conform precisely with fact, . . . free speech without evasions and circumlocution" (LE, 276).

These were of course the same questions *Le Problème du style* explored; indeed, stripped of its scientistic terminology, Gourmont's essay can be seen as the theoretical fruit of his sustained literary preoccupation with Flaubert's work. Style, as Gourmont defined it, "is feeling, seeing, thinking, and nothing more."[32] Or as Pound would echo: "the touchstone of an art is its precision," that is, "the writer says just what he means. He says it with complete clarity and simplicity. He uses the smallest number of words" (LE, 48-50). Economy, accuracy—these were precisely the classic qualities Gourmont consistently praised in Flaubert. With Flaubert, style indeed became the man: he represented the perfect synthesis of visual memory and emotive memory, he exemplified "literary exactitude" ("the conformity of narrative with the images fixed in the brain"), the perfect "symbolic connexity" of word and thing, the absolute identity of form and content, aesthetics and ethics, beauty and truth.[33]

"A false thought can never be well-written, nor a true thought poorly written" was Gourmont's Flaubertian axiom.[34] Pound marked this dictum in his own copy of *Promenades littéraires*: as he would later affirm, one could discern a man's virtue or rightness by the quality of his brushstrokes. As is often the case, Pound is his own best critic: when in the late thirties and forties he writes "kikery" or "judeocracy" as a synecdoche for usury we need go no further than the imprecision of his terminology to know he is utterly wrong, utterly in violation of his own doctrine of le mot juste or *chêng ming*. Whenever Pound's sincere social outrage overcomes his concern for exact definition, the quality of his brushstrokes accordingly declines.

Although references to Flaubert are scattered throughout the *Problème du style*, Gourmont did not analyze his style at length as he did Fénelon's, Chateaubriand's, or Taine's. However, in a chapter devoted to comparison and metaphor he contrasted Flaubertian techniques with those of Homer. The context is significant: though Pound's marginalia indicate that he quarreled with many of Gourmont's points, the juxtaposition of Homer and Flaubert nonetheless quickened his perception of their relation not only to each other but to the larger prose or realist tradition.

Gourmont's discussion was occasioned by Albalat's recommendation of Homer as an absolute stylistic prototype to be imitated. His fundamental disagreement with Albalat's doctrine of imitation was here compounded by the fact that the Homer Albalat proposed as a rhetorical model was not the original but the Homer of Leconte de Lisle's Parnassian translation. Mistaking a poor copy for the real thing, Albalat therefore rested all his theories "on this hypothetical and altogether putative, chimerical Homer who, had he written Greek the way he is made to write French, would be a heavy, grating, clumsy writer of prose" (p. 108). Gourmont spent several pages analyzing Leconte de Lisle's infelicitous attempt to render what he took to be Homer's barbarous ferocity into inert, stilted French: Pound in his essay "Early Translators of Homer" would similarly lambaste nineteenth-century versions for having "neither the concision of verse nor the virtues of direct motion" (LE, 250); in their place, he suggested the earlier translations of, among others, Divus, Chapman, Pope, or Salel (Gourmont mentioned the latter not only in *Le Problème du style* but in his essay "Les Traducteurs"[35]).

Every age, Gourmont noted in *Le Problème du style*, invented its own Homer: "We imagine we understand Homer far better today than did the seventeenth century; we understand him differently, that is all. Undoubtedly archaeology, more reliable exegeses, better methodology have modified the objective aspect of Homer's poems. But if we understand these poems in a manner quite different from that of the contemporaries of Mme Dacier, it is above all because our sensibility has changed since then" (p. 111). In a later essay entitled "La Question d'Homère" Gourmont surveyed the various historical avatars of the bard, concluding with the recent theories of Bréal, which made of Homer very nearly a contemporary. Archaeology had shown that his times were "highly civilized." "Arts flourished, luxury was refined. We know how the ladies of Mycenae dressed from the monuments recently discovered there. Their flouncy dresses, their narrow corsets, their curly coiffures make them like today's women, whose supple, serpentine air they moreover share. Homer, who reflects this civilization, is far from being the barbarian Leconte de Lisle makes him out to be . . . He was a lettered man in the fashion of Dante rather than the inspired improvisor imagined by the Romantics."[36] Whether or not Pound read this essay, the rediscovery of Homer's actuality here registered by Gourmont is, as Kenner demonstrates, basic to that modern renaissance of classical awareness which underlies both Pound's and Joyce's sense of the *Odyssey* as a living text, "composed by a real person in touch with the living details of real cities, real harbors, real bowls and cups and pins and spoons, real kings, real warriors, real houses," and as Gourmont characteristically observes and Pound would show in the *Cantos*, real women.[37]

Gourmont's "La Question d'Homère" appeared in 1912; in *Le Problème du style* of 1902, arguing against the feasibility of literally imitating Homer, he insisted not on the contemporaneity but rather on the archaic quality of the Homeric style: since it expressed a sensibility radically different from the modern, to imitate it would be merely to lapse into the kind of pastiche that he thought characterized Leconte de Lisle's "bas-relief" Homer. Indeed, as Gourmont had argued in an 1899 essay, the latter's version of the *Iliad* suffered precisely because it was too literal, too imagistic:

> Translations too well done, those which one might say possess literary literalness, in fact inevitably end up transforming into live, concrete images everything that in the original had become abstraction. Did λευκοβράχιων mean the white-armed one or had it already become a worn-out epithet? Did λευκακανϑa suggest an image of a "white thornbush" or rather some neutral idea like "hawthorn" which has lost its representational value? We cannot say. But to judge past languages by present ones, we must suppose that the majority of Homeric epithets had already become abstractions by Homer's time.[38]

One need only juxtapose Pound's admiration for Allen Upward's etymological glimpse into the live myth behind the epithet γλαυκῶπις (quoted in SP, 407) to see how profoundly the author of the first Canto would disagree with Gourmont's formulaic Homer. The very stylistic qualities that Gourmont defined as untranslatable and inimitable were to be basic to Pound's renovation of contemporary poetic technique.

Homer's manner, Gourmont observed in *Le Problème du style*, was founded on comparison, "the elementary form of visual imagination." "It precedes metaphor, which is a comparison with one of the terms lacking, unless, that is, the two terms be blended into a single one. There are no metaphors in Homer and this is an undeniable sign of primitivity" (p.

87). The primitive sensibility, Gourmont continued, was incapable of metaphor because it perceived phenomena sequentially; its senses, "well-balanced and crisp, function straightforwardly without encroaching on each other." "Since the sensations are sequential, the language is sequential. Homer describes a fact, then compares it to another analogous fact: the two images always remain distinct, although they can be roughly superimposed . . . Homer is exact because of his inability to lie. He cannot lie: impressions strike him one by one, he describes them in succession, without confusion" (p. 89).

A modern writer such as Flaubert, on the other hand, whose "general sensibility is excessively developed," perceives the world not in literal, sequential fashion but rather in a more complex simultaneous metaphoric manner:

> Flaubert, who has the ability to lie and therefore an infinite capacity for art, is not exact when he writes: "The elephants . . . the spurs of their breast-plates like prows of ships, cut through the cohorts who surged back in great gushes." If he effectively amalgamates the two images (elephants and cohorts, ships and waves), it is only because he has seized them in a single glance. What he gives us are not two pictures that can be symmetrically superimposed, but rather the confusion, visually absurd but artistically admirable, of some dim, twin sensation (p. 90).

Flaubert has here sacrificed visual precision to a more purely imaginative logic: as a result such a passage defies illustration. With Homer, on the other hand, "who presents the two pictures sequentially, there is no problem: an alternating series of panels and diptychs could render the *Iliad* line by line. Images can be translated into painting—a direct and in the end geometrical art—only if they are not metaphors" (p. 90).

Although Pound's Imagism, as we have seen, involved more than mere *ut pictura poesis*, its impulses lay much nearer to the exact visual immediacies of Homer than to the synesthetic cohorts and elephants of *Salammbô*. Indeed, one could argue that Pound's sensibility is very much akin to Gourmont's description of the "sequential mind" ("l'esprit successif")—although Roman Jakobson's account of aphasics with "similarity disorders" would perhaps go further to explain Pound's deep mistrust for metaphor and concomitant predilection for metonymic, predicational forms of ellipsis.[39]

Take for example Pound's account of the origin of his hokku-like "In a Station of the Metro": "Three years ago in Paris I got out of a 'metro' train at La Concorde, and saw suddenly a beautiful face, and then another and another, and then a beautiful child's face, and then another beautiful woman, and I tried all that day to find words for what this had meant to me" (G-B, 87). The sheer parataxis of impressions is reinforced in this account by six "ands" and three "thens" (the most frequent parti-cles in the long poem, which begins "And then . . ."). The distich Pound finally arrived at—

> The apparition of these faces in the crowd,
> Petals on a wet, black bough.

—is not a metaphor but what he called an "equation," a simile with "like" suppressed, a dynamic juxtaposition, an ideogram, "a radiant node or cluster." Though the "intellectual and emotional complex" it presents seems to happen "in an instant of time," the poem has not the simultane-ity or superposition of metaphor: we see the terms of the implied com-parison one after the other; they are no more reversible than the carefully timed order of the words, which succeed each other, as Arnold com-mented of Homer, "stroke on stroke" (LE, 267). Donald Davie confirms this as the characteristic Pound mode: "When Pound is writing at his best we seem to have perceptions succeeding one another at unusual speed at the same time as the syllables succeed one another unusually slowly. But succession, in any case, is what is involved—succession, sequacious-ness."[40]

Pound's Imagist theories had very little to say about metaphor or sim-ile: the Image was a concept that transcended grammatical or rhetorical categories, "the word beyond formulated language" (G-B, 88). He dis-agreed fundamentally, however, with Gourmont's rather Wildean notion of metaphor as a beautiful lie: "The charm of beautiful metaphors is that one enjoys them as one does lies"—to which Pound interpolated in the margin (in French): "is their exactness or their emotional violence," thus perhaps confirming Gourmont's contention that "every sequential mind is inclined to believe in the reality of metaphors" (p. 92). Similarly, when Gourmont quoted what he considered to be one of the rare metaphors in *La Chanson de Roland*—

> Tutes voz amnes ait deus li glorïus;
> En pareïs les mete en seintes flurs.

> Glorious God has all your souls;
> He places them in paradise as holy flowers.

—Pound commented, "*not* metaphor / probably conceived as actual-ity." Most clichés, Gourmont further observed, were once freshly minted metaphors; thus the image of souls/flowers from *Roland* had become so worn as to lose all power. "Exact metaphor does not wear out," was Pound's marginal retort. In sum, Gourmont's interpretation of metaphor tended to turn it into either a fiction or merely a stylistic device easily de-graded to the status of ornament or cliché. For Pound, instead, since "all poetic language is the language of exploration" (G-B, 88), true metaphor constituted, like the Image, a vital and precise mode of knowing, not a fiction, not an imitation, but a literal, permanent actuality.

Pound also disputed Gourmont's preference for *La Chanson de Roland* (whose fanatical hero he would satirize in Canto XX) over the *Iliad*. Gourmont praised the "realist precision" of the "clear-cut Homeric pictures" ("Homer describes wounds in terms that barely differ from those a surgeon might use"), but he personally found the epic similes redundant and distracting (p. 94). *La Chanson de Roland*, by comparison, seemed "more brutally realistic" because "no simile intrudes between our eye and naked fact." "*La Chanson de Roland* is not a poem, it is life itself, fixed, arrested, not in space but in time. It is not art, it is raw reality with all its light, movement, relief, and shadings" (p. 95). Though Pound agreed with Gourmont's criteria of praise, he argued with their application: not the *Chanson de Roland* but the *Poema del Cid*, he observed in the margin (as he had previously in the *Spirit of Romance*), embodied these qualities of realism. Realism—this was what ultimately constituted the true common denominator of Homer and Flaubert, according to Gourmont. If *L'Education sentimentale*, he maintained, was "our *Odyssey*" (p. 25), it was not because Flaubert, had simply imitated the stylistic procedures of Homer, as Albalat implied, but because he had "recounted in synthetic poems the day-to-day existence, be it banal or eccentric, of the men and women of his time."

"Flaubert and Homer—these two names connect in another manner, for Flaubert is our Homer just as he is our Cervantes because of the sheer amount of reality and poetry, of philosophy and anatomy of customs ("physique de moeurs") which his work contains for us" (p. 99). Pound marked this passage heavily: it is pivotal to his entire conception of the prose tradition.

Homer, *La Chanson de Roland*, Flaubert—these three examples of realism analyzed by Gourmont reappear (supplemented by Ovid, Bertran de Born, and Dante) in the same configuration and with similar import in the thumbnail history of mimesis that opens Pound's Canto VII:

> Poor old Homer blind,
> blind as a bat,
> Ear, ear for the sea surge;
>   rattle of old men's voices.
> And then the phantom Rome,
>   marble narrow for seats
> "Si pulvis nullus" said Ovid,
> "Erit, nullum tamen excute."
> Then file and candles, e li mestiers ecoutes;
> Scene for battle only, but still scene,
> Pennons and standards y cavals armatz

Not mere succession of strokes, sightless narration,
And Dante's "ciocco," brand struck in the game.

Un peu moisi, plancher plus bas que le jardin.

"Contre le lambris, fauteuil de paille,
"Un vieux piano, et sous le baromètre. . ."   (VII/24;28)

"Mere succession of strokes, sightless narration" may be, as Pearlman observes,[41] an allusion to the unflagging butchery of Homer's combat descriptions in the *Iliad*, or perhaps a contemptuous reference to the Christian fanaticism of the martial *Chanson de Roland*—at any rate, the line would seem to refract Gourmont's remarks in *Le Problème du style*. The quotations from Flaubert are drawn from a passage in "Un Coeur simple," a work that, Pound wrote in 1918," contain[s] all that anyone knows *about* writing" (L, 89):

> Un vestibule étroit séparait la cuisine de la *salle* où Mme Aubain se tenait tout le long du jour, assise près de la croisée dans un fauteuil de paille. Contre le lambris, peint en blanc, s'alignaient huit chaises d'acajou. Un vieux piano supportait, sous un baromètre, un tas pyramidal de boîtes et de cartons. Deux bergères de tapisserie flanquaient la cheminée en marbre jaune et de style Louis XV. La pendule, au milieu, représentait un temple de Vesta,—et tout l'appartement sentait un peu le moisi, car le plancher était plus bas que le jardin.

> (A narrow vestibule separated the kitchen from the parlor in which Mme Aubain spent her days seated near the casement window in a wicker armchair. Against the paneling, painted white, eight mahogany chairs were aligned. An ancient piano beneath a barometer supported a pyramidal heap of boxes and cartons. Two upholstered easy chairs flanked the yellow marble of the Louis XV mantlepiece. The clock in the middle represented a temple of Vesta—and the entire room had a musty smell to it, for the floor level was lower than the garden.)

Flaubert's paragraph is quite literally a "physique de moeurs," an anatomy of mores. Flaubert reads a room much as Homer catalogs the accoutrements of battle. A psychological analysis of Mme Aubain would be supererogatory: her entire existence, her entire social milieu can be inferred from the objects that clutter her mildewy parlor. Nor is there any need for authorial intervention or editorial comment: Flaubert's function is simply to register metonymic particulars by a "series of precise statements as to what was visible" (P/J, 248). The words, objects, characters will speak for themselves—while their author, like God in the creation, remains invisible, albeit omniscient, omnipresent. This is precisely the "objectivity and again objectivity" Pound sought to impart to contemporary verse (L, 49). Together with le mot juste, it constituted Ford's basic Flaubertian message to Pound: "Never comment: state."[42] Or as Pound defined the "presentative method" in 1913: "It is to modern verse what the method of Flaubert is to modern prose, and by that I do not mean that it is not equally common to the best work of the ancients. It means constation of fact. It presents. It does not comment. It is irrefutable because it does not present a personal predilection for any particular fraction of the truth. It is as uncommunicative as Nature. It is not a criticism of life, I mean it does not deal in opinion. It washes its hands of theories . . . It fights for a sane valuation."[43]

"Realism," Harry Levin reminds us, derives etymologically from the Latin "res."[44] Its rise in the novel coincides with that of capitalism, a system that turns people into things, things into commodities. Its most characteristic province was the nineteenth-century bourgeois interior, a senseless agglomeration of inert, dysfunctional objects, replicas of earlier styles ("la cheminée en marbre jaune et de style Louis XV") or vehicles of ersatz exoticism ("la pendule, au milieu représentait un temple de Vesta"). Pound would liken this nineteenth-century "species of surface" to "a sort of immense cardboard raft intact on, as it were, a cataract of stale sewage. A room of Madame Tussaud's as it might have been" (GK, 82). This is the claustral circle of Hell inhabited by the ghostly husks of men that wander through Canto VII "speaking a shell of speech." Its furnishings are at once those of a Henry James novel (whose "dam'd fuss about furniture," Pound observed, was "foreshadowed by Balzac") and those of the nineteenth-century French interiors inventoried by Flaubert (LE, 308):

> The old men's voices, beneath the columns of false marble,
> The modish and darkish walls,
> . . . . .
> The house too thick, the paintings
> a shade too oiled
> . . . . .
>   Paper, dark brown and stretched,
> Flimsy and damned partition.
> . . . . .
> Low ceiling and the Erard and the silver,
> These are in "time." Four chairs, the bow-front dresser,
> The panier of the desk, cloth top sunk in.
> . . . . .
> Le vieux commode en acajou [sic]   (VII/24-25;28-29)

"Acajou," mahogany—emblem of bourgeois stolidity, pretentious, lugubrious, the least workable of woods; as Pound quoted a French cabinet-maker in a footnote to his *Confucian Odes*, "Il n'y a rien de plus désagréable que l'acajou."[45] Its prevalence in middle-class salons was indicative of the sham luxury, of the debasement of design, that Pound identified as the essential trait of the nineteenth century, "The Age of Usury" par excellence. Flaubert, he stressed, had similarly discerned the degradation of craft, the commodity fetishism, the proliferation of fake art and bibelots, that resulted from a usurious economic infrastructure: "Flaubert saw 'L'art industriel,' he created the real Marxist literature and the Marxist (alleged Marxist) didn't discover it."[46] The shoddy wares of M. Arnoux's commercial art shop and porcelain factory, the inventories of Mme Arnoux's and Emma Bovary's households all attest the same tyrannical hegemony of things over people; they are the running epitaphs on lives suffocated by the sheer accumulation of bric-a-brac:

> (ÀGALMA, haberdashery, clocks, ormoulu, brocatelli,
> tapestries, unreadable volumes in tree-calf,
> half-morocco, morocco, tooled edges, green ribbons,
> flaps, farthingales, fichus, cuties, shorties, pinkies
> et cetera
>   Out of which things seeking an exit   (XL/199;207)

Pound, writing to John Quinn in 1920, considered Canto VII "the best thing I have done" to date:[47] here, for the first time in his poem, he had managed to incorporate novelistic realism and modern states of consciousness into his epic endeavor. Forrest Read has detailed just what a long and arduous struggle this integration of the epic and prose traditions entailed for Pound. His first drafts of the *Cantos*—"a new form" of "meditative / Semi-dramatic, semi-epic story"—were conceived in 1915 in the spirit of Dante's *Divina Commedia*, Whitman's *Leaves of Grass*, and, most notably, Browning's *Sordello*. Yet even as he wrote them, Pound expressed considerable uncertainty about the feasibility of modeling his "rag-bag" for the modern world "to stuff all its thought in" on these poetic models. Was Browning's dramatic and historic method adequate to the epic synthesis of modern consciousness, he asked in the original Canto I, or would he simply have to "sulk and leave the word to novelists" (P/J, 48-49)?

Pound would not fully resolve the question until he entirely revised the opening of his poem in 1923, substituting Homer for Browning and making Odysseus his central figure. Joyce, as has become increasingly apparent, played a major role in this reorganization of the *Cantos*, since his *Ulysses* seemed to come closest to providing a solution to the problems of modern epic form with which Pound had been struggling since the inception of the *Cantos*.[48] An "epoch-making report on the state of the human mind in the twentieth century" (LE, 408), as *Bouvard et Pécuchet* had been of the nineteenth, *Ulysses* conflated Homer with the modern prose tradition to achieve a major form that was at once classic and contemporary, epic and novelistic, archetypal and local.

Joyce, however, was not the sole figure to bring the modern realist novel into the context of the traditional epic. This was the major thrust of Gourmont's comments on Homer and Flaubert in *Le Problème du style:* both were realist because both were engaged in recording the mores of their contemporary ages—Pound would echo Gourmont in calling Homer a "study in moeurs" (GK, 146). Going against the prevalent tastes of his period, Gourmont accordingly preferred the Flaubert of *Madame Bovary*, *L'Education sentimentale*, and *Bouvard et Pécuchet* (which together, he noted, constituted an epic) to the author of *La Tentation* and *Salammbô*: "Flaubert's most admired books today, *La Tentation* and *Salammbô* (achievements which would nonetheless suffice to establish *two* major writers), are the least pure and least beautiful of his works. There are no books (real books) save those where an author has presented himself in presenting the customs of his contemporaries, their dreams, their vanities, their loves, and their follies" (p. 105).

Pound used this passage as the epigraph to his 1917 review of Eliot's *Prufrock and Other Observations*. Eliot, he pointed out, "has placed his people in contemporary settings, which is much more difficult than to render them with medieval romantic trappings" (LE, 420)—perhaps an allusion to the troubadour archaism that Pound was still trying to eliminate from his own verse. The antidote he prescribed for himself (the parallel with Flaubert is salient) was the "sterilized surgery" of the *Lustra* volume (PD, 72) and, specifically, the series of portraits entitled "Moeurs Contemporaines" (which were among the first poems Pound chose to have translated into French, no doubt considering them closest to the modern French prose tradition of such satirists as Tailhade).[49]

"Moeurs Contemporaines" is a key term in both Gourmont's and Pound's conception of realism. *Moeurs*—whereas two distinct English words are needed to convey the full range of the term, the strength of the nineteenth-century French novel lay precisely in its unflinching realistic synthesis of both "manners" and "morals." Neither "the Christmas spirit" of Dickens nor Henry James's "desire to square all things to the ethical standards of a Salem mid-week Unitarian meeting" (LE, 299) were capable of achieving the scientific impartiality that Pound found most concisely expressed in the Goncourts' preface to *Germinie Lacerteux*: "Now that the novel is growing and expanding and is beginning to be the serious, passionate and living form of literary inquiry and social investigation, now that, through analysis and psychological research, it is becoming the history of contemporary manners and morals ("L'Histoire morale contemporaine"), now that the novel has adopted the investigations and duties of science, it can claim a right to the latter's freedom and frankness" (LE, 417).

"L'Histoire moral contemporaine" would become another touchstone for Pound: he rendered it variously as "the history of contemporary customs" (SP, 456), "the history of contemporary ethics-in-action" (P/J, 71), "the history of contemporary moral disposition," "the history of the estimation of values in contemporary behavior" (ABC, 77). The emphasis on contemporaneity is significant: whatever its setting, the novel was to be, as nearly as possible, history in the present tense. Pound was fond of quoting Gourmont's quip to this effect: "Le roman historique. Il y a aussi la penture historique, l'architecture historique, et, à la mi-carême, le costume historique" ("The historical novel. There is also historical painting, historical architecture, and, during carnival season, historical costume": LE, 353). Flaubert's *Tentation* and *Salammbô*, Pound agreed with Gourmont, fell into this category of costume drama because they dealt not with the immediacy but with the exoticism of the past. *La Tentation de Saint Antoine* struck Pound as mere *"jettatura . . .* the effect of Flaubert's time on Flaubert," "something which matters now only as archaeology" (LE, 406-407). As for *Salammbô* (and the short story "Hérodias"), Pound translated Laforgue's *Salomé* primarily to demonstrate that "the real criticism of an author is found not in the incompetents who talk about him, but in the creating writers who follow him; thus the real criticism of *Salammbô* and "Hérodias" is found in Laforgue's *Moralités Légendaires;* and the historical, period, *costume historique*, archaeologically *rempli*, novel has never recovered from Laforgue's analysis."[50]

Pound's treatment of Hanno in Canto XL provides a concise instance of his fundamental divergence from the Flaubert of *Salammbô*. Flaubert's Carthage is so freighted with lush, antiquarian detail, so "archaeologically *rempli*," that its opulent particulars remain almost wholly static, impacted. The Hanno of the *Cantos*, by comparison, achieves universality precisely because he is *not* presented as an exotic. Pound is content simply to translate and edit Hanno's own account of his voyage (or *periplus*) down the coast of Africa: the document will speak for itself and the attentive reader will seize the rhyme with the Odyssean archetype, which makes of Hanno, like so many figures in the *Cantos*, a participant in that continuous present that includes all time and makes all history potentially "l'histoire morale contemporaine."

It was not to the *Tentation* or *Salammbô*, then, but to *Madame Bovary* and *L'Education sentimentale* that Pound, like Gourmont, looked for the resolution of the transient into the permanent, of the local into the universal, of the individual into the typical: "Flaubert gives us in each main character: *Everyman*. One may conceivably be bored by certain pages in Flaubert, but one takes from him a solid and concrete memory, a property. Emma Bovary and Frédéric and M. Arnoux are respectively every woman and every man of their period. Maupassant's Bel Ami is not. Neither are Henry James' people. They are always, or nearly always, the bibelots . . . [James] never manages the classic" (LE, 300).

Pound used very nearly the same terms in comparing James to Gourmont: whereas the former, "concerned with . . . circumvolvulous social pressures, the clash of contending conventions," had "left his scenes and his characters, unalterable as the little paper flowers permanently visible inside the lumpy glass paperweights," Gourmont's fictional characters were "all studies in different *permanent* kinds of people . . . not the results of environments or of 'social causes' " (LE, 339-340). Though James had applied the analytical techniques of "l'histoire morale contemporaine" to the upper classes of society (Pound would for this reason habitually group him with the Goncourts and Proust rather than with Flaubert), he remained incapable of generalizing his dense accumulations of social detail into universals. "James' lamentable lack of the classics" was at root "responsible for his absorption in bagatelles . . . He has no real series of backgrounds of *moeurs du passé*, only the 'sweet dim faded lavender' tone in opposition to modernity, plus nickel-plated, to the disparagement, naturally, of the latter" (LE, 323). Flaubert, on the other hand, an avid reader of the Greek classics and of Shakespeare, was so sensitive to the present because of his deep awareness of the past. He possessed what Pound called a Goethean "Weltliteratur standard" and his art therefore was "the art of 'generalization,' that is, he presumably sought conditions, facts, relations which would be unaltered by *milieu*."[51]

To Pound, one aspect of Flaubert's "art of generalization" was his "avoidance of the anecdote and accidental." He presented "the inevitable and the quotidian" with the tragic insinuation that "nothing any character will *do* will alter his case."[52] Flaubert's characters thus became Everyman inasmuch as their individual destinies were all governed by a larger fate inherent both in their milieu and in their own human limitations. Because he consistently delineated "the typical thing in timbre and quality," Flaubert, like Joyce, was therefore fundamentally "classic"—"he deals with normal things and with normal people" (LE, 303). The provincial mores analyzed in *Madame Bovary* or the city habits of *L'Education* (or of *Dubliners* or *A Portrait*) could be generalized to apply to all provinces or all metropolises: a Henry James drawing room, on the other hand, remained merely an "elaborate analysis of the much too special cases" in much too psychological a manner (LE, 323,403). Flaubert's work, by contrast, was effective as social history precisely because "he is definitely treating man, or woman, not specifically as to their own insides; by which I don't mean to imply that he neglects their subjectivity, but he is, as probably no man before him, concerned with their relation to the whole order of the age."[53]

Pound discerned similar qualities in Flaubert's *Trois Contes*. Apart from his interest in their formal compression (he conceived the modern short story as the intermediary genre between the epic sweep of the novel and the succinctness of the contemporary lyric), Pound came to see the *Trois Contes* as constructed around a single core image or motif, a kind of "great Bass" or root fact, which governed the entire design of the work. As he observed in the *Mercure de France*, they were built around a single "généralisation qui agit non seulement sur le nombre, sur la multiplicité, mais dans la permanence" (P/J, 207). They composed "un tout qui se balance sur la phrase: 'Et l'idée lui vint d'employer son existence au service des autres,' qui se trouve au milieu de 'Saint Julien' " (P/J, 201). The pivot or kernel of *Trois Contes* was thus, as Pound finely sensed, charity—the same *caritas* that he so valued in Gourmont and that would later permeate the Pisan Cantos as a leitmotif; "the work itself," Pound commented in the *Dial*, "may give the skilled reader a fairly good idea of the author, and one is not in the least surprised to find that Flaubert when over fifty, impoverished himself to save a nephew-in-law from bankruptcy. It is the kind of thing a man who wrote as Flaubert wrote, would do."[54]

Trois Contes presented three versions of sanctity, ranging from the saintly stupidity of Felicité to the more traditional hagiography of St. Julian and the martyrdom of St. John—three distinct instances of "permanent kinds of people," drawn from three historical eras, Biblical antiquity, the Middle Ages, and the contemporary world. As Read observes, Pound would employ a similar strategy in his *Poems 1918-1921*, juxtaposing *Propertius*, *Langue d'Oc / Moeurs Contemporains*, and *Mauberley* as *Three Portraits* of, respectively, Rome, Provence-London, and London, all presumably revolving around a core line, the Propertian (or Gourmontian) "My genius is no more than a girl"—that is, love as an emotional and intellectual instigation.[55] This kind of analogical staggering of historical periods around a central motif was, however, only a preliminary step towards the techniques of the *Cantos*. Though Flaubert's three lives suggested archetypes, it was Joyce who fully developed the implications of Flaubertian method into the radical synchrony of *Ulysses*. Pound wrote in the *Mercure*: "Joyce combine le moyen âge, les ères classiques, même l'antiquité juive, dans une action actuelle; Flaubert échelonne les époques" (P/J, 207). Joyce tilted the horizontal historical axis of the *Trois Contes* towards a vertical superposition of actualities, thus confirming one of Pound's earliest intuitions: "All ages are contemporaneous" (SOR, 8).

The coalescence of universal and particular into a Goethean concrete universal (*concret Allgemeine*: see VIII/31;35), the synthesis of "l'histoire morale contemporaine" with the classic art of generalization, the blending of the historical with the archetypical—all underlie Pound's maxim, "Literature is news that STAYS news" (ABC, 29).

Pound first explored this notion in a 1920 *New Age* article: "Mr Shaw is now out for journalism. He has been heard declaring that all great literature is journalism."[56] Pound found Shaw's statement too narrow, however, because it ignored the crucial fact that "literature is . . . concerned with the permanent elements of life" even though it often "bridges the gap from the profound to the trivial by contemporaneous detail." Flaubert's "Un Coeur simple," for example, was not mere journalism: "you cannot put a date on it. Among its tens of thousands of readers, there is not one to say whether it happened in the 'fifties or the 'eighties." Shaw's "yawp about journalism" was furthermore just "a one-dimensional crib from something De Gourmont once presented in three dimensions," namely: "There are no books (real books) save those where an author has presented himself in presenting the customs of his contemporaries, their dreams, their vanities, their loves, and their follies." "The hallmark of journalism," Pound contended, "is precisely that the author does not present himself." Gourmont's axiom therefore entailed far more than journalism because it placed an equal emphasis on the authorial and the reportorial, on the presentation of both subjective and objective fact.

Gourmont had made his comments in *Le Problème du style* in the context of a discussion of Flaubert's vaunted impersonality:

> Life is a sloughing-off process ("un dépouillement"). The proper end of a man's activities is to cleanse his personality, to scour it of all the stains deposited by education, to free it from all the imprints left by adolescent admirations. A time comes when the burnished coin is clean and shines with its own metal . . . Since Flaubert is one of the most profoundly personal writers who ever existed, one of those who may be read most clearly through the lacework of style, one can easily follow the man's progressive sloughing-off process throughout his work (p. 104).

Eliot quoted this passage in *The Sacred Wood*, and as several critics have shown, his "Impersonal theory of poetry" owes much to Gourmont's observations in *Le Problème du style* and other works.[57] Despite Pound's play with personae, he was ultimately far less involved than Eliot in the elaborate tactics of authorial invisibility and impersonation, nor did he entirely agree with Stephen Daedalus's Flaubertian axiom, "The artist, like the God of the creation, remains within or behind or beyond or above his handiwork, invisible, refined out of existence, indifferent, paring his fingernails."[58] Whether the author was Propertius, Villon, or John Adams, Pound remained fascinated with the intimate voice of the man in his milieu, that is, how he "presented himself in presenting the customs of his contemporaries." As Gourmont observed, "only mediocre works are impersonal . . . To be impersonal is to be personal in a special manner. In jargon one might say: the objective is one of the forms of the subjective."[59]

115

Flaubert's progressive "dépouillement" thus had little to do with depersonalization or Parnassian impassivity. Though his writing seemed, superficially, to evolve towards an increasing objectivity, its real development in fact lay in the opposite direction. Flaubert, Gourmont commented in *Le Problème du style*, "transfused himself drop by drop, down to the very dregs" (p. 107) in all of his works, and nowhere more so than in the unfinished *Bouvard et Pécuchet*, the culminating book of his epic. In the very process of recounting "the hopes and disappointments of a century," Flaubert had here laid his own heart bare: "This book is so personal, so woven as it were from nervous fibers, that one has never been able to add a page to it which did not produce the effect of a swatch of rough cloth on a tulle dress. The miracle is that this work of flesh seems entirely ethereal. At first it seems like a catalog of small experiments which any man who took the trouble could complete. But one cannot meddle with it: it is a living animal that thrashes and screams as soon as one plunges a needle into it to make the seam" (p. 106).

According to Gourmont, then, Flaubert's work was at once autobiographical and epic. Though his anatomy of mores dealt with the data of the historian or journalist, it achieved richer dimensions because so intimately pervaded and unified by Flaubert's own "powerful sensibility— excessive, domineering, extravagant" (p. 106). Gourmont's remarks on Flaubert can be compared to Pound's early definition of the epic from the personal standpoint as "the speech of a nation through the mouth of one man" (Villon or Whitman, for example) and his later, more objective formulation of it as "a poem including history." The *Cantos*, at once autobiography and epic, are in one sense the record of Pound's attempt to reconcile these two impulses.

As Pound's awareness of his vocation as economist and historian grew during the late twenties and thirties, his *Cantos* tended increasingly toward the latter, toward a more objective inclusion of history. More and more convinced that official historians were engaged in the systematic obfuscation of, among other matters, the nature of usury, Pound felt it his duty to uncover what he termed the "real" or "secret" history that had been omitted from the record (GK, 263). History became for him a plot, in both senses of the term: first, as a gigantic conspiracy on the part of the usurers and their hirelings, the historians; and second, as a logical chain of events rigorously determined by such economic causalities as interest rates.

It is in this context that Pound's later reading of Flaubert as historian should be located: "the Flaubertian concept of 'l'histoire morale contemporaine,' " he wrote in the late thirties, "arose from . . . a perception of the paucity registered in historians, the shallowness of their analysis of motivation, their inadequate measurements of causality" (SP, 149). Flaubert's social history in, say, *L'Education sentimentale* remained invaluable because he simply "set down an intelligible record of life in which things happened . . . he was thinking of history without the defects of generic books by historians which miss the pith and point of the story" (SP, 152). Indeed, "the real history of France during the age of infamy," Pound insisted in *Guide to Kulchur,* "was Flaubert and co. The intellectual struggle against political pimpery, frumpery, and finance" (GK, 264).

It would be misleading, however, to utterly dissociate Pound's later, more politicized reading of Flaubert from his earlier remarks on "l'histoire morale contemporaine." Already in 1917 he had defined realist literature as "letting the big cat out of the bag." "It is giving away the gigantic or established show, when the show is an hypocrisy; it is giving away with an ultimate precision. Shakespeare's 'Histories' gave away the show of absolute monarchy. They are the greatest indictment ever written. The realist novels let out the cats of modernity, many forms of many oppressions, personal tyrannies and group tyrannies."[60]

Realist literature (in the Gourmontian sense, by which even Shakespeare's record of contemporary mores was realist) thus appeared to Pound as primarily a literature of dissent: constatation implicitly involved contestation. And since Pound often quoted Edmond de Goncourt's triple definition of the modern novelist "as a physician, as a savant, as a historian" (P/J, 72), it is with the medical function of literature's ultimate precision that one should correlate the above passage.

> As there are in medicine the art of diagnosis and the art of cure, so in the arts, so in the particular arts of poetry and of literature, there is the art of diagnosis and there is the art of cure. They call one the cult of ugliness and the other the cult of beauty. The cult of beauty is the hygiene, it is sun, air, and the sea and the rain and the lake bathing. The cult of ugliness, Villon, Baudelaire, Corbière, Beardsley are diagnosis. Flaubert is diagnosis. Satire, if we are to ride this metaphor to staggers, satire is surgery, insertions and amputations. (LE, 45)

Although these two cults were not mutually exclusive, Pound tended to associate the art of diagnosis with prose and the art of cure with poetry; further on in this same important 1913 essay, "The Serious Artist," he extended the antithesis, linking prose with "the precisions of the intellect" and poetry with the "passionate moment" or "emotional surges" (LE, 53). By 1918, writing on Henry James, Pound had yet further generalized the root difference between the two arts of literature: "Most good prose arises, perhaps, from an instinct of negation; is the detailed, convincing analysis of something detestable; of something which one wants to eliminate. Poetry is the assertion of a positive, i.e. of desire . . . Poetry = Emotional synthesis" (LE, 324). Pound's distinction between prose and poetry, as his remarks on Joyce's scatology clearly indicate, can be reduced to an even more fundamental anatomy of style—the excremental ("something which one wants to eliminate") verses the phallic assertion of desire (P/J, 146).

Pound's definitions are a Gourmontian exercise in the dissociation of ideas: by emphasizing polarities he generates the tensions that will impel him toward a literary form large enough and flexible enough to contain, and ideally to combine, diagnosis and cure, intellectual analysis and emotional synthesis, negation and assertion, prose and poetry. Thus, although Pound, like Gourmont, conceived the motive of his art as an essentially phallic affirmation of the life-force, he also felt it his function as a social and literary critic to "construct cloacae to carry off waste matter" (LE, 191). Indeed, whenever involved in negation (or worse, vituperation), Pound's imagery frequently lapses into the scatological or visceral: the evil that obsesses him is a malign perversion of that fluid formative crystal which Pound luminously associates with Aphrodite, and, as Cantos XIV and XV most clearly demonstrate, most often takes the guise of an amorphous, viscous, clotted liquefaction which must be eliminated before the new phallic synthesis, be it poetic or economic, can be achieved.

Pound assigned literature's purgative function to prose: he saw Joyce's *Ulysses* as an "immense catharsis," a work of "diagnosis and cure" in which "the sticky molasses-covered filth of current print, all the fuggs, all the foetors, the whole boil of the European mind, had been lanced" (GK, 96). Behind Joyce's encyclopedic evacuation, however, there lay Cervantes "chewing up the Spanish Romances," Rabelais "chewing up scholastic bunk and the idolatry of written words in his own day" (P/J, 250), and, more immediately, the "great engineering feat," the "huge labour of drainage and sanitation" that constituted Flaubert's encyclopedia in farce, *Bouvard et Pécuchet*.[61]

Henry James had found the "drollery" of *Bouvard et Pécuchet* "about as contagious as the smile of the keeper showing you through the ward of a madhouse."[62] The Paterians, interested primarily in Flaubert's exotic opalescences, passed over the work in silence. Even such a Flaubertian as Pound's and Yeats's friend, Sturge Moore, made little more than peripheral reference to it in his studies of the master.[63] True, Ford had spoken occasionally of *Bouvard et Pécuchet* and of accepted ideas in *The Critical Attitude*, but he remained too much the Pre-Raphaelite to fathom the novel's formal implications.

Gourmont, almost alone among French and English critics of the period, was much more prescient in his appreciation of the work, which in *Le Problème du style* he called "this book which can only be compared to *Don Quixote* and which . . . will remain the item in the archives whereby posterity will be able to read clearly the hopes and disappointments of an entire century" (p. 106). Pronouncing it "a work beyond which there is nothing, a unique work, without visible style, without imagination, without ornament of any sort, a work stripped of everything that makes a novel pleasing, and yet is the most moving of novels,"[64] Gourmont astutely grasped the revolutionary nature of Flaubert's experiment: he had gone beyond the structures of the traditional novel to write "the book *par excellence*, the book for the strong-minded" ("le livre pour les forts").[65]

Pound and Eliot no doubt considered themselves among the select circle of "forts" to whom the work appealed. Eliot would express their mutual admiration for *Bouvard et Pécuchet* (and for each other) in his 1917 parody, "Eeldrop and Appleplex."

> Both were endeavouring to escape not the commonplace, respectable or even the domestic, but the too well pigeonholed, too taken-for-granted, too highly systematized areas, and, —in the language of those whom they sought to avoid—they wished "to apprehend the human soul in its concrete individuality."
>
> . . . It may be added that Eeldrop was a sceptic, with a taste for mysticism, and Appleplex a materialist with a leaning towards scepticism; that Eeldrop was learned in theology and that Appleplex studied the physical and biological sciences.[66]

Eeldrop-Eliot was, in certain respects, the more Gourmontian of the two:

> "The artistic temperament—" began Appleplex.
> "No, not that." Eeldrop snatched away the opportunity. "I mean that what holds the artist together is the work which he does; separate him from his work and he either disintegrates or solidifies. There is no interest in the artist apart from his work."[67]

Eeldrop had obviously been reading the observations on Flaubert in *Le Problème du style:* "Outside of his books into which he transfused himself drop by drop down to the very dregs, Flaubert is not very interesting. He remains nothing but dregs: his intelligence clouds over, exasperated by incoherent fantasies . . . Far from being impersonal in his works, the roles are here reversed: it is the man who is vague and woven with incoherences; whereas it is the work that lives, breathes, and smiles with nobility" (p. 107). Appleplex ("who had the gift of an extraordinary address with the lower classes of both sexes" whereas Eeldrop "preserved a more passive demeanor") possessed the greater talent for sociological fieldwork and, with Eeldrop's help, was working on a massively documented "Survey of Contemporary Society"—an allusion to Pound's 1917 *New*

Age series, "Studies in Contemporary Mentality," an investigation of the current British periodical press.

Pound explained the impulse behind his survey in the second install-ment of the series: "A passion to convey realism further than Zola has led me to record the details of human utterance as carefully as he recorded the newspaper details relative to 'La Débâcle.' "[68] Pound's true mentor in this nineteen-part series, however, was not Zola but Flaubert who in the process of documenting *Bouvard et Pécuchet* had ploughed through some 1500 subliterary texts in order to prepare what Pound called "his immense diagnosis of the contemporary average mind."[69] Pound's excur-sion into the literary sociology of the contemporary average mind was journalistic hackwork to be sure, but it nevertheless netted him some valuable insights.

Pound vented his greatest contempt on such serious periodicals as *Blackwood's* and the *Edinburgh Review* (which had taken up "with Claudel and that kind of messiness," though they did "seem to have been aware of the French XVIIIth century"[70]). He reserved his more Voltairean scorn for publications like *The Christian Herald* and proffered against their fanaticism his own "CREED OF ANTICHRIST" ("Intellectual Hon-esty, the Abolition of Violence, the Fraternal Deference of Confucius, and Internationalism"[71]). More sympathetic was his treatment of the fic-tion of pulp magazines, whose romantic stories about young typists (compare *The Wasteland*?) were based on an "abstract sort of writing" not unlike that of the Morality Plays and their figure of Everyman.[72] "The no-man's land of the unexplored popular heart" had not lost touch with the older spirit of romance: "The most wildly romantic and melo-dramatic writer always has this one advantage over the professed 'real-ist,' that whenever anything 'happens' in real life it is often in excess of 'fiction,' of the patterns of life already portrayed . . . The 'unlikely' ele-ment in romance has a profound value, a value that no aesthetic, no theory of literature can afford to omit from its scheme of things."[73] The worship of Sherlock Holmes, Pound observed of *The Strand*, was simi-larly a degradation of an essentially mythic impulse: "whenever art gets beyond itself, and laps up too great a public, it at once degenerates into religion."[74]

Despite his mandarin mask, Pound had a keen appreciation for the mythos preserved in popular or folk culture, for "Disney against the metaphysicals" (CXVI/796). In fact, during his Rapallo years he would become, with Yeats, an avid reader of detective novels: "some day the novelists will admit that the technique of the 'tec' is just as serious a part of the total novelist's technique as any other. For 20 years we have looked for the criminal," he wrote in 1939[75]—and the Cantos he was composing during this period often seem like some immense detective story, with Sherlock-Pound sleuthing out the root of evil; "19 years on this case," he reported in Canto XLVI, "I have set down part of / The Evidence" (XLVI/234;245).

Pound learned a great deal about the art of setting down evidence from Flaubert. Gourmont had described and quoted at length from the "Dictionnaire des idées reçues" (the *sottisier* appended to *Bouvard et Pécuchet*) in his "Flaubert et la Bêtise humaine" (included in *Promenades littéraires*, 4th series). As early as 1914 Pound was using the stratagem Gourmont had made available to him in the *Egoist*, culling a medley of snippets from the current press (the *Times Literary Supplement* was a favorite source) and printing them, without comment, under such rubrics as "Revolutionary Maxims," "Revelations," "Inconsiderable Imbecilities." In 1917, again in the *Egoist*, he published a satirical compendium of Joyce criticism, consisting solely of a string of excerpts from adverse reviews of *Dubliners* and *A Portrait* (P/J, 118). Quotation, be it in *sottisier* form or, as more frequently in the *Cantos*, in the shape of a cento, is simply the doctrine of constatation or presentation carried to its purest extreme. To indict one need only cite: the evidence will speak for itself. As Kenner makes clear, Flaubert ideally hoped that the French bourgeois, after reading the "Dictionnaire des idées reçues," would no longer dare open his mouth for fear of uttering one of the phrases it contained—diagnosis here entails what he calls a "feedback loop,"[76] although medically one should perhaps rather speak of homeopathy, like curing like.

The art of quotation, however, should not be confused with mimesis: it is a mode not merely of copying or reflecting but of including the real— much as a cubist collage includes a metro ticket or newspaper headline. In a larger sense yet, quotation involves shifting the emphasis from language as a means of representation to language as the very object of representation. To quote is thus to adduce words as facts, as exhibits, as documents, to lift them out of context, to isolate them, to make them self-evident. It is a technique basic to the strategy of much modern art. When Duchamp exhibited a urinal at the Armory Show as a "readymade," he was engaged in quotation: by displaying his objet trouvé in a museum he was in essence placing quotation marks around it, ironically citing the functional as the aesthetic (and thus subversively devalorizing both). It would become a standard tactic of Dadaist and Surrealist antiart, exemplified in their found poems.

Pound's important essays on *Bouvard et Pécuchet* and *Ulysses* coincided with his association with the Parisian avant-garde of the early twenties. Seen in the light of their analogous experiments, his extensive and multifaceted use of quotations in the *Cantos* no longer appears an idiosyncratic aberration but rather a logical development of a modernist aesthetic that can be traced back to those techniques of constatation and subversive juxtaposition that Flaubert applied at almost every level of his art. Word placed against word, detail against detail, phrase against phrase, interact within invisible quotation marks to build the intricate rhythmic and tonal nuances of the Flaubertian paragraph—or perhaps one should say stanza, for as Pound observed in the *Dial*, Flaubert "was the first prose writer, perhaps, who dared to write a paragraph of prose presentation with the economy and 'perfection' that songsters had before him reserved for the lyric, the sonnet, the triolet."[77] What Pound called these "series of island paragraphs marvellously clear and condensed"[78] are, as in the famous Agricultural Fair scene of *Madame Bovary*, in turn juxtaposed to elicit subtle ironic incongruities between narrative empathy and detachment, between elation and deflation, between lyric epiphany and crushing cliché. Pound would equally define "such swift alternation of the subjective beauty and external shabbiness, squalor and sordidness" and "the bass and treble" of Joyce's method (LE, 412). The *Cantos*, too, abound with examples of this kind of cinematic montage in which the poet cuts, without copula or transition, from one structural component to the next (be it a single word, a line, a strophe, an entire Canto, or block of Cantos), alternating "subjective beauty" and "external shabbiness," ideogrammically "presenting one facet and then another until at some point one gets off the dead surface of the reader's mind onto a part that will register" (GK, 51).

The significant action of a Flaubert novel, as Kenner observes with contemporary French structuralists, does not reside so much in a diagrammable plot as in the interaction of the various tensions he sets up between words, tones, moods, things: one can no more paraphrase *L'Education sentimentale* or *Bouvard et Pécuchet* than a Symbolist poem—or for that matter, a plotless epic such as the *Cantos*.[79] "Relations are more real and important than the things which they relate," insisted that theorist of natural and verbal patternings, Ernest Fenollosa, almost echoing Flaubert's comment to Maupassant, "Il n'y a de vrai que les rapports" ("Only relations are true").[80] In Flaubert's hands, however, such relations are frequently vehicles less of metaphor or revelation than of destructive irony. He associates ideas (or words or objects) only in order to heighten their incongruities; the items thus set side by side, as in the description of Charles' hat at the beginning of *Madame Bovary* or the countless dreary inventories of *L'Education sentimentale*, seem merely senseless agglomerations, interacting incoherently in their contiguity to cancel each other out. Details, facts, events assume no hierarchical relationship or order among themselves but rather are leveled to an essential (democratic) sameness and meaninglessness. Particulars are isolated only to be dissolved into a single amorphous fluidity that permeates everything with the monotony of ennui. Juxtaposition becomes a mode of subversive equation, the key operation in what Anthony Thorlby calls "an immensely complex and comprehensive mathematical formula which makes everything equal zero."[81]

Flaubert achieved this encyclopedic nullity most devastatingly in *Bouvard et Pécuchet*, which is perhaps why Gourmont called it his "livre pour les forts." Though Pound had reread the work in late 1918, he did not fully grasp its implications until his essays of 1922—the year of Flaubert's centenary and "the first of a new era," as he labeled it, for it coincided with the epoch-making publication of *Ulysses*, true successor to the "new form in literature" initiated by *Bouvard et Pécuchet* (P/J, 201). Summarizing the major outlines of Flaubert's oeuvre, Pound wrote in the *Mercure* (my translation):

> Although *Bouvard et Pécuchet* does not pass for the master's "finest work," one can maintain that *Bovary* and *L'Education* are but the apogee of an earlier form, and that the *Trois Contes* give a kind of summary of everything Flaubert had acquired while writing his other novels . . . *Bouvard et Pécuchet* carries on the thought and art of Flaubert but does not perpetuate the tradition of the novel or short story. One can consider the "Encyclopedia in farce," whose subtitle is "Lack of method in the sciences," the inauguration of a new form, a form without precedent. (P/J, 201)

One aspect of what Pound called Flaubert's "radical progress in method" was that *Bouvard et Pécuchet* seemed, as Gourmont had remarked, "without visible style, without imagination, without ornament of any sort . . . stripped of everything that makes a novel pleasing."[82] Of plot it apparently had little, of characterization even less; its verbal medium was created out of the subliterary flotsam and jetsam of contemporary culture; its subject was not so much any external action as the nature and process of thought itself. Flaubert had accordingly substituted for the traditional conventions of the novel a form derived from the very structure of the modern average mind, that is, an encyclopedic inventory of *idées reçues*, a comic catalog of platitudes, repeatable ad infinitum.

Though the form of *Bouvard et Pécuchet* distinguished it from the rest of Flaubert's oeuvre, it carried to their logical reduction (ad absurdum) the diagnoses undertaken in his previous major novels. *Madame Bovary* had been a book about the dangers of books, an antinovel, "a sort of specific for literary diabetes" (P/J, 252), despite the fact that Flaubert, like Cervantes, had attacked "only one form of hyperbole," "only one literary folly, the folly of chivalry" (or in Emma Bovary's case, the folly of Romanticism).[83] The analysis of the failure of political and amatory ideals in *L'Education sentimentale* had been yet broader in import; in a 1917 article Pound compared it to Joyce's *Portrait*: "Flaubert pointed out that if France had studied his work they might have been saved a good deal in 1870. If more people had read the *Portrait* and certain stories in Mr. Joyce's *Dubliners* there might have been less recent trouble in Ireland. A clear diagnosis is never without its value" (P/J, 90). (Pound often returned to this Flaubertian anecdote, which he had probably heard from Ford.[84] Later, as World War II loomed, he would see his own works, both economic and poetic, as having a similar diagnostic, preventive function.) In *Bouvard et Pécuchet*, Flaubert's attempt "to make humanity aware of itself" (LE, 297) achieved its ultimate exasperated generalization: he was diagnosing not the pathology of Romanticism nor of modern political ideology, not the mores of the provinces nor those of city life, but the very bankruptcy of culture itself.

Flaubert's disconsolate reaction to the debacle of 1870 in a sense paralleled the intellectual nihilism that overtook the postwar avant-garde: before the Dadaists, he had inaugurated a literature of aftermath. As Pound put it:

> Civilization, as Flaubert had known it, appeared to be foundering. Gautier died, as Flaubert wrote, "suffocated by modern stupidity," and Flaubert thinking of Gautier feels "as if a tide of filth" were rising around him and submerging him. This tide of *immondices* must be considered as messy thought, general muddle. "We pay for the long deceit in which we have lived, everything was false, false army, false politics, and false credit." "The present is abominable, and the future ferocious." So run the phrases of his correspondence. And the old man's last stand against this tide is his "dictionnaire des idées reçues," his encyclopedia *en farce;* his gargantuan collection of imbecilities, of current phrases . . . Thus Flaubert goes about making his immense diagnosis of the contemporary average mind. And this average mind is our king, our tyrant, replacing Oedipus and Agamemnon in our tragedy.

Pound added a typically political twist to this tragedy "of democracy, of modernity."

> It is this human stupidity that elects the Wilsons and Ll. Georges and puts power into the hands of the gun-makers, demanding that they blot out the sunlight, that they crush out the individual and the perception of beauty. This flabby blunt-wittedness is the tyrant.[85]

The tyranny of stupidity affected far more than the political realm, however. As Gourmont's investigations into the association and dissociation of ideas had shown, this same human stupidity ("la bêtise humaine, la seule chose qui donne une idée de l'infini"—Pound quoting Gourmont quoting Renan) penetrated "the whole mental structure" of the age and underlay the paralysis of live thought into inert accepted ideas, the collapse of ordered knowledge into encyclopedic clutter.[86] Gourmont had observed, alluding to Bouvard and Pécuchet's incoherent horticultural endeavors, that "an average brain today resembles those experimental gardens that cultivate specimens of every kind of flora"—such gardens having as their only principle that haphazard encyclopedism that Flaubert keenly sensed was the major mode of knowledge in his time.[87] An encyclopedia, as Kenner describes it, "takes all that we know apart into little pieces, and then arranges those pieces so that they can be found one at a time. It is produced by a feat of organization, not a feat of understanding."[88] Its effect is thus at once a fragmentation, a sorting of knowledge into arbitrary pigeonholes, and at the same time the wholesale lumping of discrete facts into one indiscriminate bolus. The categories into which it distributes its omnivorously amassed data are not organic, but merely alphabetical—no wonder then that Flaubert's novel of ideas took the form of comedy, for as Bergson demonstrated, the comic is integrally involved with the mechanical. Modern thought, for Flaubert, had become a version of slapstick.[89]

Flaubert's immense negation of the contemporary average mind thus paradoxically adopted the form of the very disease it sought to diagnose and cure; if *Madame Bovary* was a novel written against novels, so *Bouvard et Pécuchet* was an encyclopedia compiled to end all uncritical encyclopedism. Though Rabelais, as Pound pointed out, had similarly attacked an entire age and "an entire idiotic encyclopedia" in his fiction, Flaubert's use of the encyclopedia (or dictionary) form as a vehicle of social and intellectual critique derived more directly from the Enlightenment strategies of Bayle and Voltaire (whose *Dictionnaire philosophique* he reread in preparation for *Bouvard et Pécuchet*[90]). In his attempt to "to affect the whole of a civilization, to modify the net mass of human outlook," Flaubert was the true heir of the philosophes.[91] Like the Encyclopedists, Pound wrote in the late thirties, the whole of Flaubert's work was a "protest," "a fight against maxims, against abstractions, a fight back toward a human and/or total conception" (SP, 155). Though he might have satirized the opportunistic debasement of Enlightenment principles in the person of M. Homais, the Flaubert of Pound (and of the later Gourmont) remained in many ways a descendent of Voltaire: behind Flaubert's indignation against bourgeois stupidity, behind his desire to "vomir ma bile" over contemporary society, behind the desolate rictus of *Bouvard et Pécuchet*, there lay the philosophe's rage against l'infâme, against the credulity of the contemporary average mind let loose in the junkheap of modern mass culture.

In his 1922 essays, Pound interpreted the intent of *Ulysses* in the same manner: Bloom, for example, provided a "rapid means of summarizing the normal stupidity of the age," he had "emitted what appear to be all the clichés of the English language in a single volcanic eruption," his mind was an inventory of "toute la bouillabaisse pseudo-intellectuelle des prolétaires."[92] Pound's narrow, mandarin reading of *Ulysses* as a derogatory "report on the state of the human mind in the twentieth century"

(LE, 408) grew out of a gradual redefinition of the direction of his own *Cantos*. Like *Bouvard et Pécuchet*, like the nihilistic pranks of such Dadaists as Picabia ("a sort of Socratic or anti-Socratic vacuum cleaner"[93]), *Ulysses* was the testimony of the breakdown of culture, that "old bitch gone in the teeth" (P, 191). Following Flaubert's and Joyce's diagnoses, Pound therefore now conceived his *Cantos*, as Forrest Read observes, not as "a poem written from within modern civilization, but a poem about a break with modern civilization and a search for a new basis."[94] *Bouvard et Pécuchet* and *Ulysses* had, in short, been the analyses, the negations, the purgations. The *Cantos* would continue these critical labors while at the same time pursuing the quest for affirmation, the Odyssean journey toward a new synthesis.

This new synthesis would be, as Pound later designated it, "totalitarian" (GK, 95); that is, it would take a dynamic, open form based on the encyclopedic principle of inclusion, of plenitude. Pound was haunted, as Valéry remarked of Flaubert, by the Faustian "demon of encyclopedic knowledge";[95] although his Odyssean voyage through history, philology, theology, economics, music, politics, and on and on—his own *periplus* (to use a term he adopted)—often seems to resemble the madcap intellectual tourism of Bouvard and Pécuchet (just as Flaubert's own obsessive documentary expeditions and researches bear a complex affinity to those of his two "bonshommes"), the *Cantos* nevertheless represent a radically different mode of encyclopedism. Against Bouvard and Pécuchet's travesty of scientific method, Pound posits the ideogrammic method which is the core of his "New Learning" or "New Paideuma"—based not on "simply abridging extant encyclopedias" but rather on an organic "correlation of learning" through "general equations of real knowledge" (GK, 27, 54). Such real knowledge, he insisted in *Guide to Kulchur*, "does NOT fall off the page into one's stomach" (GK, 107). It was not a knowledge "that has to be acquired by particular effort" but rather the "knowing that is in people, 'in the air' " (GK, 57), inrooted in the tradition, in mythos. It had nothing to do with Bouvard and Pécuchet's indiscriminate and bookish ingurgitation of facts: "Knowledge is or may be necessary to understanding, but it weighs as nothing against understanding, and there is not the least use or need of retaining it in the form of dead catalogues once you understand process. Yet, once the process is understood it is quite likely that the knowledge will stay by a man, weightless, held without effort" (GK, 53).

Rather than pretend omniscience ('No man can carry an automobile factory on his back"), Pound wanted to devise "an efficient tool kit" for the organic and ideogrammic ordering of available knowledge into some sort of usable, active shape (GK, 70). It was a question, as Montaigne had put it, of having "la tête bien faicte plutôt que bien pleine," of learning to elicit meaningful patterns from the welter of fact, of discerning forms in flux, of seeing "the rose in the steel dust" (LXXIV/449;477). If

one had the right method and correct understanding of "the process," if
one possessed a few basic truths (perhaps reducible, Pound
hypothesized, to a single Confucian principle, to one unwobbling pivot),
one might be able to erect a new mental structure, a new civilization, out
of the ruins of the old—"To build the city of Dioce whose terraces are the
colour of stars" (LXXIV/425;451).

Deriving (via Joyce) their archetypal scaffolding from the *Odyssey*, the
Cantos enact Pound's quest for what he unhappily called the new totalitarian synthesis. As in *Bouvard et Pécuchet*, their epic hero and subject is
ultimately the intelligence itself—not the paralyzed contemporary average mind but rather that permanent, universal intelligence which, in its
sundry metamorphoses, acts simultaneously in various ages and cultures. *Polumetis* Pound made his form open enough and elastic enough
to accommodate, at least potentially, any kind of experience, material,
or style, in short, any kind of discovery made in the process of his *periplus*. The diverse strands would, by sheer force of will (*directio volun-
tatis*), be woven into intricate ideogrammic patterns, into a musical "universe of interacting strains and tensions."[96]
Encyclopedic in scope but not in method, the *Cantos* resemble what
Friedrich Schlegel, speaking of the novel, had called "progressive Uni-
versalpoesie," a poetry capable of integrating art, science, history, philosophy, myth into a single organic whole, a summa capable of encompassing live, active mind, past and present, in its simultaneous totality.
Spawned by Renaissance and Enlightenment encyclopedism, these Romantic ambitions inform many of the nineteenth century's ventures into
inclusive, "totalitarian" forms based on the principle of the plenum, ventures as various as the epics of Blake or Hugo, the metaphysics of Hegel,
Balzac's *Comédie Humaine*, Wagner's notion of the total artwork (*Ge-
samtkunstwerk*), or that ultimate Book which Mallarmé dreamt would
provide "the Orphic explanation of the world," an ambition Yeats would
pursue in his ideal "Sacred Book of the Arts" and in the systematics of *A
Vision*.
The formal risks involved in these kinds of wholistic, encyclopedic endeavors loom large, as their twentieth-century descendents *Finnegans
Wake* and the *Cantos* demonstrate. Pound was not unaware of them;
Flaubert, he realized, had run similar risks in *Bouvard et Pécuchet*: "[he]
does, let us admit, pack so much into a 'novel' that many readers find it
indigestible." Yet, Pound added, "no method is justified until it has been
carried too far; and perhaps only great authors dare this."[97] Flaubert, he
observed elsewhere, "never stopped experimenting" (ABC, 74). The
flaws of the unfinished *Bouvard et Pécuchet*—its lumbering pace, its rep-
etitiousness, its lack of architectonics (P/J, 207)—could therefore be
forgiven, since "the rights of experiment include the right to be unsatisfactory . . . Errors, i.e. wanderings in search of truth have their rights"

(GK, 252). Pound might have characterized *Bouvard et Pécuchet* the way he did his own great undertaking: "It has the defects or disadvantages of my Cantos . . . the defects inherent in a record of struggle" (GK, 135).

Flaubert's struggle trailed off into a complex despair. As for his two retired Faustian clerks, the drafts and fragments appended to the unfinished work inform us: "Ainsi tout leur a craqué dans la main. Ils n'ont plus aucun intérêt dans la vie" ("Thus everything went to pieces in their hands. They have no more interest in life"). Their tragicomic odyssey of the mind ends in shipwreck—and yet in a way comes full circle, for in the end the two scribes resolve to return to their former copywork. Like Saint Antoine who, at the close of his phantasmagoric combat with the specters of the mind, cries out in pantheistic fervor his desire to be nothing more than matter, so Bouvard and Pécuchet, deciding to resume their places at their scrivener's desk, finally learn with their creator, "Penser, c'est le moyen de souffrir" ("To think is the way to suffer").

Perhaps the silence Pound discovered at the end of his own intellectual odyssey grew from the same tragic awareness:

> But the beauty is not the madness
> Tho' my errors and wrecks lie about me.
> And I am not a demigod,
> I cannot make it cohere.   (CXVI/796)

The *Cantos* conclude, like Flaubert's unfinished masterwork, with an ambiguous affirmation of both the grandeur and the vanity of the mind's enterprise:

> I have tried to write Paradise.
>
> Do not move.
>   Let the wind speak.
>   That is Paradise.   (CXX/803)

5

THE NATURAL PHILOSOPHY OF LOVE

Pound's 1922 essays on Flaubert coincided with the publication of his translation of Gourmont's *Physique de l'amour*. Though ostensibly a textbook of biology (LE, 343), Gourmont's work not only provided scientific confirmation of the phallic synthesis towards which Pound was then still striving, but also a further critique of those underlying "Xtian taboos" which permeated both the manners and morals of the time, "moeurs contemporaines."

In the eyes of Pound and Gourmont, the most pernicious of all Christian tyrannies involved its theological debasement of the natural into a fallen world and its consequent repressive attitude towards human sexuality. One of Gourmont's most effective exercises in the dissociation of ideas had gone straight to the heart of the matter: unlike the Greeks, who had managed to sunder the idea of sexual pleasure from that of procreation, Christian moralists had narrowly equated the two—outside of the progenerative conjugal act all sex was sin. Furthermore, through its notion of pure, divine love (which Gourmont perceived as merely the solipsistic intelligence "adoring itself in the infinite idea it conceives of itself"), Christianity had schizophrenically dissociated Amor from Eros, and, indeed, had substituted for the latter an exaltation of pain and sexual abnegation particularly repugnant to Gourmont's Epicurean sensibilities.[1]

As a philosophe, Gourmont was an ardent libertarian—and he included sexual emancipation on the same plane as religious, political, social, or intellectual freedom. He consistently ridiculed the nineteenth century's hypocrisy toward sex: its double-faced condemnation of prostitution and adultery, its cult of virginity, its censure of homosexuality. "One must fight for freedom of manners and morals as for every other freedom," he proclaimed, for "every infringement on the freedom of love is a protection granted to vice."[2] His novels and short stories explored a wide spectrum of sexual experiment and sensation, often with an explicitness unusual for the age. Karl Uitti remarks that much of Gourmont's popularity in England and America no doubt derived from the libertine tenor of these works: such writers as Havelock Ellis, Aldous Huxley (who translated *Un Coeur virginal* in 1921), Richard Aldington, and even D. H. Lawrence could enlist Gourmont in their battle against the sexual puritanism of Anglo-Saxon culture.[3]

Pound was fighting on the same front. His poems of the middle teens are full of what Marianne Moore called an overemphasis on unprudery.[4] "Fratres Minores," more snide and adolescent than most of them, strikes out against those contemporary sexual obsessions and hypocrisies that hampered the healthy acceptance and exercise of "natural fact / long since fully discussed by Ovid."

> With minds still hovering above their
>   testicles
> Certain poets here and in France
> Still sigh over established and natural fact
> Long since fully discussed by Ovid.
> They howl. They complain in delicate and ex-
>   hausted metres
> That the twitching of three abdominal nerves
> Is incapable of producing a lasting Nirvana.   (P, 148)

The first and last two lines of this poem were canceled in most copies of *Blast*; Pound ran into similar censorship problems in the publication of *Lustra*—all due to that same "local pudibundery" (L, 107) that had brought Flaubert to trial and would later obstruct the publication of Joyce's *Ulysses*. Gourmont had warned: "Times are serious: a new law has just rendered books liable to denunciation; the moralists will have one year to meditate their vile legal suits and to choose their victims; no bookseller will be invulnerable to the hate of some competitor; no painter will know for sure whether the nude bather he exhibits will land him in prison or not."[5]

The question ran deeper than censorship, however. At bottom, as Pound observed as early as 1912, it reduced itself to the conflict between the "mosaic or Roman or British Empire type" of religion—fanatical, repressive of the "life-force"—and "ecstatic" religion, benevolent, dynamic, life-asserting (SOR, 95; GK, 223). The former, as we have seen, Pound came increasingly to associate with monotheistic Protestantism, nowhere more oppressive than in its puritanical aversion to sensuality. "The puritan is a pervert," Pound wrote in *Guide to Kulchur*, "the whole of his sense of mental corruption is squirted down a single groove of sex

... the whole of protestant morals, intertwined with usury-tolerance, has for centuries tended . . . to degrade all moral perceptions outside the relation of the sexes, and to vulgarize the sex relation itself" (GK, 185, 282). Gourmont had similarly expressed the opinion that "moral hypocrisy" and "contempt for style" (the apposition is significant) were "Anglican vices."[6]

In Canto XII Pound linked the Protestant ethic of "the ranked presbyterians, / Directors, dealers through holding companies, / Deacons in churches, owning slum properties, / *Alias* usurers in excelsis" with a ribald account of an ex-sodomite turned magnate—the implication clearly being that usury and sodomy are equally "contra naturam," equally against natural increase. The contemporary Hell Cantos (XIV-XV) similarly indict the "perverts, who have set money-lust / Before the pleasures of the senses." And the image of "the vice crusaders fahrting through silk / waving the Christian symbols" culminates in "Episcopus, waving a condom full of black beetles" (XIV/63;67). Like "naked" Blake who emerges from this Hell "Shouting, whirling his arms, the swift limbs / Howling against the evil" (XVI/68;72), Pound correlates oppressive capitalism with the defilement and prostitution of the sexual act: "sadic mothers driving their daughters to bed with decrepitude" (XIV/62; 66).

In less obvious fashion, "l'histoire morale contemporaine" of Canto XXIX deals with Protestant repression of desire in small-town America:

> Languor has cried unto languor
>   about the marshmallow roast
> (Let us speak of the osmosis of persons)
> The wail of the phonograph has penetrated their marrow
> . . . . .
> With a vain emptiness the virgins return to their homes
> With a vain exasperation
> The ephebe has gone back to his dwelling
> . . . . .
> The gentleman of fifty has reflected
>   That it is perhaps just as well.   (XXIX/143;148)

Again the perspective is Blakean. Compare Blake's condemnation of the life-denying tyranny of puritanical religious codes: forbidding the young the lineaments of gratified desire, such (Urizenic) moral systems drive their guilt-ridden victims to create a spectral universe of futile masturbatory fantasies:

> The virgin
> That pines for man shall awaken her womb to enormous joys
> In the secret shadows of her chamber: the youth shut up from
> The lustful joy shall forget to generate & create an amorous image

In the shadows of his curtains and in the folds of his silent pillow.
Are not these the places of religion, the rewards of continence,
The self enjoyings of self denial?

> ("Visions of the Daughters of Albion")[7]

To such wretched "self enjoyings of self denial" Pound opposed the
ecstatic world of the gods, the transfiguring powers of

> Cydonian Spring with her attendant train,
> Maelids and water-girls,
> Stepping beneath a boisterous wind from
> Thrace,
> Throughout this sylvan place
> Spreads the bright tips,
> And every vine-stock is
> Clad in new brilliancies.
> >   And wild desire
> Falls like black lightning.   (P, 87)

This kind of exultation in the life-force (associated, as Guy Davenport
points out, with the cyclical resurgence of Persephone in springtime)[8] informs the entire range of Pound's work from the early poems of *Hilda's
Book* to the final paradisal visions of the *Cantos*.

In Gourmont's "complicated sensuous wisdom," similarly attuned to
natural energies, Pound therefore recognized his own "emotional timbre," his own "modality of apperception"—and this is the reason Gourmont spoke to Pound in a way Henry James never could, for "the gods
had not visited James, and the Muse, whom he so frequently mentions,
appeared doubtless in corsage, the narrow waist, the sleeves puffed at the
shoulders, à la mode 1890-2" (LE, 340-342). Gourmont, "in contradiction
to, in wholly antipodal distinction from, Henry James," was "an artist of
the nude" and his notion of "love, passion, emotion as an intellectual instigation" (LE, 343) was rooted in a sensuality as anti-Christian and as
exuberantly pagan as Pound's: "Tartuffe casting his filthy handerkerchief
over the immortal breasts of goddesses must be countered by the gesture
which tears away the gown and displays woman in all her nakedness: the
Faun will then whinny in broad daylight. Let us cover all the walls with
Corregio's *Antiope* and *Leda*, and Titian's *Venus*, along with the poems
of Théophile Gautier."[9] "Faun's flesh is not to us," Pound complained in
Hugh Selwyn Mauberley, borrowing his chiseled stanzas from Gautier—
John Espey has shown to what extent he drew on his reading of Gourmont not only for the intricate sexual imagery of the poem, but for its
larger structural dissociation between the muses of Gourmont and James,

the former an instigation of active passion "phallic and ambrosial," the latter a "mere invitation to perceptivity" in the exquisite, passive manner of the fin-de-siècle aesthete.[10]

"Qu'est-ce qu'ils savent de l'amour et qu'est-ce qu'ils peuvent en comprendre," asked Caid Ali (alias Pound) in the epigraph to the second Mauberley poem. It was undoubtedly with a similar question in mind that Gourmont undertook his most scientific investigation of love, the *Physique de l'amour*, published in 1903, just a year after the physiological theories of *Le Problème du style*. In the following year Gourmont founded *La Revue des Idées* with Edouard Dujardin (Wagnerian and proto-Joycean), Arnold Van Gennep (ethnographer and folklorist), and Jules de Gaultier (philosopher of "bovarisme"). The review, centered around the zoologist René Quinton, was intended to build a bridge between literature and science.[11]

Gourmont inherited his fascination with science not only from the philosophes but from the Symbolists who, unlike their British contemporaries, were on the whole quite open to possible syntheses of art and science (hence the admiration for Poe). Although Gourmont ridiculed the bourgeois adulation of science, Burne notes that the scientific *method* appealed to him—its empiricism, its tentativeness, its experimental attitude toward human problems.[12] Above all, however, the scientific method was congenial to Gourmont's associative-dissociative mind because of its fundamentally comparative approach to phenomena. Pound would similarly insist at the beginning of *ABC of Reading*: "The proper METHOD for studying poetry and good letters is the method of contemporary biologists, that is careful first-hand examination of the matter, and continual COMPARISON of one 'slide' or specimen with another" (ABC, 17). This method he came to call (after Fenollosa, who had observed "Poetry agrees with science and not with logic"[13]) "the ideogrammic method or the method of science," based not on abstraction or generalization, but rather (like the Chinese character itself) on the dynamic juxtaposition of immediate, discrete sensorial facts. This scientific empiricism, Gourmont pointed out in *Le Problème du style*, was also basic to any effective style: "Buffon is in no way a rhetorician. He used to say: 'One can only acquire transmissible knowledge by looking with one's own eyes.' "[14] He went on to illustrate how Buffon invariably abridged the verbose taxonomies of his collaborators on *L'Histoire naturelle*, commenting, "Nothing leads to concision like an abundance of ideas; of which Buffon has many" ("Rien ne pousse à la concision comme l'abondance des idées"). Pound was quite fond of this quotation; it is basic to his later equation: "Dichten = Condensare" ("Poetry = condensation") (ABC, 92).

Science, then, provided Gourmont with "an entire method and ethics" —and for his *Physique de l'amour* he turned to a stylistic heir of Buffon, the nineteenth-century entomologist Henri Fabre. He described his first encounter with Fabre's *Souvenirs entomologiques* as nothing less than a revelation: "What I glimpsed there dazzled me. I took the book with me, hardly suspecting . . . that it would give birth in me to an idea of philosophy in which man would no longer take up all the space, but would rather occupy a place in the middle of the animal series".[15] Gourmont's comment clearly indicates that he saw Fabre not only as a naturalist but as a *moraliste*. His own *Physique de l'amour* (and Pound's decision to translate it) grew largely out of this impulse to strip man of his (Christian) sovereignty and to reintegrate him into "le milieu vital," not as "alpha and omega" of nature, but as a participant in a larger totality.[16] He wrote at the opening of his *Physique de l'amour* (I follow Pound's 1922 translation): "Man is not the culmination of nature, he is *in Nature*, he is *one* of the unities of life, that is all. He is the product of a partial, not of total evolution; the branch wherein he blossoms parts like a thousand other branches from a common trunk."[17]

Gourmont's anti-Darwin bias (derived in part from Quinton and Fabre) is evident. Darwin's "scale of creatures with man at the summit, as the culmination of universal effort," he commented, "is of a too theologic simplicity" (p. 19). The evolutionists had merely superimposed the bourgeois teleology of progress, with *homo victorianus* as its crowning achievement, onto the processes of nature. Gourmont instead suggested a more synchronic approach, akin to the radical ahistoricism of Pound's "all ages are contemporaneous." "We must chuck the old ladder, whose rungs the evolutionists ascended with such difficulty. We will imagine, metaphorically, a center of life, with multiple lives diverging from it . . . On reflection, one will consider the different love-mechanisms of all the dioicians as parallel and contemporary. Man will then find himself in his proper and rather indistinct place in the crowd, beside the monkeys, rodents and bats" (p. 20).

Gourmont's purpose was not to degrade man, but rather to venture "a theory as to the psychological unity of the animal series," to give "man's sexual life its place in the one plan of universal sexuality," to consider "human love as one form of numberless forms, and not perhaps, the most remarkable of the lot, a form which clothes the universal instinct of reproduction" (p. 19). Darwin, on the contrary, "truckling to the religiose pudibundery of his race," had almost wholly neglected "the actual facts of sex," just as "Christian prudery" had hampered the development of sexual ethnography, theologically committed as it was to conceal "all that unites, sexually, man and animal, everything that proves the unity of origin for all that lives and feels" (p. 63). Gourmont insisted on the ecological totality and reciprocity of natural forces: "We are animals, we live on animals, and animals live on us. We both have and are parasites. We are predatory, and we are the living prey of the predatory. And when we follow the love act it is truly, in the idiom of theologians, *more bes-tiarum*. Love is profoundly animal; therein is its beauty" (p. 22).

Approached in this manner, the Christian dichotomy between man and nature evaporated, "there being everywhere the same matter animate with the same desire: to live, to perpetuate life" (p. 21). Gourmont ex-claimed enthusiastically at the perspectives opened up by this kind of en-lightened organic vision: "Quelle clarté alors, que de lumière venant de tous les côtés."[18] Or as Pound translated it: "And what clarity from the process, lights showering in from all corners" (p. 20). All of these terms, clarity (*claritas*), process (*tao*), and liquid light (*e lo soleills plovil*: IV/15; 19), in conjunction—chthonic, sexual forces joined with love, luster, and fluidity—form an epiphanic ideogram absolutely central to the *Cantos*.

Gourmont's title, *Physique de l'amour*, carries many resonances: the work is an anatomy in both the scientific and older literary sense; a com-pendium of the sexual behavior of the birds, the beasts, and the bees (one critic has called it "une chanson de gestes du rut"[19]), the book resembles medieval bestiaries as well as the physiologies that returned to vogue in the nineteenth century (Brillat-Savarin's *Physiologie du goût*, Balzac's *Physiologie du mariage*, and Stendhal's *De l'Amour*, originally entitled *Physiologie de l'amour*). Pound's translation of the title, *The Natural Philosophy of Love*, educed a yet wider scope for the work, its implica-tions at once classic (the "natural philosophy" of Renaissance or eigh-teenth-century naturalists) and romantic (the *Naturphilosophie* that Agassiz and the American Transcendentalists inherited from such Ger-man thinkers as Goethe and Schelling).

Underlying what Pound called Gourmont's textbook of biology lay a broader social and philosophic purpose: "For clarity one must proceed from the known to the unknown; man is the figure to whom one may compare necessarily the observations on other animals" (p. 56). The pur-port of Gourmont's natural philosophy was hence humanistic, inasmuch as it involved reestablishing the harmony between man and nature: "Far from wishing to impart human logic to nature, one attempts here to in-troduce a little natural logic into the old classic logic" (p. 49), for "one must place natural logic above our human logic, derived from mathe-matical logic. Facts in nature are connected by a thousand knots of which no one is solvable by human logic" (p. 121). Fenollosa had similarly assailed the inert "brickyard" of medieval logic that walled man off from the natural world "full of homologies, sympathies and identities" in which all processes were ecologically interrelated.[20] Whereas Fenollosa sought to define the possibilities of natural language (which, like Chi-nese, would be based on active verbs, "since motion and change are all that we can recognize" in nature[21]), Gourmont the philosophe turned to nature as a corrective to the incoherence and hypocrisy of society's moral and sexual codes.

At first glance Gourmont's notion of nature seems much more akin to Nietzsche's than, say, to Fenollosa's (or Agassiz's) sense of natural design: "It does not seem as if anything in nature were ordered in view of some benefit; causes blindly engender causes; some maintain life, others force it to progress, others destroy it; we qualify them differently, according to the dictates of our sensibility, but they are non-qualifiable; they are movements and nothing else" (p. 87). And yet this anarchic dynamism of nature ("her imagination always active invents, ceaselessly, new forms"), though amoral, is ultimately not unjust: "Nature is neither good, nor evil, nor altruist, nor egoist; she is an ensemble of forces whereof none cedes save under superior pressure. Her conscience is that of balance; being of a perfect indifference, it is of an absolute equity" (p. 131).

The artificial human order imposed by society is, in Gourmont's view, "often a disorder worse than spontaneous disorder, because it is a forced and premature finality, an inopportune turning of the vital river out of its course" (p. 127)—one thinks of the misdirected passions and the moral, political, and aesthetic disorder that Pound presented in his early Renaissance Cantos. For Gourmont this specious human order was nowhere more evident than in society's condemnation of sexual aberrations as immoral or abnormal—"from the microscopic beasts to man, aberration is everywhere; but one should, rather, call it, at least among animals, impatience" (p. 127). If seen in the light of animal habits, "debauchery" or "perversion" loses "all its character and all its tang, because it loses all immorality . . . there is no lewdness which has not its normal type in nature, somewhere" (p. 85). Indeed, if one had to isolate the most pernicious of sexual "aberrations" it would be chastity—not because it is antinatural ("nothing is anti-natural") but because its pretexts are utterly fallacious, utterly abstract (p. 128). In similar fashion Gourmont could, through the comparative examination of the female "love-organs" of mammals, subversively erode the shibboleth of virginity: "The maidenhead is, therefore, not peculiar to human virgins, and there is no glory in a privilege which one shares with the marmoset" (p. 58).

As a philosophe, then, Gourmont appealed to the full range of animal sexuality, to the "ingenuity of total fauna" in order to show the artificiality and arbitrariness of society's sexual mores and taboos—he had planned a companion volume, *Physique des moeurs*, which would have applied the same method to "l'histoire morale contemporaine." Gourmont's aim, however, was not a Rousseauistic return to nature, but rather a reevaluation of man's relation to the rest of the animal world: only by studying the life of nature could he become fully aware of his distinctive place within that totality. Man was more than an animal, of course, but his superiority lay merely "in the immense diversity of his aptitudes" (p. 12). Gourmont thus elegantly solved the conflict between freedom and biological determinism, between intelligence and instinct:

> Free will is only the faculty of being guided successively by a great number of different motives. When choice is possible, liberty begins, even though the chosen act is rigorously determined and when there is no possibility of avoiding it. Animals have a smaller liberty, restricted in proportion as their aptitudes are more limited; but when life begins liberty begins. The distinction, from this view-point, between man and animal is quantitative, and not qualitative. One must not be gulled by the scholastic distinction between instinct and intelligence; man is as full of instincts as the insect most visibly instinctive; he obeys them by methods more diverse, that is all there is to it. (pp. 21-22)

The exceptional diversity of man's sexual aptitudes Gourmont termed *luxure*. Pound, finding no English equivalent other than "the exercise of pleasant lusts," translated it by the Latin *luxuria* (Freud would have called it the pleasure principle). According to Gourmont, *luxuria*, like the surplus energy aimlessly discharged in the sexual play of birds, was the base of all human art, and indeed of the highest achievements of civilization (p. 100). "All is but *luxuria*," began his invocation in the *Physique de l'amour*—one need only typographically rearrange the litanylike cadences of Gourmont's prose to elicit its remarkable affinities to Pound's Usura Canto:[22]

All is but *luxuria*.
Luxuria, the variety of foods, their cooking, their seasoning, the culture
    of special garden plants;
luxuria, the exercises of the eye, decoration, the toilet painting;
luxuria, music;
luxuria, the marvelous exercises of the hand, so marvelous that direct
    hand work can be mimicked by a machine but never equalled;
luxuria, flowers, perfumes;
luxuria, rapid voyages;
luxuria, the taste for landscape;
luxuria, all art, science, civilization   (p. 143)

Usura is the malign perversion of Gourmont's *luxuria*. If the latter accounts for "the marvelous exercises of the hand" and eye, so Usura

> blunteth the needle in the maid's hand
> and stoppeth the spinner's cunning. Pietro Lombardo
> came not by usura
> Duccio came not by usura   (XLIV/229;239)

The antithesis between *luxuria* and Usura, however, can be seen to include also diversity versus uniformity (or polytheism versus monotheism), the pleasure principle versus self-denial, charity versus avarice, or in more economic terms, free exchange versus monopoly, or natural increase, abundance, surplus versus the artificial shortages engineered to their own profit by scarcity economists. This sense of *luxuria* as dynamic surplus was, in Pound's mind, fundamental not only to civilized arts but also to love.[23] In Canto XXVI he translated Cavalcanti's meticulous analysis of the onset of Amor:

> Cometh he to be
>   when the will
> From overplus
> Twisteth out of natural measure   (XXXVI/178;183)

This same "overplus" recurs in connection with the Sienese Monte dei Paschi bank whose credit was based on "the abundance of nature / with the whole folk behind it" (LII/257;267) and all of whose profits were to be recycled into the community it served:

> To pay 5% on its stock, Monte dei Paschi
> and to lend at 5 and 1/2
> Overplus of all profit, to relief works   (XLI/205;213)

Pound also used the term *luxuria* in a much more pejorative (Dantesque) sense to signify the perversion of what he termed the prolific "jocundity and *gentilezza*" of nature into the mere manufactured clutter so characteristic of modern commodity fetishism. The culprit here again was Usura, "always trying to supplant the arts and set up the luxury trades, to beat down design, which costs nothing materially and which can come only from intelligence, and to set up richness as a criterion" (GK, 282). It is in this context, then, and not the Gourmontian, that Pound's account of the decadence of Renaissance Venice must be read:

> And hither came Selvo, doge,
>   that first mosaic'd San Marco,
> And his wife that would touch food but with forks,
> Sed aureis furculis, that is
>   with small golden prongs
> Bringing in, thus, the vice of luxuria   (XXVI/122;127)

In a later Canto Pound explicitly rhymes the decline of early nineteenth-century America into gross (European) materialism with the decadence of Venice:

Tip an' Tyler
We'll bust Van's biler.....
brought in the vice of luxuria, sed aureis furculis
which forks were
b[r]ought back in the time of President Monroe
by Mr Lee our consul in Bordeaux.   (XXXVII/183;189)

The subtitle of Gourmont's *Physique de l'amour* was *Essai sur l'instinct sexuel*—and the relation of instinct to intelligence provides the basic arguments and ambiguities of the book. If Bergson had maintained an absolute opposition between the two, Gourmont, following Ribot, Rabier, and Fabre, instead posited instinct as "merely a mode of intelligence" (p. 46).

> We will attribute to instinct the series of acts which tend to conserve the present condition of a species; and to intelligence, those which tend to modify that condition. Instinct will be slavery, subjection to custom; intelligence will represent liberty, that is to say, choice, acts which while being necessary, since they occur, have yet been determined by an ensemble of causes anterior to those which govern instinct. Intelligence will be the deep, the reserve, the spring which after long digging emerges between the rocks. In everything that intelligence suggests, the consciousness of the species makes a departure; what is useful is incorporated in instinct, enlarging and diversifying it; what is useless perishes—or perhaps flowers in extravagances, as it does in man, in dancing and gardening birds, or the magpies attracted by a jewel, larks by a mirror! (p. 135)

There exists no dichotomy between the two—Gourmont similarly argued against the (Hartmannian or Freudian) dualism of conscious and unconscious—but rather a dynamic interplay: instinct crystallizes the useful discoveries of intelligence; it is, as Pound observed in the *Guide to Kulchur*, "the result of countless acts of intellection, something after and not before reason" (GK, 195). This reference to Gourmont occurred in the context of Pound's definition of culture as "what is left after a man has forgotten all he set out to learn"—the notion derived from Frobenius's concept of *paideuma*, "the tangle or complex of the inrooted ideas of any period," the "knowing that is in the people, 'in the air' " as opposed to "knowledge that has to be acquired by particular effort" (GK, 57).[24] *Paideuma*, then, is culture-as-instinct, the collective accumulation of innumerable individual innovations into habits of mind—or as Gourmont phrased it, "the sum of intellectual acquisitions slowly crystallized in the species" (p. 139).

In *Jefferson and/or Mussolini*, Pound applied those Gourmontian definitions of instinct and intelligence to his own increasingly political concern with "ideas into action." "Let us deny that *real* intelligence exists until it comes into action. A man in desperate circumstances, let us say, Remy de Gourmont in pre-war France, might get to the point of thinking that an idea is spoiled by being brought into action, but Gourmont also got to the point of cursing intelligence altogether, *vide* his remarks on the lamb. (*Chevaux de Diomède*)" (J/M, 18). The passage to which Pound alludes concludes Gourmont's "romance of possible adventures" (LE, 342):

> I shall adopt Lamb . . . I will make of him a ram who will perpetuate his race, without perpetuating the thought which corrupts races and breaks up the harmony of unity. Lamb is a creature whose acts will always be pure, since their rhythm can never be troubled by a single scruple. What is evil, what deforms everything, is thought—with all its temptations, its labyrinths from which no one has returned, unless maimed by battle, feverish with intellectual anguish . . . A curse on you, Thought—creator of everything, but a deadly creator, an incompetent mother who has only brought into the world creatures whose shoulders are the footstools of chance and whose eyes are the laughing-stock of life.[25]

The conflict between action and intellection is basic to the dynamic contradictions in much of Gourmont's work; like *Bouvard et Pécuchet*, *Les Chevaux de Diomède* concludes with an ambivalent assertion of the immense potentialities and liabilities of human thought. A similar stress can be felt in much of Pound's work, perhaps most vividly in his political writings of the thirties. Searching for the bases of a new civilization, a new *paideuma*, he attempts, following Gourmont, to define the kind of intelligence-in-action that might bring the new social, economic, and ethical order about:

> [Gourmont] then got round to defining intellect as the fumbling about in the attempt to create instinct, or at any rate on the road towards instinct. And his word instinct came to mean merely PERFECT and complete intelligence *with a limited scope* applied to recurrent conditions (*vide* his chapters on insects in *La Physique de l'Amour*).
> The flying ant or wasp or whatever it was that I saw cut up a spider at Excideuil may have been acting by instinct, but it was not acting by reason of the stupidity of instinct. It was acting with remarkably full and perfect knowledge which did not have to be chewed out in a New Republic article or avoided in a London *Times* leader.
> When a human being has an analogous completeness of knowledge, or intelligence carried into a third or fourth dimension, ca-

pable of dealing with NEW circumstances, we call it genius. (J/M, 18)

Such "intelligence carried into a third or fourth dimension" evokes the close of Canto XLIX:

> The fourth; the dimension of stillness.
> And the power over wild beasts   (XLIX/245;256)

This is the Confucian axis of the unwobbling pivot or unmoved mover, time (Einstein's fourth dimension) and motion brought towards stasis. Yet this centripetal still point of a turning world is balanced by a centrifugal "outspread process," which, branching out from the root, establishes social order (*to kalon*) "and the power over wild beasts."[26] "Perfect" knowledge or genius in like manner achieves, through action, harmony between instinct and intelligence, between the collective and the individual, between inherited wisdom and the innovative dealing with "NEW circumstance." Pound's economic mentor, C. H. Douglas, had offered a similar definition of the "increment of association," that is, those "tools and processes" that form "the cultural inheritance of the community" and, transmitted from generation to generation like instinct, constitute our true capital.[27] All these notions converge in Pound's celebrated homage to the tradition behind the individual talent:

> What thou lov'st well shall not be reft from thee
> What thou lov'st well is thy true heritage
> . . . . .
> To have gathered from the air a live tradition
> or from a fine old eye the unconquered flame
> This is not vanity.   (LXXXI/522;556)

"Fabre and Frazer," Pound wrote in one of his Gourmont essays, "have been essentials in the mental furnishings of any contemporary mind qualified to write of ethics or philosophy or that mixed molasses religion" (LE, 343). Both had attempted, by using the comparative method, to reimmerse man in the total design of nature—Fabre, by demonstrating the identities between human and animal instinct, Frazer, by collocating myth with such natural processes as the cyclical recurrence of seasons. Myth, like instinct, could thus be seen as the collective compendium of chthonic natural wisdom, rooted in the primordial rhythms of birth, death, and resurrection. The same intuition controls the mythopoeia of the *Cantos*, perhaps nowhere more so than in Canto XLVII. A reprise of the *Nekuia* of the first Canto, where Odysseus's archetypal descent "to the bower of Ceres' daughter Proserpine" rhymes with the seasonal disappearance of the Frazerian vegetation god Tammuz-Adonis into the underworld, Canto XLVII is at the same time a Whitmanesque celebration of the universal force that drives the almond bough to put forth flame and impels man toward woman:

> The light has gone down into the cave,
> Splendour on splendour!
> By prong have I entered these hills:
> That the grass grow from my body,
> That I hear the roots speaking together,
> The air is new on my leaf   (XLVII/238;248)

"Prong" was Pound's English for the French term "verge" in his translation of the *Physique de l'amour*. Gourmont's definitions of the sexual act as the "integration of one force in another force" (p. 24), as both a "renewal" of form and "a perpetual return to the unity" (p. 20) are equally fundamental to these lines.

Gourmont's and Pound's celebrations of sexuality are not without their ambivalences, however. Gourmont spoke of the inexorable tyranny of the sexual instinct: "What one sees clearly is a necessity: the act must be accomplished; to this end, all obstacles, whatever they are, will be overcome. Neither distance, nor the difficulty of the voyage, nor the danger of the approach can drive back the instinct" (p. 103). He cited the "long courageous voyages" of the great peacock moth who "covers several leagues of country in the attempt to satisfy his desire" (p. 102) and also adduced the example of the bull: "The bull merely enters and leaves, and it is a spectacle for philosophers, for one understands immediately that what drives the fiery beast at his female is not the lure of a pleasure too swift to be deeply felt, but a force exterior to the individual although included in his organism" (p. 65). Pound would remember this passage in one of his final fragments:

> And the bull by the force that is in him—
>   not lord of it,
>   mastered.   (CXIII/789)

The most explicit application of Gourmont's remarks and examples, however, occurs again in Canto XLVII:

> Two span, two span to a woman,
> Beyond that she believes not. Nothing is of any importance.
> To that is she bent, her intention
> To that art thou called ever turning intention,
> Whether by night the owl-call, whether by sap in shoot,
> Never idle, by no means by no wiles intermittent

The Natural Philosophy of Love

> Moth is called over mountain
> The bull runs blind on the sword, *naturans*
> To the cave art thou called, Odysseus,
> By Molü hast thou respite for a little   (XLVII/237; 247)

Molü frees Odyssean man from the sexual bondage that leads to Circe's pigsty. As Daniel Pearlman explains it, *molü* is "the effective will, the refined intelligence, the sense of proportion man needs for creative action."[28] It enables him to come into a new and more harmonious relation with nature. No longer nature's slave, but moving from lover to husband, from Eleusinian sexual ecstasy ("sacrum, sacrum, inluminatio coitu": XXXVI/180;185) to a broader social and cultural wisdom, man is released from Circe to regain Penelope:

> By Molü art thou freed from the one bed
>   that thou may'st return to another   (XLVII/237;247)

Molü, then, is akin to Gourmont's *luxure*, that diversification of instinct which enables man to transmute organic energies into civilization: "Man even in the humblest species has mastered love and made it his daily slave, at the same time that he has varied the accomplishments of his desire and made possible its renewal after brief interval. This domestication of love is an intellectual work" (p. 64).

Canto XLVII clearly implies that Pound sees this intellectual work as the province of the male. As for woman,

> The stars are not in her counting,
>   To her they are but wandering holes. (XLVII/237;247)

"Conservatrix of Milesien" Pound had dubbed her in *Mauberley*, lifting the epithet ("conservatrices des traditions milésiennes") from Gourmont's *Histoires magiques*.[29] Pound's vision of woman as an agent both of disorder (the Sirens, Helen, Eleanor, among others) and of revelation (Aphrodite and Artemis, for example) is so broad and so complex as to require a monograph in itself; suffice it here merely to examine its more Gourmontian dimensions. "The female is primordial," Gourmont wrote in his *Physique* (p. 52). Physically her shape is purer and more primitive than the male's, whose sexual organs distinguish themselves from hers by their "supplementary development, which is moreover useless, for the penis is a luxury [sic] and a danger" (p. 33)—masculinity, in short, is "an augmentation, an aggravation of the normal type represented by femininity; it is a progress, and in this sense it is a development" (p. 44). The drift of Gourmont's natural logic should be clear, for the distinction he draws between male and female is merely an elaboration of his definitions of instinct and intelligence. Instinctual, "sexed thoughout all her parts: *tota femina sexus*," woman's intelligence, "less spontaneous, inclines in general to activities entirely practical" (p. 46). Similarly, her function is to conserve the useful traditions of the species or civilization—in her role as child-rearer and educator, it is she who transmits the cultural heritage, above all its language. Man, on the other hand, functions as intelligence, for he "has centralized in himself most of the activities independent of the sexual motor. He alone is capable of disinterested works, that is to say of aims unconnected with the physical conservation of the race" (p. 52).[30]

Pound summarized Gourmont's distinctions in his "Translator's Postscript" to the *Physique*: "One offers woman as the accumulation of hereditary aptitudes, better than man in the 'useful gestures,' the perfections; but to man, given what we have of history, the 'inventions,' the new gestures, the extravagance, the wild shots, the impractical" (p. 150). Gourmont had cited the Aristotelian apposition of male with active form and female with passive matter (p. 68); Pound pursued the analogy in his "Postscript"—"man really the phallus or spermatozoide charging, head-on, the female chaos" (p. 150). One might juxtapose this with Canto XXIX:[31]

> Wein, Weib, TAN AOIDAN
> Chiefest of these the second, the female
> Is an element, the female
> Is a chaos
> An octopus
> A biological process   (XXIX/144;149)

Against this female "chaos" Pound posited the form-giving energy contained in the spermatozoide, which "compels the ovule to evolve in a given pattern" (p. 152). Noting that this "power of exteriorizing a form" was equally characteristic of "the brain as maker or presenter of images," Pound postulated a "physique de la pensée" that radically equated the two: "the brain itself, is, in origin and development, only a sort of great clot of genital fluid held in suspense or reserve" (p. 149). With the brain "thus conceived not as a separate and desiccated organ, but as the very fluid of life itself" (p. 158), intelligence and sexuality were resolved into a single biological totality: "Even oneself has felt it, driving any new idea into the great passive vulva of London, a sensation analogous to the male feeling in copulation" (p. 150). If genius, as Gourmont had suggested, "fecundates the generation of minds," so Pound defined "creative thought" as "an upspurt of sperm" or as a new "up-jut" or "outpush of a demand," which, "striking matter, forced it into all sorts of forms, by gushes" (pp. 53, 150). He offered a Dantesque analogy: "Three channels, hell, purgatory, heaven, if one wants to follow yet another terminology:

digestive excretion, incarnation, freedom in the imagination, i.e. cast into an exterior formlessness, or into form material, or merely imaginative visually or perhaps musically or perhaps *fixed* in some other sensuous dimension, even of taste or odor" (p. 156).

Although man was "the sum of the animals, the sum of their instincts," precisely this imaginative ability to exteriorize energies in forms was what distinguished him from other species: his "great divergence has been in the making of detached, resumable tools"—be they pure thought (which, once born, leads "an independent life much like a member of the vegetable kingdom, blowing seeds, ideas from the paradisal garden at the summit of Dante's Mount Purgatory") or such inventions as fire and the club, which enabled him to detach his digestion, to free his brain from his own limited body, thus multiplying his physical potential by sheer intellection (pp. 152, 154). These new faculties, Pound argued, were not developed over a long, evolutionary process, but rose with the suddenness of revelation. Against Darwin, he offered Ovid: "I believe that the species changes as suddenly as a man makes a song or a poem, or as suddenly as he *starts* making them, more suddenly than he can cut a statue in stone, at most as slowly as a locust or long-tailed Sirmione false mosquito emerges from its outgrown skin" (p. 153).

Of all the new "organs" or "faculties" that man had a "protean capacity to grow," none fascinated the ex-Imagist Pound more than the possible extension or intensification of his powers of visualization:

> You have the visualizing sense, the "stretch" of imagination, the mystics, —for what there is to them—Santa Theresa who "saw" the microcosmos, hell, heaven, purgatory complete, "the size of a walnut"; and you have Mr. W., a wool-broker in London, who suddenly at 3 A.M. visualizes the whole of his letter-file, three hundred folios; he sees and reads particularly the letter at folder 171, but he sees simultaneously the entire contents of the file, the whole about the size of two lumps of domino sugar laid flat side to flat side. (p. 155)

He would recall this passage in Canto LXXXVII, a meditation on visions of paradise (the passage follows the "phallic heart" ideogram, which Pound also associated with Gourmont: "leading to Remy?"):

> Monsieur F. saw his mentor
>   composed almost wholly of light.
> (Windeler's vision: his letter file
>   the size of 2 lumps of sugar,
> but the sheet legible. Santa Teresa . . .
>   (LXXXVII/573;609)

It was natural, then, that Pound, like the medieval theologian Grosse-teste (LE, 160), would attempt to hypothesize a "physique de la lumière" as corporeal and as esemplastic as "spermatozoic thought" itself. He wrote in his "Postscript": "Let us say quite simply that light is a projection from the luminous fluid, from the energy that is in the brain, down along the nerve cords which receive certain vibrations in the eye. Let us suppose man capable of exteriorizing a new organ, horn, halo, Eye of Horus" (p. 154).

Pound found support for his theory in Dr. Louis Berman's *Glands Regulating Personality*, which he reviewed for the *New Age* in early 1922 under the title "The New Therapy." Berman's book, he wrote, offered a "chemistry of the soul" ("a comforting relief from Freudian excess") which correlated the diverse endocrine glands with various physiological and psychological functions: particular personality traits could, for example, be explained by the predominance of one gland or another. Berman's description of the pineal gland as containing "cells filled with a pigment like that in the eye's retina" caught Pound's attention, for here, he thought, was scientific evidence for the Cartesian location of the soul in the extinct pineal eye.[32] "Light, or the sensation of light," Pound suggested, "may well be the combustion or encounter of this retina-pigment either, as in the eye, with exterior vibrations, or in the pineal with the emanation of brain cells, or even with the cells themselves."[33] Light could thus be defined as both a physical and mental energy, as both external and internal, as both received and projected—the notion is analogous to Pound's definitions of the impressionist artist "as the plastic substance *receiving*" and the Vorticist "as directing a certain fluid force against circumstance, as *conceiving* instead of merely reflecting and observing" (G-B, 89).

Pound distinguished, however, between "the orderly visualization which I presume to be pineal, but which neither confuses or annoys the vision," and "the D.T.s, or any sort of hallucination," which was rather the product of "post-pituitary phantasma" (and to which, he claimed, the female was much more susceptible than the male).[34] It was not the Rimbaldian "derangement of all the senses" at which Pound's poetics aimed, but rather this "orderly visualization" which would have the intensity of the visionary but none of that phantasmagoric incoherence by which the seer becomes not the shaper but the passive victim of his vision.

The pineal gland, Pound summarized, was therefore the gland of "lucidity," of "the sense of light flowing along the nerves," of "luminosity in vision, 'gates of beryl and chrysophase' effect"; it was equally the "gland of metamorphosis, of original thought," whose secretions caused "the *new* juxtaposition of images."[35]

The *Cantos* provide any number of examples of this "pineal" and paradisal light of the mind, fluid and metamorphic, but perhaps one of the finest instances occurs at the close of the first Pisan Canto. Here the spermatozoic imagery of Pound's "Postscript" reappears, mingled with memories of the ecstatic "jets d'eau" of Verlaine's "Clair de Lune."[36] The liquid "upjut" of creative thought, which exteriorizes form (expressed, as so often in Pound, as a luminous sphere crystallized out of flux), is equated with that force by which the magnet elicits a rose pattern from random iron filings. Nature (or for that matter, woman) is no longer seen as an "exterior formlessness" onto which shape must be cast, but rather as integral to the process: "stone knowing the form which the carver imparts it" (LXXIV/430;457):

> Serenely in the crystal jet
>   as the bright ball that the fountain tosses
> (Verlaine) as diamond clearness
>   How soft the wind under Taishan
>   where the sea is remembered
>   out of hell, the pit
>   out of dust and glare evil
>   Zephyrus / Apeliota
> This liquid is certainly a
>   property of the mind
> nec accidens est but an element
>   in the mind's make-up
> est agens and functions dust to a fountain pan otherwise
>   Hast 'ou seen the rose in the steel dust
>   (or swansdown ever?)
> so light is the urging, so ordered the dark petals of iron
> we who have passed over Lethe.   (LXXIV/449;477)

Although never named, Gourmont the naturalist is an indirect presence throughout the Pisan sequence. In these Cantos Pound, his ideological landscape devastated, turns his vigilant eye to the natural world about him, reproportioning, as Pope's *Essay on Man* or Fabre's *Souvenirs entomologiques* had suggested, his own place in the great chain of being, "au milieu de la série animale."

> The ant's a centaur in his dragon world.
> Pull down thy vanity, it is not man
> Made courage, or made order, or made grace,
>   Pull down thy vanity, I say pull down.
> Learn of the green world what can be thy place
> In scaled invention or true artistry,
> Pull down thy vanity,

Paquin pull down!
The green casque has outdone your elegance.
(LXXXI/521;556)

Kenner identifies the Bible as Pound's source for vanity and the ant ("All is vanity," Eccles. I:2; "Go to the ant, thou sluggard; consider her ways, and be wise," Prov. VI:6);[37] yet the metamorphosis of ant into Greek centaur in an oriental "dragon world"[38] is consonant with the animistic entomology of the *Physique de l'amour*—where a butterfly is said to wear a "nymph's corset" (p. 25), a plant-louse is described as this "milch-cow of the ants" (p. 30), and the male tachyte wasp sports a "citron-colored diadem" (p. 36) or the dragon-fly a "steely-blue helmet" (p. 89). Gourmont had drawn particular attention to the headgear of soldier ants ("noncoms in close rank"), noting "the development of their mandibles and the largeness of their heads" (p. 122). As for the natural elegance of the "green casque" (compare VII/26;30) that outdoes that of the Parisian dressmaker's haute couture, Gourmont had commented that "in the insect world the male is the frail elegant sex, gentle and sober, with no employment save to please and to love" (p. 35).

Pound's translation of the *Physique de l'amour* had taught him not only an exact attention to natural processes and designs, but a descriptive technique that supplemented the lesson of Flaubert. Take, for example, Gourmont's account of the amatory customs of wild bees:

> Among all solitary bees, scolies, masons, bembex, and anthopores, the males, born soonest, range about the nests awaiting the birth of the females. As soon as these appear they are seized and fecundated, knowing, thus, life and love in the same shiver. The female osmies and other bees are keenly watched by the males who nab and mount them as they emerge from the natal tube, the hollow stalk of a reed, flying at once with them into the air where the love-feast is finished. Then while the male, drunk with his work, continues his death-flight, the female feverishly hollows the house of her offspring, partitions it, stores the honey for the larvae, lays, whirls for an instant and dies. The year following: the same gestures above the same reeds split by the reed-gatherers; and thus in years following, the insect permitted never the least design save the conservation of one fragile form: brief apparition over flowers. (p. 25)

The stylistic precision of this passage, its humor, its subtle aligning of the micro- with the macro-cosmic, of natural with mythic patterns of love, life, and death, are equally characteristic of Pound's portrait of wasp life, and of the infant vespa's Odyssean descent to greet the chthonic powers of the underworld:

and Brother Wasp is building a very neat house
of four rooms, one shaped like a squat indian bottle
La vespa, *la* vespa, mud, swallow system
. . . . .
and in the warmth after chill sunrise
an infant, green as new grass,
has stuck its head or tip
out of Madame La Vespa's bottle
. . . . .
    The infant has descended,
    from mud on the tent roof to Tellus,
like to like colour he goes amid grass-blades
    greeting them that dwell under XTHONOS XΘONOΣ
OI XΘONIOI; to carry our news
    εἰς χϑονίους to them that dwell under the earth,
begotten of air, that shall sing in the bower
    of Kore,   Περσεφόνεια
and have speech with Tiresias, Thebae   (LXXXIII/532-533;568)

Insect imagery pervades the entire Pisan sequence. Pound himself becomes

    As a lone ant from a broken ant-hill
    from the wreckage of Europe, ego scriptor
                            (LXXVI/458;487)

The mere presence of the minute purposes and coherences of nature are enough to stave off insanity:

    When the mind swings by a grass-blade
        an ant's forefoot shall save you   (LXXXIII/533;568)

Alone in his cage at dawn, he notices the effects of light on the tiny gait of centaur ants (one of the central motifs of the Pisan Cantos is quite simply the question of scale, the ratios and proportions between animal, man, landscape, elements, gods, history):

    if calm be after tempest
    that the ants seem to wobble
        as the morning sun catches their shadows
                            (LXXX/513;548)

    And now the ants seem to stagger
        as the dawn sun has trapped their shadows
                          (LXXXIII/531;566)

Following Italian folk tradition, Pound invokes luck (or rather that larger design behind his own predicament, fate or *fortuna*) from the spider—"Arachne mi porta fortuna"—and greets a new guest at tentside:

> being given a new green katydid of a Sunday
> emerald, paler than emerald
> > minus its right propeller   (LXXIV/435;462)

Speculating as to whether the grasshopper's incessant music was a "love-call" or merely a "physiological exercise at once necessary and disinterested," Gourmont had cited Fabre's *Souvenirs entomologiques* in his *Physique de l'amour*: "Fabre, who lived all his life among the implacable noises of the Provençal countryside, sees in 'the violin of the locust, in the bag-pipe of the tree-toad, in the cymbals of the cacan only a means suitable to expressing the joy of living, the universal joy which each animal species celebrates in its own fashion' " (p. 38). This is the same Provence in whose natural music Pound exulted with the troubadours: its birds can still be heard singing in the Jannequin of Canto LXXV. Like Fabre, Pound welcomes the Mozartian sonorities of the cricket's viola da gamba (again, wittily, the naturalist's precision) as against the cacophonies of the camp's martial "bumm drum" and "tubas."

> Be welcome, O cricket my grillo, but you must not
> > sing after taps.
> . . . . .
> So Salzburg reopens
> > Qui suona Wolfgang grillo
> > > Po viola da gamba   (LVIII/480;511)

In his *Physique de l'amour*, Gourmont had on several occasions described the aerial mating of hymenoptera: "Fecundation takes place in the air; the lovers fly up, join, fall enlocked, a golden cloud which the death of the male disperses, while the females, losing their wings, re-enter the house for egg-laying" (p. 37). Pound witnesses the same scene in Canto LXXIV:

> nor is it for nothing that the chrysalids mate in the air
> > color di luce
> green splendour and as the sun thru pale fingers
> > > > > (LXXIV/432;459)

At the back of these lines probably lies Gourmont's explanation of the physiological reason for these airy amours: "Copulation takes place in the air . . . it is only possible after a long flight has filled with air the pouches which cause the male's organ to emerge. Between these pockets, or aeriferous bladders shaped like perforated horns, emerges the penis, a small white body, plump and bent back at the point" (p. 116).[39]

Although Pound's memory of this small detail is precise, his use of the term "chrysalids" would seem in this instance wholly inexact—pupae would hardly be capable of flight, or, for that matter, of mating. Nonetheless, Pound's numenous glimpse of this diaphanous intercourse, "color di luce,"[40] again recalls his vision of that "radiant world" of Cavalcantian or Dantesque love "where one thought cuts through another with clean edge, a world of moving energies . . . magnetisms that take form, that are seen, or that border the visible . . . the body of air clothed in the body of fire" (LE, 153-154). Gourmont had in like fashion conceived the ethereal, ephemeral existence of the butterfly, mediator of earth, air, and fire, as "a symbol for pure thought" (p. 101). Of the mating of dragonflies he observed: "It is so pure, so immaterial, one would say that two ideas joined in the limpidity of ineluctable thought" (p. 90).[41] Classical tradition, moreover, had associated the butterfly with psyche, the soul—all these resonances converge in Canto LXXVI as Pound is vouchsafed an epiphanic glimpse of Aphrodite, a moment of splendor too fleeting to last:

> that butterfly has gone out thru my smoke hole
> AΘANATA, saeva.   (LXXVI/461;491)

Pound's blending of the visionary with the naturalist's precise observation of flora and fauna, his respect for "the vegetal powers / or 'life however small' " (LXXXVIII/582;617) governs the remaining Cantos, *Rock-Drill, Thrones,* and the final *Drafts and Fragments.* His mentor in these matters here is no longer Gourmont but Louis Agassiz, though for his rediscovery of the American naturalist Pound was clearly indebted to the author of *Physique de l'amour,* as he wrote his old friend Natalie Barney in the early fifties: "I take it Remy knew his Agassiz, tho dont recall direct reference. I got Agassiz via Remy."[42] Gourmont's writings yield no allusion to Agassiz (although they do include several pieces on the naturalist Ruskin); several salient affinities nevertheless link the two men's natural philosophies.

Like Gourmont, Agassiz sought to "remplacer l'homme dans la série animale," to demonstrate "the psychological unity of the animal series."

The psychological history of animals shows that as man is related to animals by the plan of his structure, so are these related to him by the character of those very faculties which are so transcendent in man as to point at first to the necessity of disclaiming for him completely any relationship with the animal kingdom. Yet the natural history of animals is by no means completed after the somatic side of their nature has been thoroughly investigated; they, too, have a psychological individuality, which, though less fully studied, is never-theless the connecting link between them and man. I cannot there-fore agree with those authors who would disconnect mankind from the animal kingdom and establish a distinct kingdom for man alone.[43]

Agassiz argued in favor of an "immaterial principle" which, "whether it be called soul, reason, or instinct . . . presents in the whole range of or-ganized beings a series of phenomena closely linked together; and upon it are based not only the higher manifestations of the mind, but the very permanence of the specific differences which characterize every organ-ism."[44] Agassiz's insistence on permanence is clearly antievolutionary: if Gourmont opposed Darwin's implicit ideology of progress, so Agassiz's celebrated quarrel with the evolutionists was based on his theological conviction as to the immutability of divine design—though its members might change, the species was an invariable, quasi-transcendental form that could only be altered by the sudden intervention of God. Change (or phylogeny) was therefore not a teleological, evolutionary process, but rather a recurrent cycle of growth, such as characterized the metamor-phic development (or ontogeny) of the individual. Against Darwin, then, Agassiz posited Ovidian metamorphosis within a cosmic synchrony:

> Taking nature as exhibiting thought for my guide, it appears to me that while human thought is consecutive, Divine thought is simul-taneous, embracing at the same time and forever, in the past, the present, and the future, the most diversified relations among hun-dreds of thousands of organized beings, each of which may present complications again, which, to study and understand even imper-fectly, as for instance, Man himself, Mankind has already spent thousands of years. And yet, all this has been done by one Mind, must be the work of one Mind only, of Him before whom Man can only bow in grateful acknowledgement of the prerogative he is al-lowed to enjoy in the world, not to speak of the promises of a future life.[45]

The Platonic strain in Agassiz is not unlike that vision of an ideal, per-manent order—at once ethical and metaphysical, at once in the mind of man and "in nature / rooted" (XCIX/709;738)—which dominates the *paradiso* of Pound's later Cantos. Pound turned to Agassiz, as he had previously to Gourmont, not only for his stylistic precision ("Agassiz could teach a litteratus to write," he wrote Hugh Kenner[46]) but, even more crucially, for his elucidation of the "signatures" in nature (LXXXVII/573;609) and of the intelligent "design in the Process" (XCV/645;678). Pound placed him among the fixed stars beside Confucius, both thinkers being necessary to that organic (and visual) correlation of moral with natural science which Gourmont had also attempted:

Nine knowledges about

> 止 chih³
> chih

. . . . .

The 8th being natural science, 9th moral
8th the concrete, 9th the agenda,
Agassiz with the fixed stars, Kung to the crystaline

. . . . .

From the sea-caves   Risplende
       degli occhi
Manifest and not abstract   (XCIII/625;658)

In these late Cantos the natural world is apprehended with a paradisal serenity and a new order of descriptive exactness, the taxonomic nomenclature derived from Agassiz and Linnaeus. We are in an Adamic universe of sheer naming.

> Box hedge, the garden in form,
>   heliotrope, kalikanthus, basilicum
> the red bird, that is a cardinal
>   lark almost out of season
> had been a field full at Allègre
>   as 40 rising together
>   the short tails.   (CVII/760;785)

> The great acorn of light bulging outward,
>   Aquileia, caffaris, caltha palistris,
>   ulex, that is gorse, heryx arachnites:
> Scrub oak climbs against cloud-wall—   (CVI/753;779)

The "great acorn of light" here may be taken as a dense emblem of Pound's *paradiso*. It is akin to the "great ball of crystal" (CXVI/795), which, as Pound remarked in reference to Brancusi, is "an approach to the infinite *by form*, by precisely the highest possible degree of consciousness of formal perfection; as free of accident as any of the philosophical demands of a 'Paradiso' can make it" (LE, 444). The acorn of light is also the visionary eye, Emerson's "transparent eyeball," casting its light outward—"God's eye art 'ou, do not surrender perception" (CXIII/790). There is still another, more Gourmontian meaning here, though, for the acorn (Latin *glans*) is a traditional sexual symbol and thus rejoins the "spermatozoic" light ("bulging outward") of Pound's "Postscript" to the *Physique de l'amour*. Elsewhere, coining his image from the shape of the Chinese ideogram, he would in like fashion fuse Amor and Eros into "the phallic heart" (XCIX/697;727). The acorn is finally and most literally the seed of the oak; like thought itself—Pound now calls it "Gestalt seed"—it is the repository of potential patterns of energy waiting to be released, to be blown from Mount Purgatory, to take root:

> And from this Mount were blown
> seed
> and that every plant hath its seed
> so will the weasel eat rue
> and the swallows nip celadine   (XCII/618;651)

These last phrases derive from another "secretary of Nature," the neo-Platonist and astrologer John Heydon,[47] decipherer of the ecological reciprocities and homologies in nature; Gourmont, in an essay entitled "Une science d'autrefois: La phytognomique" (which dealt with acorns and other plants as fertility symbols), had similarly explored the Renaissance fascination with natural analogies and homeopathies.[48]

In these late Cantos Gourmontian dissociation of ideas is linked with the Confucian principle of "sorting things into organic categories"[49] and with the ability of such naturalists as Agassiz to distinguish "throstle's note from banded thrush / by the wind in the holly bush" (XCVI/652; 684). Like Agassiz, Pound asserts the coherence and purposiveness of nature ("but there is something intelligent in the cherry-stone": CXIII/788) and the continuities of pattern, or phyllotaxis,[50] within change:

> The clover enduring,
> basalt crumbled with time.
> "Are they the same leaves?"
> that was an intelligent question.   (XCIV/634;667)

As in the Pisan sequence, Pound's eye seizes the most subtle of natural manifestations:

> Flora Castalia, your petals drift thru the air,
> the wind is 1/2 lighted with pollen
> diafana
> (XCIII/632;665)

Through Gourmontian feats of attention he notices the "shingled flakes on a moth's wing" (C/717;745) or how "the water-bug's mittens / petal the rock beneath" (XCI/616;650). The butterflies of Pisa similarly reappear, now more explicitly Dantesque:

The Natural Philosophy of Love

> But in the great love, bewildered
>   farfalla in tempesta
> under rain in the dark:
>   many wings fragile
>
> Nymphalidae, basilarch, and lycaena,
> Ausonides, euchloe, and erynnis
> And from afar
>   il tremolar della marina   (XCII/619;652)

In Canto CVI his vision of a flock of king butterflies (their wings perhaps
likened both to the "veined phyl[l]otaxis" of leaves and to a "faun's ear")
coincides with an ecstatic glimpse of Artemis:

> Gold light, in veined phyl[l]otaxis.
> By hundred blue-grey over their rock-pool,
>   Or the king-wings in migration
>   And in thy mind beauty, O Artemis
> Over asphodel, over broom-plant,
>   faun's ear a-level that blossom.   (CVI/754;779)

Compare, for example, Gourmont's eye-witness account of the courtship
of dragonflies in his *Physique de l'amour;* the "Vierge" he refers to, however, is not the virgin huntress Artemis, but the peasant nickname for
these Libellulas. "It was on the surface of a pond among the border flowers, a morning of July, a flaming morning. The 'Vierge,' corselet of blue
green, almost invisible wings, fluttered in great numbers, slowly, as if
seriously; the hour of parade had arrived. And everywhere couples
formed, rings of azure hung from the grass blades, trembled on leaves of
the water-lentil, everywhere green arrows and blue arrows played at
flight, and wing-brushing, at joining" (p. 90). Although the phenomena
described are not identical, clearly Pound's and Gourmont's modalities
of apperception are very close.

These "king-wings in migration" once again alight, "as to enter arcanum," in the penultimate fragment of the *Cantos:*

> La faillite de François Bernouard, Paris
> or a field of larks at Allègre,
>   "es laissa cader"
> so high toward the sun and then falling,
>   "de joi sas alas"
> to set here the roads of France.

155

Two mice and a moth my guides—
To have heard the farfalla gasping
    as toward a bridge over worlds.
That the kings meet in their island,
    where no food is after flight from the pole.
Milkweed the sustenance
    as to enter arcanum.
To be men not destroyers.   (CXIX/802)

Gourmontian resonances are present even in the first line, for the printer François Bernouard was, as Pound knew, a close friend, disciple, and sometime publisher of Gourmont—as late as 1946, he was still planning to reissue the out-of-print works of "le dernier humaniste français," as he called his "cher maître" Gourmont.[51] Although Bernouard seems to have consistently encountered economic difficulties in his publishing ventures, the "faillite" to which Pound refers is probably his bankruptcy in late 1929. Bernouard had in 1927 undertaken his ambitious magnum opus—the publication of an elegant series of the *Oeuvres complètes* of Barbey d'Aurevilly, Georges Courteline, Gérard de Nerval, Jules Renard, Marcel Schwob, and Emile Zola. Apparently it was the fifty-volume Zola edition that finally brought on the financial debacle. He described it as follows in an interview: "I was printing over five thousand volumes, many of which ran more than five hundred pages . . . My press was worth two and a half million (old francs). I had an inventory of quality books worth ten million, and only some two million worth of debts. My creditors forced my liquidation; some wanted to attach my house, others wanted damages. I didn't mince words with them and there were days when I would wake up like Job naked on the dungheap. Everything got sold at a ridiculously low price."[52]

Bernouard, artisan and visionary publisher, is, then, the final victim of the serpent "neschek" in the *Cantos:* his bankruptcy provides the ultimate instance of the Usura that "had made printing a midden, a filth, a mere smear, bolted down by the bank racket, which impedes the use of skill and implements for the making of proper books or of healthy populations" (GK, 184). The first major block of the *Cantos* has ended with the "die-cutter for greek fonts and hebrew (XXX/148;153) whom Hieronymus Soncinus imported to Fano, thus initiating that translation of the classics to the present (Divus, for example) so basic to any Renaissance. Another major section, the dynastic Cantos, had concluded with John Adams requesting Otis to print his work on Greek prosody for the New World (LXXI/420;442: "He said there were no Greek types in America / and if there were, no typesetter cd / use 'em")—Pound explicitly rhymes these two Renaissance gestures at LXXXII/524;559: "Otis, Soncino."[53] In this penultimate Canto Bernouard completes the chord, though dissonantly: his bankruptcy implies not only the collapse of what

Kenner has called the "Paris Printing Vortex"[54] but also, if we follow the structural analogies above, the larger botch of that twentieth-century Renaissance, both artistic and political, in which Pound had so energetically believed.

Having presented Bernouard's "faillite" as a luminous detail of a wider bankruptcy (which, we learn in *Drafts and Fragments*, may also be that of the *Cantos* themselves), Pound moves in the next line (through a crucial "or") toward that paradisal landscape "dove sta memoria"[55]—Paris, the failed urban vortex giving way to the rural "roads of France," the memories of Pound's early walking tours in Provence "now in the heart indestructible." The interspliced Provençal of Ventadorn dates as far back as the 1910 *Spirit of Romance:*

> When I see the lark a-moving
> For joy his wings against the sunlight,
> Who forgets himself and lets himself fall
> For the sweetness which goes into his heart;
> Ai! what great envy comes unto me for him whom I see so
> rejoicing!   (SOR, 41)

Now, half a century later, in Canto CXIX the full Icarian resonance hits home:

> so high toward the sun and then falling

Ventadorn's precise visual and musical notation of lark flight is exemplary of that tender reverence towards nature, of that *humanitas*, or Confucian *jên*, of that active, apperceptive love which Pound also discerned in Gourmont. It is the key to entering the arcanum:

> Two mice and a moth my guides—

This triad of minute psychopomps (guiding the soul, psyche) modulates effortlessly into the butterfly ("farfalla") of the next line, a reprise of the "farfalla in tempesta" Pound had seen in Canto XCII and possible intimation of *Purgatorio* X, 120-130, the Dantesque parallel to Pound's "Pull down thy vanity." "O superbi cristian, miseri lassi . . .

> non v'accorgete voi che siam vermi
>   nati a formar l'angelica farfalla,
>   che vola alla giustizia sanza schermi?
> Di che l'animo vostro in alto galla,
>   poi siete quasi entomata in difetto,
>   sì come vermo in cui formazion falla?

157

Instigations

> Perceive ye not that we are worms, designed
>   To form the angelic butterfly, that goes
>   To judgement, leaving all defence behind?
> Why doth your mind take such exalted pose,
>   Since ye, disabled, are as insects, mean
>   As worm which never transformation knows?[56]

And yet:

> To have heard the farfalla gasping

—again the visionary blended with Gourmontian delicacy and precision: seeing, hearing the half-alighted butterfly's breath by its wing-beats, almost as one would listen to incense,

> as toward a bridge over worlds.

And the "king-wings in migration" of Canto CVI, the Odyssean moths of Canto XLIX, called over mountain, *naturans*, anima into aura, at last reach shore:

> That the kings meet in their island
>   where no food is after flight from the pole.
> Milkweed the sustenance
>   as to enter arcanum.

> To be men not destroyers.

Appendix
Selected Works by Gourmont
Notes
Index

Appendix: Marginalia to "his true Penelope"

Chapter 4 examines various aspects of Pound's reading of Flaubert, particularly the Flaubert of *Bouvard et Pécuchet* disclosed by Gourmont. Although it was primarily Flaubert's fiction that shaped Pound's conception of the prose tradition, he was also familiar with Flaubert's correspondence, a veritable mine of aesthetic, political, and personal pronouncements often written in a prose whose verbal exuberance and orthographic high jinks are not entirely without resemblance to Pound's own epistolary style. The Flaubert who emerges from these letters—he often refers to himself as a "vieux troubadour"—is a figure rather different from the supposedly invisible, impassible author of the novels, for here we are allowed a privileged glimpse of Flaubert *intime*, a man capable of considerable cantankerousness toward his age, great tenderness toward his friends, and a moving reverence for the past and present masters of his craft. In short, the passionate, disheveled personality these letters reveal merely corroborated Pound's initial admiration for Flaubert the artist. As he observed in the *Dial* in 1922: "The work itself may give the skilled reader a fairly good idea of the author, and one is not in the least surprised to find that Flaubert when over fifty impoverished himself to save a nephew-in-law from bankruptcy. It is the kind of thing a man who wrote as Flaubert wrote would do."[1]

It remains unclear when exactly Pound first read Flaubert's correspondence; various scattered remarks and allusions would seem to indicate that he was familiar with it by the late teens or early twenties, that is, around the time he declared Flaubert Mauberley's "true Penelope." Pound's library at Brunneburg contains the first volume (the 1830-1850 series) of the 1887 Charpentier edition of Flaubert's *Correspondance* with

161

various marginal markings and annotations in Pound's hand. The second, third, and fourth volumes of the set are missing, but a loose sheet found in the first volume contains Pound's page references to various passages in the third volume (the 1854-1869 series) of this edition. The particular nature of Pound's markings would seem to suggest, however, that most were made during the late twenties and thirties, for they reflect his overriding interests of the period—history, and political and economic theory.

It was apparently during these same years that Pound also reread *L'Education sentimentale* (his two-volume Charpentier edition of the work bears the publication date 1925). Here again the marginalia and underlinings clearly indicate that Pound approached the novel less as a masterpiece of fiction than as a work of historical and sociological analysis. It was not the tale of Frédéric's love for Mme Arnoux nor the lyric flights that interested the historian Pound (he commented in the *Dial*, "when Flaubert gets into a moonlit passage he so eminently shows the abundant *sensibilité* of his epoch that . . . it is quite certain Flaubert in prescribing the Flaubertian discipline for himself, committed no error whatsoever"),[2] but rather the novel's detailed dissection of the political, economic, and moral roots and reverberations of the failed 1848 Revolution—the passages Pound marked in the book tend for the most part to deal with such questions as electoral corruption, monopoly capitalism, usury, stock market profiteering, unemployment, and so forth.

Pound was probably drawn to *L'Education sentimentale* for, above all, its implicit critique of modern political ideologies, be they leftist or rightist. Perhaps thinking of contemporary parallels, Pound underscored, for example, a celebrated passage in which Flaubert compared the 1848 Revolution and its bloody repression to a virulent outbreak of collective insanity, equal in enormity to some vast cataclysm of nature:

> C'était un débordement de peur. On se vengeait à la fois des journaux, des clubs, des attroupements, des doctrines, de tout ce qui exaspérait depuis trois mois; et, en dépit de la victoire, l'égalité (comme pour le châtiment de ses défenseurs et la dérision de ses ennemis) se manifestait triomphalement, une égalité de bétes brutes, un méme niveau de turpitudes sanglantes; car le fanatisme des intérêts equilibra les délires du besoin, l'aristocratie eut les fureurs de la crapule, et le bonnet de coton ne se montra pas moins hideux que le bonnet rouge. La raison publique était troublée comme après les grands boulversements de la nature. Des gens d'esprit en restèrent idiots pour toute leur vie.[3]

In his copy of the correspondence, Pound marked a letter that amplified Flaubert's contempt for what he considered the intellectual dimness of nineteenth-century egalitarian ideologues:

Je viens d'avaler Lamennais, Saint-Simon, Fourier et je reprends
Proudhon d'un bout à l'autre. Si on veut ne rien connaître de tous
ces gens-là, c'est de lire les critiques et les resumés faits sur eux; car
on les a toujours réfutés ou exaltés, mais jamais exposés. Il y une
chose saillante et qui les lie tous: c'est la haine de la liberté, la haine
de la Révolution française et de la philosophie. Ce sont tous des bonshommes du moyen âge, esprits enfoncés dans le passé. Et quels
cuistres! quels pions! Des séminaristes en goguette ou des caissiers en
délire.[4]

Pound no doubt found Flaubert's fulminations against modern socialist
theory congenial, for a similar bias underlay his own irascible rejection
of the entire leftist (and in his case, specifically Marxist) tradition.

As Pound went back through "Papa" Flaubert's letters during the late
twenties or thirties, his various marginalia indicate that he found his own
political and cultural assumptions echoed in many portions of the correspondence. Pound the aesthete found his elitism confirmed by such Flaubertian axioms as "le vrai beau n'est pas pour la masse, surtout en
France."[5] The economist Pound noted with approbation Flaubert's similar interest in this emerging science: "Vous vous préoccupez beaucoup
des injustices de ce monde, de socialisme et de politique. Soit. Eh bien!
Lisez d'abord *tous ceux* qui ont eu les mêmes aspirations que vous. Fouil-
lez d'abord les utopistes et les rêveurs secs. —Et puis, avant de vous permettre une opinion définitive, il vous faudra étudier une science assez
nouvelle dont on parle beaucoup et que l'on cultive peu, je veux dire
l'Economie politique." Pound the philosophe, convinced that many of
the world's ills stemmed from fanaticism and provincialism in all their
guises, shared Flaubert's espousal of Voltaire as a civilizing agent: "On va
envoyer contre les musulmans des soldats et du canon. C'est un Voltaire
qu'il leur faudrait et l'on criera de plus belle au fanatisme! A qui la faute?
Et puis tout doucement la lutte va venir en Europe. Dans cent ans d'ici
elle ne contiendra plus que deux peuples, les catholiques d'un côté et les
philosophes de l'autre." Pound the mandarin was convinced with Flaubert that the profound crisis affecting modern society could be largely as-
cribed to the corruption and incompetence of its ruling classes; the Confucian solution lay not in instructing the masses but rather in truly edu-
cating the governing elite: "Si l'on se fut préoccupé davantage de l'in-
struction des classes *supérieures* en reléguant pour plus tard les comices
agricoles; si on avait mis enfin la tête au-dessus du ventre, nous n'en
serions pas là probablement."[6]

Pound's exasperation with the leftist intelligentsia of the thirties was
corroborated by Flaubert's choleric reaction to circumambient *bêtise*—
nowhere more evident than in the dogmas of the socialist intellectuals of
his day: "Mais il me semble que notre malheur vient *exclusivement* des
gens de notre bord. Ce que je trouve de christianisme dans le socialisme

est énorme . . . Quand je serai vieux, je ferai de la critique; ça me soul-
agera, car souvent j'étouffe d'opinions rentrées. Personne, mieux que
moi, ne comprend les indignations de ce brave Boileau contre le mauvais
goût: 'Les bêtises que j'entends dire à l'Académie hâtent ma fin.' Voilà un
homme." Indeed, Flaubert's savage indignation against *la bêtise* led him
to indulge in a scatalogical vehemence not unrelated to the excremental
imagery into which Pound frequently lapses when vituperating against
contemporary evil. Pound marked the following passage, the ferocity of
which recalls some of his own Hell Cantos: "Je sens contre la bêtise de
mon époque des flots de haine qui m'étouffent. Il me monte de la m[erde]
à la bouche comme dans les hernies étranglées. Mais je veux la garder, la
figer, la durcir; j'en veux faire une pâte dont je barbouillerai le dix-neu-
vième siècle, comme on dore de bouse de vache les pagodes indiennes, et
qui sait? cela durera peut-être."[7]

Although Pound's notations in the *Correspondance* occasionally seem
to hint that he was merely foraging through Flaubert's letters for confirmation of what were rapidly becoming his own political and economic
idées fixes, he also marked a number of passages that provide concrete
proof of the bond between Poundian and Flaubertian aesthetics to which
such critics as Kenner, Espey, Schneidau and de Nagy have alluded.
Pound's 1913 pronouncements on the "presentative method" ("It means
constation of fact. It presents. It does not comment.") can be aligned with
a passage he noted in a letter where Flaubert insists on the importance of
impartial observation and representation while warning against facile
conclusions. Flaubert's identification of history as the muse of the
modern age no doubt also struck a responsive chord in the poet who defined his epic *Cantos* as a "poem including history."

> On fausse toujours la réalité quand on veut l'amener à une conclu-
> sion qui n'appartient qu'à Dieu seul. Et puis, est-ce avec des fictions
> qu'on peut parvenir à découvrir la verité? l'histoire, l'histoire et
> l'histoire naturelle! Voilà les deux muses de l'âge moderne. C'est avec
> elles que l'on entrera dans des mondes nouveaux. Ne revenons pas
> au moyen âge. *Observons,* tout est là. Et après des siècles d'études il
> sera peut-être donné à quelqu'un de faire la synthèse? La rage de
> vouloir conclure est une des manies les plus funestes et les plus
> stériles qui appartiennent à l'humanité. Chaque religion et chaque
> philosophie a prétendu avoir Dieu à elle, toiser l'infini et connaître
> la recette du bonheur. Quel orgueil et quel néant. Je vois au contraire
> que les plus grands génies et les plus grandes oeuvres n'ont jamais
> conclu. Homère, Shakespeare, Goethe . . . se sont bien gardés de
> faire autre chose que *représenter.*[8]

Pound singled out a famous letter in which Flaubert enunciated his
doctrine of impersonality; the artist was to be in his work like God in cre-

ation, everywhere present but nowhere visible: "L'illusion (s'il y en a une) vient au contraire de l'*impersonnalité* de l'oeuvre. C'est un de mes principes: qu'il ne faut pas *s'écrire*. L'artiste doit être dans son oeuvre comme Dieu dans la Création, invisible et tout-puissant, qu'on le sente partout mais qu'on ne le voie pas."[9] Flaubert's statement can be juxtaposed with a comment of Coleridge's Pound was fond of quoting: "As Coleridge has wisely said, the distinguishing mark of the serious artist will be a sort of undercurrent everywhere present and yet nowhere visible as a separate excitement. No fragment of his work will, apart, have the full significance that it has when considered in relation to the whole sum of his work" (SP, 110-111). Flaubert, in another passage Pound marked, had similarly insisted on the crucial relation of part to whole in the creation of an artistically unified work: "travaille, médite surtout, condense ta pensée, tu sais que les beaux fragments ne font rien; l'unité, l'unité, tout est là. L'ensemble, voilà ce qui manque à tous ceux d'aujourd'hui, aux grands comme aux petits." Flaubert's emphasis on condensation as a mode of achieving formal impact and unity corresponds quite closely to Pound's axiom "Dichten = condensare," an axiom he found rephrased in another portion of the correspondence: "et puis l'imagination est plutôt une faculté qu'il faut, je crois, condenser pour lui donner de la force, qu'étendre pour lui donner de la longueur."[10] As for the entire question of style that had been the focus of *Le Problème du style*, Pound discovered further confirmation of Gourmont's arguments in Flaubert's observation to Feydau: "Car je ne crois pas que l'on puisse *tout* bien dire. Il y a des idées impossibles (celles qui sont usées, par exemple, ou foncièrement mauvaises?) et comme *le style n'est qu'une manière de penser*, si votre conception est faible, jamais vous n'écrirez d'une façon forte . . . Le style est autant *sous* les mots que *dans* les mots."[11]

Although all these various marked passages relating to the craft of writing begin to indicate just what Pound meant when, as late as 1941, he defined himself as an "orthodox Flaubertian," other, more personal, aspects of Flaubert's artistic temperament apparently also seized his attention. For example, he noted down the page reference to a letter in which Flaubert speaks of the soul's disquieting voracity for knowledge: "Notre âme est une bête féroce; toujours affamée, il faut la gorger jusqu'à la gueule pour qu'elle ne se jette pas sur nous"—Pound would similarly quip in *Guide to Kulchur*, "Discoveries are made by gluttons and addicts" (GK, 100). Hard work, scholarly or scientific research, Flaubert continued in this same letter, were perhaps the only trustworthy means of satiating such devouring appetite—the parallel with Pound's own encyclopedic drive is salient: "Rien n'apaise plus qu'un long travail. L'érudition est chose rafraîchissante. Combien je regrette souvent de n'être pas un savant, et comme j'envie ces calmes existences pasées à étudier des pattes de mouche, des étoiles ou des fleurs. Faites de grandes lectures, tout est là." In both authors this genuine taste for scholarship and documentation often became a way of escaping the rage the present day inspired in them. As Flaubert explained in a letter Pound marked: "C'est en haine de tout cela, pour fuir toutes les turpitudes qu'on fait, qu'on dit et qu'on pense que je me réfugie en désesperé dans les choses anciennes. Je me fiche une bosse d'antiquité comme d'autres se gorgent de vin."[12]

Whereas Pound's phrenological "bump of antiquity" led him back to Confucian China, Flaubert's drew him to the Carthage of *Salammbô*. In the course of his massive background research for this work, Flaubert had of course come across mention of the Carthaginian explorer Hanno, but as he wrote Sainte-Beuve after having read the latter's rather pedantic review of *Salammbô*, he neither admired the Greek account of Hanno's voyage down the western coast of Africa (the *Hannonis Periplus*) nor believed in the document's authenticity. Although Canto XL clearly shows that Pound did not agree with Flaubert, he was evidently struck by the letter to Sainte-Beuve:

> Dès le debut, je vous arrête à propos du *Périple* d'Hannon, admiré par Montesquieu, et que je n'admire point. A qui peut-on faire croire aujourd'hui que ce soit là un document *original?* C'est évidemment traduit, raccourci, échenillé et arrangé par un Grec. Jamais un Oriental, quel qu'il soit, n'a écrit de ce style. J'en prends à temoin l'inscription d'Eschmounazar, si emphatique et redondante! Des gens qui se font appeler fils de Dieu, oeil de Dieu (voyez les inscriptions d'Hamaker) ne sont pas simples comme vous l'entendez.—Et puis vous m'accorderez que les Grecs ne comprenaient rien au monde barbare. S'ils y avaient compris quelque chose, ils n'eussent pas été des Grecs. L'Orient répugnait à l'hellénisme. Quels travestissements n'ont-ils pas fait subir à tout ce qui leur a passé par les mains d'étranger![13]

Indeed, the only mention of Flaubert's *Correspondance* that surfaces in the *Cantos* involves *Salammbô*'s reconstruction of Carthaginian history:

> "Pige-moi le type" said old Gustav
>   qui vous peindra un fauteuil carthaginois.
> Henry J. had Coburn take photographs. (LXXXIX/602;636)

Like much in the late *Cantos*, the reference is highly elliptic. Pound is alluding to a letter Flaubert wrote to his friend Jules Duplan complaining that *Salammbô*'s publisher, Lévy, was pestering him for illustrations both impossible to execute and wholly superfluous to the written text: "Mais la persistance que Lévy met à demander des illustrations me f[out] dans une fureur *impossible à décrire*. Ah! qu'on me le montre, le coco qui fera le portrait d'Hannibal, et le dessin d'un fauteuil carthaginois! il me rendra grand service. Ce n'était guère la peine d'employer tant d'art à laisser tout dans le vague, pour qu'un pignouf vienne démolir mon rêve par sa précision inepte."[14] Pound ideogrammically juxtaposes "old Gustav" with "Henry J." because in the preface to *The Golden Bowl* Henry James speaks of Coburn's photographic frontispieces to the New York edition of his works. Like Flaubert, James argues that the written text should be free from the distracting literalness of illustrations: "Anything that relieves responsible prose of the duty of being, while placed before us, good enough, interesting enough and, if the question be of picture, pictorial enough, above all *in itself*, does it the worst of services, and may well inspire in the lover of literature certain lively questions as to the future of that institution." If James had Coburn take photographs for the frontispieces, it was largely because he hoped "the reference [of photography] to Novel or Tale should exactly be *not* competitive and obvious, should on the contrary plead its case with some shyness, that of images always confessing themselves mere optical symbols or echoes, expressions of no particular thing in the text, but only of the type or idea of this or that thing."[15] Canto LXXXIX, from which these references to Flaubert and James are drawn, deals in its own way with the problem of illustration and relates the illustrative use of quotations, facts, statistics, and documents to the broader question of historiographical honesty and accuracy.

Selected Works by Gourmont

Le Chemin de velours. Paris: Mercure de France, 1902.

Les Chevaux de Diomède. Paris: Mercure de France, 1897.

Un Coeur virginal. Paris: Mercure de France, 1907.

Couleurs. Contes nouveaux suivis de choses anciennes. Paris: Mercure de France, 1908.

Le Culture des Idées. 1900; reprint ed., Paris: Mercure de France, 1964.

D'un Pays lointain. Paris: Mercure de France, 1898.

Dante, Béatrice, et la poésie amoureuse. Essai sur l'idéal feminin en Italie à la fin du XIIIe siècle. Paris: Mercure de France, 1908.

Dialogues des amateurs sur les choses du temps, 1905-1907 (Epilogues IV). Paris: Mercure de France, 1907.

Epilogues [I], Réflexions sur la vie (1895-1898). Paris: Mercure de France, 1903.

Epilogues II (1899-1901). Paris: Mercure de France, 1904.

Epilogues III (1902-1904). Paris: Mercure de France, 1905.

Esthétique de la langue française. Paris: Mercure de France, 1899.

Histoires magiques. Paris: Mercure de France, 1894.

Le Joujou patriotisme. Suivi de la Fête nationale. Introduction and notes by Jean-Pierre Rioux. Paris: J. J. Pauvert, 1967.

Le Latin mystique: Les Poètes de l'antiphonaire et la symbolique au moyen âge. 2nd ed., Paris: Mercure de France, 1892.

Lettres à l'Amazone. Paris: Crès, 1914.

Lettres intimes à l'Amazone. Paris: La Centaine, 1926.

Lilith, suivi de Théodat. Paris: Mercure de France, 1906.

Le Livre des masques. 1896; reprinted ed., Paris: Mercure de France, 1963.

The Natural Philosophy of Love. Trans., Ezra Pound. 1922; reprinted ed., New York: Collier, 1972.

Nouveaux Dialogues des amateurs sur les choses du temps (Epilogues V, 1907-1910). Paris: Mercure de France, 1910.

Une Nuit au Luxembourg. Paris: Mercure de France, 1906.

Le Pèlerin du silence, rev. ed. Paris: Mercure de France, 1911.

Pensées inédites. Preface, G. Apollinaire. Paris: Ed. de la Sirène, 1920.

Physique de l'amour. Essai sur l'instinct sexuel. Paris: Mercure de France, 1903.

Le Problème du style. Paris: Mercure de France, 1902.

Promenades littéraires, 1st series. Paris: Mercure de France, 1905.

Promenades littéraires, 2nd series. Paris: Mercure de France, 1906.

Promenades littéraires, 3rd series. Paris: Mercure de France, 1909.

Promenades littéraires, 4th series. Paris: Mercure de France, 1912.

Promenades littéraires, 5th series. Paris: Mercure de France, 1913.

Promenades philosophiques. Paris: Mercure de France, 1904.

Promenades philosophiques, 2nd series. Paris: Mercure de France, 1908.

Promenades philosophiques, 3rd series. Paris: Mercure de France, 1909.

Remy de Gourmont: Selections from All his Works, chosen and trans., Richard Aldington. 2 vols. New York: Covici-Friede, 1929.

Selected Writings. Trans. and ed., Glenn S. Burne. Ann Arbor: University of Michigan Press, 1966.

Sixtine. Roman de la vie cérébrale. Paris: Savine, 1890.

Le Songe d'une femme. Paris: Mercure de France, 1899.

Notes

Introduction

1. T. S. Eliot, *The Sacred Wood* (London: Methuen, 1960), p. 14.
2. E. J. H. Greene, in *T. S. Eliot et la France* (Paris: Boivin, 1951), p. 146, af-_ firms, presumably on the basis of conversations with Eliot, that "c'est d'ailleurs sur un conseil de Pound qu'Eliot s'est mis a lire Gourmont."
3. Karl Uitti, *La Passion litteraire de Remy de Gourmont*, (Paris: Presses Universitaries, 1962), pp. 3-4.
4. Glenn Burne, *Remy de Gourmont: His Ideas and Influence in England and America* (Carbondale: Southern Illinois University Press, 1963). Remy de Gourmont, *Selected Writings*, ed. and trans. Glenn Burne (Ann Arbor: University of Michigan Press, 1966).
5. See Burne, *Remy de Gourmont*, pp. 111-153; Garnet Rees, *Remy de Gourmont: Essai de biographie intellectuelle* (Paris: Boivin, 1940), pp. 271-278, René Taupin, "The Example of Remy de Gourmont," *Criterion* (July 1931), pp. 614-625. For Hulme and Gourmont see T. E. Hulme, *Speculations*, ed. Herbert Read (London: Gollancz, 1960); Michael Roberts, *T. E. Hulme* (London: Faber and Faber, 1938). For Eliot and Gourmont see F. W. Bateson, "Contribution to a Dictionary of Critical Terms: Dissociation of Sensibility," *Essays in Criticism* (July 1951), pp. 302-312; E. J. H. Greene, *T. S. Eliot et la France*, pp. 143-170; F. W. Bateson, "The Poetry of Learning" and John Chalker, "Authority and Personality in Eliot's Criticism," in *Eliot in Perspective*, ed. Graham Martin (New York: Humanities Press, 1970), pp. 35-38, 199-202. For Aldington and Gourmont see D. Mossop, "Un disciple de Gourmont: Richard Aldington," *Revue de littérature comparée* (Oct.-Dec. 1951), pp. 403-435; Richard Aldington, *Life for Life's Sake* (New York: Viking Press, 1941), pp. 172-175. For Huxley and Gourmont see R. E. Temple, "Aldous Huxley et la littérature française," *Revue de littérature comparée* (Jan.-Mar. 1939), pp. 99-102. Cyrena N. Pondrom, *The Road from Paris* (Cambridge: Cambridge University Press, 1974), gives Gourmont a prominent place in her survey of the French influence on English poetry 1900-1920.
6. John Espey, in *Ezra Pound's Mauberley* (Berkeley: University of California Press, 1955), pp. 62-83, concentrates exclusively on Gourmont's impact on specific themes and images of *Mauberley*. Donald Davie, in *Ezra Pound: Poet as Sculptor* (New York: Oxford University Press, 1964), pp. 65-76, devotes a rather summary chapter to Pound's reading and translation of Gourmont. N. Christophe de Nagy's *Ezra Pound's Poetics and Literary Tradition* (Bern: Francke, 1966), pp. 72-77, provides a brief theoretical discussion of the relation of *Le*

171

Problème du style to Pound's Imagist poetics. Hugh Kenner's *The Poetry of Ezra Pound* (New York: New Directions, 1951) and *The Pound Era* (Berkeley: University of California Press, 1971) mention Gourmont only in passing. More recently, Ronald Bush's *The Genesis of Ezra Pound's Cantos* (Princeton: Princeton University Press, 1976), pp. 153-175, provides an excellent if somewhat specialized discussion of Gourmont's part in Pound's discovery of a new dramatic narrative voice in the early stages of the *Cantos*.

7. Background information on Huneker for this page and the following ones is from Arnold T. Schwab, *James Gibbons Huneker* (Stanford: Stanford University Press, 1963); and Burne, *Remy de Gourmont*, pp. 111-112. See also Harry Levin, "America Discovers Bohemia," *Grounds for Comparison* (Cambridge: Harvard University Press, 1972), pp. 272-275.

8. Quoted in Schwab, pp. 196-197.

9. Ibid., p. 197.

10. Ibid.

11. Ibid. See also Kenneth Burke, "Approaches to Remy de Gourmont," *Dial* (Feb. 1921), pp. 125-128, and "De Gourmont on 'Dissociation' " in his *A Rhetoric of Motives* (New York: Prentice-Hall, 1950), pp. 149-154. In *Grounds for Comparison*, p. 276, Harry Levin provides an excellent summary of the achievement of Huneker and other such Bohemian American literary figures as Lafcadio Hearn and Edgar Saltus: "The opinions Huneker imported, the books Hearn and Saltus translated, did much to eradicate the taint of provinciality that Henry James had detected in Poe. Though traditionalists had kept in touch with England, the current stimulus came largely from France. And, though the importers and translators were equally versatile as creative writers, their accomplishment was largely critical. Its results may be counted in educated audiences, rather than achieved masterpieces. Where literature had been traditionally connected with oratory and theology, it could now be envisaged through its relation to purely artistic disciplines; hence the old-fashioned didactic presuppositions gave way to estheticism. Art for art's sake was never a very positive credo, but it aided in releasing the artist from ulterior constraints—particularly the taboos of sexual reticence. Sometimes, it may seem to us, the prudery of the moralists was outmatched by the prurience of the esthetes; the struggle between them, at all events, would be prolonged and embittered before the subject could be faced in frank simplicity. To turn from subject matter to technique is to note the paradoxical devotion of a group of journalists to the cult of style. Affectation and mannerism did not obscure their genuine feeling for the cadence and the nuance. If they no longer excite us, it is because their successors reaped the benefits of their imitations and experiments."

12. "Interesting French Publications," *Book News Monthly* (Sept. 1906), pp. 54-55. For Pound's interest in Péladan, see Leon Surette, "A Light from Eleusis," *Paideuma* (Fall 1974), pp. 191-200. Pound mentions reading Anatole France in Paige Typescript #29, 11 Feb. 1905, at the Pound Center, Beinecke Library, Yale University.

13. "I have always felt that the soul has two movements primarily: one to transcend form, and the other to create form. Nietzsche, to whom you have been the first to introduce me, calls these the Dionysian and the Apollonic, respectively." Quoted by Monroe K. Spears, *Dionysus and the City: Modernism in Twentieth-Century Poetry* (New York: Oxford University Press, 1970), p. 48.

14. Schwab, p. 240. Huneker's "James Joyce" is reprinted in his *Unicorns* (New York: Scribner's, 1917), pp. 187-194.

15. Paige Typescript #200, 2 March, and #207, 26 March, 1911. Pound Center, Beinecke Library, Yale.

16. Paige Typescript #210, May 1911.

17. Noel Stock, *The Life of Ezra Pound* (New York: Avon, 1974), p. 240. Stock's book has supplied much of the biographical background for these pages.

18. Wallace Martin, *The New Age under Orage* (Manchester: Manchester University Press, 1967), p. 91. Martin's study provides an excellent account of the literary and political dimensions of the *New Age*.

19. F. S. Flint, "Book of the Week: Remy de Gourmont," *New Age*, p. 220. See also L. C. Breunig "F. S. Flint, Imagism's 'Maître d'Ecole,' " *Comparative Literature* (Spring 1952), pp. 118-136.

20. Arthur Symons, "Some French Stories," *Saturday Review* (17 July 1897), p. 71. Edmund Gosse, "Two French Critics, Emile Faguet and Remy de Gourmont," *Aspects and Impressions* (New York: Scribner's, 1922), pp. 203-223. Havelock Ellis, "Remy de Gourmont," *From Rousseau to Proust* (Boston: Houghton Mifflin, 1935), pp. 307-327.

21. F. S. Flint, "The History of Imagism," *Egoist* (1 May 1915), p. 71.

22. Paige Typescript, #238, 21 Feb. 1912.

23. Kenner, *The Pound Era*, p. 555.

24. René Taupin, *L'Influence du symbolisme français sur la poésie américaine (1910-1920)* (Paris: Champion, 1929), p. 30.

25. Donald Gallup, *A Bibliography of Ezra Pound* (London: Hart-Davis, 1969), p. 53.

26. De Nagy, *Ezra Pound's Poetics*, p. 118, affirms, on the basis of conversations with both Pound and H. D., that they began reading *Le Problème du style* in the early months of 1912.

27. Ibid., p. 76.

28. The source of Pound's misleading analogy is perhaps Flint's paraphrase of Tancrède de Visan's *L'Attitude du lyrisme contemporain* (1910) in his "Contemporary French Poetry," *Poetry Review* (Aug. 1912), p. 357: "A symbol is a sign used in place of a reality, as in algebra; but the symbolist poet attempts to give you an intuition of the reality itself and of the forces, vague to us, behind it, by a series of images which the imagination seizes and brings together in its effort to insert itself into and express that reality, and to evoke at the same time the infinity of which it is the culminating point in the present." Although Pound is at pains to dissociate Imagism from Symbolism in this passage, the terms he uses echo Yeats's Coleridgean distinctions between symbol and allegory: "A symbol is indeed the only possible expression of some invisible essence, a transparent lamp about a spiritual flame; while allegory is one of the many possible representations of an embodied thing, or familiar principle, and belongs to fancy and not to imagination: the one is a revelation, the other an amusement." *Essays and Introductions* (New York: Collier, 1968), p. 116. The "variable significance" that Pound ascribes to the image can be correlated with Yeats's insistence on the polysemous functions of "symbols that have numberless meanings besides the one or two the writer lays an emphasis upon . . ." (*Essays and Introductions*, p. 87). It would seem, in short, that Pound's distinction between Imagism and allegory merely substitutes the term "image" for Yeats's "symbol."

29. Paige Typescript #243, May 1912, and #251, Aug. 1912.

30. Paige Typescript #269, 29 Nov. 1912.

31. See Breunig, "F. S. Flint," pp. 122-123.

32. See my "Ezra Pound: Letters to Natalie Barney," *Paideuma* (Fall 1976) pp. 279-299.

33. Paige Typescript #522, Spring 1919. As for the plans to publish *Les Chevaux de Diomède* in *The Glebe*, see Alfred Kreymborg, *Troubadour* (New York: Sagamore Press, 1957), p. 157.

34. "The Approach to Paris, I," *New Age* (4 Sept. 1913), p. 551.

35. "Paris," *Poetry* (Oct. 1913), p. 27.

36. "The Approach to Paris, V," *New Age* (2 Oct. 1913), p. 662.

37. Quoted in William Wees, *Vorticism and the English Avant-Garde* (Toronto: University of Toronto Press, 1972), p. 127.

38. "A Blast from London," *Dial* (16 Jan. 1915), p. 41.

39. William Carlos Williams, "Prologue to Kora in Hell," *Selected Essays* (New York: New Directions, 1969), pp. 23-24.

40. Paige Typescript #323, 25 March 1914.

41. Paige Typescript #389, 21 May 1915.

42. *Confucius*, trans. and commentary by Ezra Pound (New York: New Directions, 1969), pp. 20-22.

43. Paige Typescript #400, 1 Nov. 1915.

44. Richard Aldington, "Remy de Gourmont," *Egoist* (11 Nov. 1915). J. G. Huneker, *Unicorns*, pp. 18-32. John Cowper Powys, *Suspended Judgements* (New York: Arnold Shaw, 1916), pp. 225-257. Havelock Ellis also contributed an obituary to the *New Republic* (18 Dec. 1915).

45. Rees, *Remy de Gourmont*, p. 265.

46. "Dust for Sparrows" ran for nine installments in the *Dial* from September 1920 through May 1921. They are included in Pound's *Translations* (New York: New Directions, 1963), pp. 363-400.

47. Richard Aldington, *Remy de Gourmont: A Modern Man of Letters* (Seattle: University of Washington Bookstore, 1928), p. 10. Havelock Ellis, *From Rousseau to Proust*, p. 311.

48. *Physique de l'amour*, p. 5.

49. What remains of Pound's personal library at Brunnenburg includes the following works by Gourmont, all published by the Mercure de France: *Histoires magiques* (1894), *Le Pèlerin du silence* (1896), *D'Un Pays lointain* (1898), *Le Problème du style* (1902), *Epilogues* [I] (1902), *Promenades littéraires*, 1st series (1904), *Une Nuit au Luxembourg* (1906), *Un Coeur virginal* (1907), *Dialogues des amateurs sur les choses du temps* (1907), *Promenades philosophiques*, 3rd series (1909), *Lettres intimes à l'Amazone* (1926).

50. Quoted in Charles Norman, *Ezra Pound*, revised ed. (New York: Minerva, 1969), p. 290.

51. "Mr. Aldington's Views on Gourmont," *Dial* (Jan. 1929), p. 71. A review of *Remy de Gourmont: Selections from all his Works*, chosen and trans., Richard Aldington (Chicago: Covici, 1928), 2 vols.

52. "Appunti: Il Mal francese," *L'Indice* (Nov. 1930), p. 1.

53. "Arretrati e snobisti," *Meridiano di Roma* (7 March 1943), p. 1.

54. "A French Accent," *If This Be Treason* (Siena: Printed privately for Olga Rudge, 1948), pp. 21-22. During his association with the *Little Review* and the *Dial*, Pound apparently tried to find authors who might supply the magazines with a monthly coverage of French literature—Jules Romains was for a while the *Little Review*'s French editor, Clément Pensaers and Paul Morand supplied the *Dial* with "Letters from Paris" after Pound ceased contributing them. Concerning Pound's admiration for Mockel as an editor, see his "Albert Mockel and 'La Wallonie,' " *Little Review* (Oct. 1918), pp. 51-64. Pound mentions Vallette's offer of a rubric at the *Mercure* in LE, 81, and in Paige Typescript #532, 3 Sept. 1919: "Have also seen Vallette (Edtr. Mercure de France), he talked for about an hour in a very small quiet voice. Intelligent but resigned. Knows what is wrong but also knows that even a disproportionate effort would probably fail to rectify it very much. He has done a big job in making the Mercure and his personality explains the result."

55. Letter to E. E. Cummings (circa 1947) at Houghton Library, Harvard University.

56. Ibid.

57. Letter to Natalie Barney, 17 Nov. 1952, at the Bibliothèque littéraire Jacques Doucet, Paris.

58. Letters to Cummings at Houghton Library.

1. *"Amas ut facias pulchram"*

1. Donald Hall, "Ezra Pound, An Interview," in *Ezra Pound: A Collection of Criticism*, ed. Grace Schulman (New York: MacGraw-Hill, 1974), p. 30.

2. "Status Rerum," *Poetry* (Jan. 1913), p. 125.

3. "The Approach to Paris, II," *New Age* (11 Sept. 1913), p. 578.

4. Donald Davie, *Ezra Pound: Poet as Sculptor*, p. 58.

5. As for Symbolism's " 'sin,' satanism, rosy cross, heavy lilies" to which Pound alludes, here is Mario Praz's description of Gourmont's *Litanies*: "However much disgust Gourmont may have shown later (in *Epilogues*) for Sade . . . he made consummate use, at one period, of the litany of sacrilege, the sadistic mingling of obscene and religious themes. Thus, in the *Litanies de la rose* . . . he evokes false, cruel women under the image of various kinds of roses; in the *Correspondances* he twists the phraseology of mysticism to lascivious meanings, and in the *Fantôme-duplicité* . . . he provides a detailed initiation into the Black Mass . . . Gourmont went further than any one in this employment of sacred and mystical texts for the purpose of adding a new flavour to erotic adventure, but as he was not a believer like Huysmans, his pages lack that sense of revolt and horror which breathes in all the sadistic abandonments of *Là-bas*." Mario Praz, *The Romantic Agony* (New York: Oxford University Press, 1951), pp. 352-353.

6. "The Approach to Paris, II," p. 577.

7. Pound was introduced to the Duhamel and Vildrac *Notes sur la technique poétique* by F. S. Flint's influential "Contemporary French Poetry" issue of the *Poetry Review* (Aug. 1912), p. 361. Pound's March 1913 "A Few Don'ts," published in *Poetry*, alludes to their *Notes*, especially the section devoted to rhyme. As for the question of the "constant rythmique," see Stanley K. Coffman, *Imagism: A Chapter for the History of Modern Poetry* (Norman: University of Oklahoma Press, 1951), pp. 92ff.

8. Henri de Régnier's prefatory poem to *Les Médailles d'Argile* (Paris: Mercure de France, 1900) makes similar use of a four-syllable rhythmic constant to pattern its free-verse evocation of the return of the gods. Pound's 1912 poem on the same subject, "The Return," transforms Régnier's four-syllable unit into the recurrent rhythmic figure: $-\cup\cup/-\cup/-$. See René Taupin, *L'Influence du symbolisme français sur la poésie américaine (de 1910 à 1920)* (Paris: Champion, 1929), p. 30, and Hugh Kenner, *The Pound Era*, pp. 189-190.

9. "The Approach to Paris, II," p. 578.

10. René Taupin, "The Example of Remy de Gourmont," *Criterion*, p. 619.

11. "French Poets," *Make It New* (New Haven: Yale University Press, 1935), p. 188. Pound's critical anthology of contemporary French verse first appeared as "A Study in French Poets," *Little Review* (Feb. 1918).

12. "The Approach to Paris, II," p. 578.

13. "The Approach to Paris, VII," *New Age* (16 Oct. 1913), p. 728.

14. "Rabindranath Tagore," *Fortnightly Review* (1 Mar. 1913), p. 571. Also quoted in Davie, p. 68.

15. Davie, p. 58.

16. Ibid., p. 45.

17. René Taupin in his *L'Influence du symbolisme* has suggested the "Martagon" section of Gourmont's 1893 *Fleurs de jadis* as the model for the "Midonz" section of Pound's 1912 "The Alchemist." Burne quotes the relevant passage in his *Remy de Gourmont*, p. 126:

Martagon dont les têtes se dressent par centaines,
monstre odorante, hydre azurée,
Martagon dont le front porte un turban de pourpre,

Martagon dont les yeux sont jaunes, lys byzantin,
joie des empereurs décadents, fleur
favorite des alcôves, parfums des Saintes Images,

Martagons, multiples Martagons, je vous préfère à
d'autres monstres dont je pourrais dire le nom, fleurs
trépassées, fleurs de jadis.

18. *Make It New*, p. 187.

19. Rapprochement suggested by Karl Uitti, *La Passion littéraire de Remy de Gourmont*, p. 235. William York Tindall also points out the possible debt of this passage in *Ash Wednesday* to the *Litanies* (in *Forces in Modern British Literature*, New York: Vintage Books, 1956, p. 281).

20. "The Approach to Paris, II," p. 578. Pound's reference to the drunkenness induced by Gourmont's "naming over of beauty" and to the trancelike vision of "the procession of all women that ever were" has strong Yeatsian overtones. Compare Yeats's description of such "systematic mystics" and symbolists as Rossetti and Wagner in his 1898 essay "Symbolism in Painting": "Such men often fall into trances, or have waking dreams. Their thought wanders from the woman who is Love herself, to her sisters and her forebears, and to all the great procession; and so august a beauty moves before the mind that they forget the things which move before the eyes" (*Essays and Introductions*, New York: Collier, 1968, p. 150).

21. Mary de Rachewiltz has kindly allowed me to examine Pound's own annotated copies of Gourmont's works, currently in the library of the Schloss Brunnenburg, Merano.

22. See Guy Davenport, "Persephone's Ezra," in *New Approaches to Ezra Pound*, ed. Eva Hesse (London: Faber and Faber, 1969), p. 149.

23. *Le Latin mystique*, p. 8.

24. Richard Aldington, *Remy de Gourmont*, pp. 222-223.

25. The *Oxford English Dictionary* defines "sequence" as "A composition in rhythmical prose or accentual meter said or sung, in the Western Church, between Gradual and the Gospel. Also called *prose*." At the risk of forcing their etymological relation, one might relate Pound's interest in the sequence to his espousal of the "prose tradition in verse."

26. *Le Latin mystique*, p. 120.

27. Hugh Kenner, *The Poetry of Ezra Pound*, p. 115.

28. *Le Latin mystique*, p. 163. Also quoted in R. Murray Schafer, "The Developing Theories of Absolute Rhythm and Great Bass," *Paideuma* (Spring 1973), p. 25.

29. *Le Latin mystique*, p. 121.

30. Ibid., p. 123.

31. *Dante, Béatrice et la poésie amoureuse, Essai sur l'idéal féminin en Italie à la fin du XIIIe siècle*, p. 62. This monograph is merely a slight revision and conflation of "Béatrice, Dante et Platon" (1883) and "La Béatrice de Dante et l'idéal féminin" (1885). For further discussion of Dante, Gourmont, and the latter's discovery and definition of "idealism" see Karl Uitti, *La Passion littéraire de Remy de Gourmont*, pp. 60-72.

32. Pound never specifically alludes to Gourmont's work on Dante, but T. S. Eliot's comments in his unpublished Clark Lectures are illuminating. They exist in

French in the essay "Deux Attitudes mystiques: Dante et Donne," *Chroniques*, 3 (1927), p. 151. "Une des meilleures vulgarisations de la *Vita Nuova* est la plaquette de Remy de Gourmont intitulée *Dante, Béatrice et la poésie amoureuse.* Gourmont s'y applique à montrer que la Béatrice de Dante n'est en définitive qu'une construction, lors même que son nom n'aurait pas été choisi tout exprès pour le sens qu'il renferme. Argument propre à convaincre pleinement tous ceux pour qui la *Vita Nuova* est le récit fidèle d'une ancienne passion; mais je ne sache pas qu'un lecteur intelligent en ait jamais douté. Gourmont en souligne l'arbitraire et le symbolisme chronologique, et, à l'appui, compare la vision de Dante à d'autres visions de la littérature apocalyptique, entre autres au *Pasteur d'Hermas.* Mais Gourmont ne doit jamais être accepté sans réserves. Ce critique de talent n'était pas philosophe; et, n'étant pas philosophe, nourrissait quantités de préjugés philosophiques, notamment sur l'amour. Sa brochure pourrait nous faire accroire que la *Vita Nuova* n'est qu'une sèche allégorie, privée de toute vie. Il n'en est rien. A mon avis, la *Vita Nuova* rapporte une actualité vécue, moulée dans une forme particulière."

33. *Le Livre des masques*, p. 11.

34. "L'Idéalisme," in *Le Chemin de velours*, p. 227.

35. *Le Chemin de velours*, pp. 144-145.

36. G. R. S. Mead, editor of the *Quest*, a quarterly devoted to gnosticism, theosophy, and pagan mystery religions. Pound's "Psychology and Troubadours," published in the magazine in Oct. 1912 and later included in *The Spirit of Romance*, was originally a lecture delivered to Mead's Quest Society in the spring of that year.

37. Pound observed in the surrealist periodical *Minautaure*, 3-4 (1933), p. 112: "Mais ma rencontre avec Guido Cavalcanti décédé, porte (à leur insu) sur le problème des surréalistes: état de conscience et (ou) force morale." "The XIIth century had surrealism in plenty," he later observed in "the Coward Surrealists," *Contemporary Poetry and Prose* (Nov. 1936), p. 136.

38. *Dante, Béatrice et la poésie amoureuse*, p. 48.

39. Ibid., p. 39. Compare Eliot, "Deux Attitudes mystiques," p. 158: "Gourmont note dans sa plaquette que, chez les *trecentisti* l'amour n'implique point l'idée de possession; et, pour hasardée que soit cette généralisation, il est exact de dire que les *trecentisti* se soucient plus de la contemplation de l'objet aimé que des sentiments d'union; ce qu'ils rapportent, ce sont les sensations et les sentiments de l'amant qui contemple l'objet de son amour . . . 'Chi e questa che vien, ch'ogni uom la mira, / Che fa tremar di claritate l'aere?' dit Cavalcanti dans son célèbre sonnet; et on constatera que ce vers n'est pas qu'une flatteuse hyberbole, mais la notation exacte de l'impression visuelle de l'être aimé sur l'amant. Ce fait est très significatif." Pound makes a similar argument in his "Cavalcanti" piece in *Literary Essays.*

40. Ronald Bush, *The Genesis of Ezra Pound's Cantos* (Princeton: Princeton University Press, 1976), pp. 159-161.

41. *Lettres à l'Amazone*, p. 202. Quoted in part in LE, 419.

42. John Espey, *Ezra Pound's Mauberley* (Berkeley: University of California Press, 1974), pp. 68-71.

43. John Peck, "Pound's Lexical Mythography," *Paideuma* (Spring-Summer 1972), p. 17.

44. "Le Roman de Guillaume de Machaut et de Peronne d'Armentières," in *Promenades littéraires*, 5th series, pp. 5-36.

45. *Lettres à l'Amazone*, pp. 47, 60, 69, 71, 105, 109, 241.

46. Praz's chapter "Byzantium," which discusses, among other things, the fatal woman, sadism and Catholicism in the French Decadents, the theme of the androgyne, lust and death, includes a short chapter on Gourmont's fiction and its

relation to the contemporary works of Huysmans, Lorrain, Schwob, and D'Annunzio. Praz points out, however, that Gourmont's use of these themes is in many cases ironic: "Belated *Encyclopédiste* as he is, Gourmont mocks at religious superstition; but he is also a Decadent and as such makes use of religion in order to extract sensations from it. It is from this twofold nature that his particular half-humoristic, half-serious tone is derived." *The Romantic Agony*, p. 352.

47. *Le Songe d'une femme*, 5th ed. (Paris: Mercure de France, 1916), p. 19.

48. "Three Cantos," *Poetry* (June 1917), p. 119.

2. The Problem of Style

1. T. S. Eliot, *The Sacred Wood*, p. 44.

2. Ibid., p. 14.

3. T. S. Eliot, "Isolated Superiority," *Dial* (Jan. 1928), p. 7.

4. Garnet Rees, *Remy de Gourmont*, p. 208. Karl Uitti, *La Passion littéraire de Remy de Gourmont*, p. 289, calls Gourmont the "Sainte-Beuve du modernisme."

5. See his "Arthur Symons," *Athenaeum* (21 May 1920), pp. 663-664.

6. "Paris Letter," *Dial* (Jan. 1923), p. 87.

7. *Le Livre des masques* (1963), p. 10. For a further discussion of Gourmont's definitions of Symbolism, see Glenn S. Burne, "Remy de Gourmont and the Aesthetics of Symbolism," *Comparative Literature Studies*, vol. 4, nos. 1-2 (1967), pp. 161-175, and John Porter Houston, "Proust, Gourmont and the Symbolist Heritage," in *Modern French Criticism from Proust and Valéry to Structuralism*, ed. John. K. Simon (Chicago: University of Chicago Press, 1972), pp. 41-60.

8. Cited in Glenn S. Burne, *Remy de Gourmont*, p. 148. Aldington quoted this same passage of Gourmont's in the *Bruno Chap Book* (1915); it also appeared in the preface to *Some Imagist Poets* (1916) as part of the Imagist manifesto.

9. I have been unable to locate Gourmont's obituary of Gaudier-Brzeska.

10. *Sacred Wood*, p. 44. Though it is not entirely clear when Pound first encountered *Le Livre des masques*, his reading of *Le Problème du style* in the early months of 1912 is affirmed by de Nagy on the basis of conversations with both Pound and H.D. See N. Christoph de Nagy, *Ezra Pound's Poetics and Literary Tradition*, p. 118.

11. "An 'Image' is that which presents an intellectual and emotional complex in an instant of time. I use the term 'complex' rather in the technical sense employed by the newer psychologists, such as Hart, though we might not agree absolutely in our application" (LE, 4). As Hugh Witemeyer explains in *The Poetry of Ezra Pound: Forms and Renewal, 1908-1920* (Berkeley: University of California Press, 1969), p. 33: "Bernard Hart, a distinguished Cambridge psychologist, used the term 'complex' in an orthodox Freudian sense, as 'a system of connected ideas, with a strong emotional tone, and a tendency to produce actions of a definite character.' He went on in his popular primer, *The Psychology of Insanity* (1912), to explain that complexes become active 'in the presence of a 'stimulus' occurring whenever one or more of the ideas belonging to a complex is roused to activity, either by some external event, or by a process of association occurring within the mind itself.' "

12. "The Revolt of Intelligence, IV," *New Age* (1 Jan. 1920), p. 139.

13. "America: Chances and Remedies, VI," *New Age* (5 June 1913), p. 143.

14. Davie, *Ezra Pound: Poet as Sculptor*, p. 69.

15. *Le Problème du style.*

16. Ibid., p. 31. Hereafter, all references to *Le Problème du style* will be cited in the body of the text by page number.

17. Guillaume Pauthier, *Confucius et Mencius. Les Quatre Livres de philoso-phie morale et politique de la Chine* (Paris: Charpentier, 1858), p. 44. Pauthier's translation was the source for Pound's Canto XIII. Though he had by then ac-quired Legge's bilingual edition of the *Four Books*, Pound would again use Pau-thier's French version as the basis for his own 1928 rendering of the *Ta Hio*. His translation of this particular passage ran: "Renovate, dod gast you, renovate!"—though in a footnote he observed that "Pauthier with greater elegance gives in his French the equivalent to: 'Renew thyself daily, utterly, make it new, and again new, make it new.' " It would appear, then, that Pound's celebrated motto, Make It New, is an inspired misprision of Pauthier's "fais-le de *nouveau*." *Ta Hio* (Seat-tle: University of Washington Book Store, 1928), p. 12.

18. Remy de Gourmont, "Tradition and Other Things," *Egoist* (15 July 1914), pp. 262-263. See also Burne, pp. 145-147.

19. *The Sacred Wood*, p. 51.

20. *Promenades littéraires*, 1st series, p. 43.

21. *Promenades philosophiques*, 2nd series, p. 42.

22. *The Sacred Wood*, p. 49.

23. Burne, p. 41.

24. *Promenades philosophiques*, 2nd series, p. 25.

25. Ibid., p. 31.

26. *The Sacred Wood*, p. 31.

27. "Tradition and Other Things," p. 262.

28. Ibid., p. 261.

29. Commenting on the codification of French literary tradition into a static pantheon of "gloires littéraires," Gourmont quipped: "Armed with the four rules of literature, the professors have examined various talents and classified them. They have awarded prizes and honorable mentions. There is the first order and then the others ranked down to the fourth and fifth order. French literature has become as hierarchically arranged as an apartment house. 'Villon,' one of the classifiers told me one day, 'is not of the first order.' Admiration is to be shaded according to the seven notes on the university scale. Serious flautists excel at this game." *Le Chemin de velours*, p. 119.

30. Pound's own copy of *Le Problème du style* (currently in the library at Schloss Brunnenburg) is heavily marked in the margins. In quoting from Gour-mont's work I have emphasized those passages specifically noted by Pound in or-der to follow more closely his particular reading of the text.

31. See the 1st, 3rd, and 6th series of Gourmont's *Promenades littéraires.*

32. "Les Traducteurs," *Promenades littéraires*, 5th series, pp. 163-164. Also quoted in de Nagy, *Ezra Pound's Poetics*, pp. 42-43.

33. "The Approach to Paris, II," *New Age* (11 Sept. 1913), p. 577.

34. Hulme and Eliot quoted in Burne, pp. 117 and 133. Burne's book contains a good account of the debt of Hulme's *Speculations* to *Le Problème du style*, which Hulme probably read around 1909 or 1910. See also Alun R. Jones, *The Life and Opinions of T. E. Hulme* (Boston: Houghton Mifflin, 1960), for Hulme's reading of both Bergson and Gourmont.

35. See Uitti, pp. 257-259.

36. Pound's first combined usage of the terms "melopoeia" and "logopoeia" occurs in his "A List of Books," *Little Review* (March 1918), p. 57.

37. See de Nagy, pp. 76-86. De Nagy's book provides a dense analysis of the theoretical impact of *Le Problème du style* on Pound's Imagist precepts.

38. Quoted in Davie, *Ezra Pound*, p. 65.

39. Ernest Fenollosa, *The Chinese Written Character as a Medium for Poetry*, ed. Ezra Pound (San Francisco: City Lights, n.d.), p. 25.

40. Ibid., p. 26.

41. Ibid., p. 22.

42. Herbert Schneidau, *Ezra Pound: The Image and the Real* (Baton Rouge: Louisiana State University Press, 1969), p. 48. Pound, like Eliot, would also disagree fundamentally with Gourmont's emphasis on the role of the subconscious in the creative process (see the latter's "La Création subconsciente" in *La Culture des idées*). Gourmont's theory of subconscious creation implied a passivity on the part of the artist vis à vis his material that was unacceptable to Pound's factive, voluntaristic temper. He would vehemently object to Freudian theory and to surrealist automatism for similar reasons.

43. Schneidau, p. 22. It should be pointed out, however, that in *Le Problème du style* Gourmont cautioned against an exclusively visual style: "The style of the pure visual . . . composed entirely of unprecedented images, would be absolutely incomprehensible" (p. 47). Pound later noted a similar flaw in Ford Madox Ford's theories of style: "I think Hueffer goes wrong because he bases his criticism on the eye, and almost solely on the eye." "On Criticism in General," *Criterion* (Jan. 1923), p. 146.

44. See Schneidau, p. 56, on the "transubstantial" nature of the Image as the basis of Pound's poetry of reality. The Olson phrase is the title of one of the essays included in *Selected Writings of Charles Olson*, ed. Robert Creeley (New York: New Directions, 1966).

45. Burne, p. 97.

46. Remy de Gourmont, "Du Style ou de l'écriture," *La Culture des idées* (1964), p. 22. Gourmont also used the term *verbalisme* frequently in his *Epilogues* to define the dissociation of the world of sensations from the world of words.

47. "A List of Books," *Little Review* (March 1918), p. 57.

48. T. S. Eliot, *The Complete Poems and Plays 1909-1950* (New York, Harcourt Brace, 1952), p. 121.

49. Schneidau, p. 159.

50. "Editorial," *Little Review* (May 1917), p. 6.

51. T. S. Eliot, "Eeldrop and Appleplex," *Little Review* (May 1917), p. 10. Compare Pound: "The genius can pay in nugget and in lump gold: it is not necessary that he bring up his knowledge into the mint of consciousness, stamp it into either the coin of conscientiously analysed form-detail knowledge or into the paper money of words, before he transmit it." *New Age* (Nov. 27, 1919), p. 60.

3. Dissociations

1. "The New Sculpture," *Egoist* (16 Feb. 1914), p. 68.

2. "Mr. Aldington's Views on Gourmont," *Dial* (Jan. 1929), pp. 70-71.

3. See Garnet Rees, *Remy de Gourmont*, p. 144, for Gide's comments on Gourmont.

4. Both passages quoted in Rees, p. 148.

5. Ibid., p. 144.

6. Noel Stock, *The Life of Ezra Pound*, pp. 114-115.

7. See my "Ideas Into Action: Pound and Voltaire," *Paideuma* (Winter 1977), pp. 365-390.

8. Donald Davie, *Ezra Pound: Poet as Sculptor*, p. 71.

9. Remy de Gourmont, *Epilogues* [I], *Réflexions sur la vie 1895-1898*, pp. 151-152.

10. Charles Baudelaire, *Oeuvres complètes* (Paris: Bibliothèque de la Pléiade, 1961), p. 1179.

11. "The Bourgeois," *Egoist* (2 Feb. 1914), p. 53.

12. "The New Sculpture," *Egoist* (16 Feb. 1914), p. 68.

13. "The Bourgeois," pp. 53-54.
14. "Pastiche: The Regional, XVII," *New Age* (13 Nov. 1919), p. 32.
15. Charles Norman, *Ezra Pound*, revised ed. (New York: Minerva Press, 1969), p. 32.
16. Quoted in *Ezra Pound: The Critical Heritage*, ed. Eric Homberger (London: Routledge and Kegan Paul, 1972), p. 144.
17. Ibid., pp. 146-147.
18. Ibid., p. 151.
19. Rees, p. 144.
20. Remy de Gourmont, *Nouveaux Dialogues des amateurs sur les choses du temps (Epilogues V, 1907-1910)*, p. 127. Quoted in Rees, p. 138.
21. Paul Rosenfield, reminiscing about meeting Pound in Paris during the twenties, records the following conversation: "What are you writing on now Mr Pound?" inquired Tennessee Anderson. "Dante composed the Poem of Faith. I am writing the Poem of Doubt," said he. In *Ezra Pound: The Critical Heritage*, p. 355.
22. Remy de Gourmont, *Les Chevaux de Diomède*, p. 232.
23. Remy de Gourmont, *Epilogues III, 1902-1904*, p. 205, and *Promenades philosophiques*, 2nd series, p. 158.
24. T. S. Eliot, "The Hawthorne Aspect," *Little Review* (Aug. 1918), p. 46. Compare Gourmont: "Once they have entered us, ideas either remain inert, unknown, or else they disintegrate. In the first case, it is not long before they are expelled from the mind, somewhat like an indigestible fragment from the intestines. Their sojourn can produce a certain irritation, even lesions—that is to say, they can provoke absurd acts, manifestly without logical relation to the normal physiology of the patient. This effect is very apparent in different nations, but especially in France, at the time of great political or moral crises. We see people tormented by the presence of a parasitic idea in their brains, like sheep by the lodging of a trumpet fly's larva in their frontal sinuses. Man, like the sheep, has an 'inflammation.'" *Promenades philosophiques* (Paris: Mercure de France, 1904), p. 90.
25. "On the Imbecility of the Rich," *Egoist* (15 Oct. 1914), p. 389. Richard Ellmann in *Eminent Domain* (London: Oxford University Press, 1970), p. 176, notes that Yeats demoted Pound from Phase 12 to Phase 23 of *A Vision* because of "the sight of Pound feeding all the stray cats in Rapallo in 1928. This undifferentiated pity, pity 'like that of a drunken man,' was quickly connected by Yeats to the hysterical pity for general humanity left over from the romantic movement. He had observed and blamed it in other writers, notably Sean O'Casey and Wilfred Owen. All three seemed to belong to Phase 23, the theme of which is Creation through Pity."
26. Remy de Gourmont, *Epilogues II, 1899-1901*, p. 88.
27. *La Culture des Idées* (Paris: Mercure de France, 1964), p. 63.
28. *Epilogues* [I], p. 245. See also *Le Chemin de velours*, p. 86: "Definitions . . . contain of reality what a badly retrieved fishnet contains of the obscure and swarming life of the sea where it has awaited its prey—some snarled seaweed, some scrawny creatures waving their translucent limbs about, and all sorts of sea-snails and bivalves clamped shut by a mechanical sensibility. But reality, that sizeable fish, has, with a flip of its tail, slipped away. In general, clear and distinct phrases have no meaning whatsoever—they are affirmative gestures that suggest dutiful acquiescence, and that is all. The human mind is so complex and things are so tangled up with each other that, to explain a blade of straw, one would have to take the entire universe apart."
29. Remy de Gourmont, *Le Chemin de velours*, p. 144.
30. "The method was clearly a companion discovery to symbolism, which

sought its effects precisely by utilizing, more programmatically than in any previous movement, the clusters of associations surrounding the important words of a poem or fiction." Kenneth Burke, *Counterstatement* (Los Altos: Hermes Publications, 1953), p. 23.

31. "What America Has to Live Down, I," *New Age* (22 Aug. 1918), p. 266.

32. On Pound's "parataxis of sound" see Hugh Kenner, *The Pound Era*, pp. 77-83.

33. Ibid., p. 423.

34. Remy de Gourmont, *L'Esthétique de la langue française*, p. 302.

35. "Pastiche. The Regional, VII," *New Age* (21 Aug. 1919), p. 284.

36. "Pastiche. The Regional, XIV," *New Age* (23 Oct. 1919), p. 432.

37. "The Revolt of Intelligence, VI," *New Age* (15 Jan. 1920), p. 177.

38. "What America Has to Live Down, II," *New Age* (29 Aug. 1918), p. 281.

39. "Pastiche, The Regional, XVII," *New Age* (13 Nov. 1919), p. 32. Compare Gourmont: "Form passes, it is true, but it is hard to see how form could survive the matter which is its substance. If the beauty of a style becomes effaced or falls to dust, it is because the language has modified the aggregate of its molecules— words—as well as the molecules themselves, and because this internal work has not been effected without swellings and disturbances. If Fra Angelico's frescos have 'passed,' it is not because time has rendered them less beautiful; it is because humidity has swollen the cement where the paint has dulled. Languages swell like cement and flake apart; or rather they are like plane trees which live only by constantly changing their bark and which, early each spring, shed on the moss below the names of lovers engraved on their very flesh." *La Culture des idées*, p. 25.

40. *Epilogues* [I], pp. 35, 135.

41. "Pastiche. The Regional, VII," *New Age* (21 Aug. 1919), p. 283.

42. *Epilogues* [I], p. 145. Quoted in LE, 347.

43. *Promenades philosophiques*, p. 116.

44. "Studies in Contemporary Mentality, XVI," *New Age* (20 Dec. 1917), p. 148.

45. *Epilogues* [I], p. 195. Quoted in LE, 348.

46. Ibid., pp. 142, 52.

47. Ibid., p. 211.

48. *Epilogues II, 1899-1901*, p. 83. My italics.

49. *Epilogues III, 1902-1904*, p. 68.

50. Ibid., p. 162.

51. "Studies in Contemporary Mentality, XIV," *New Age* (29 Nov. 1917), p. 89.

52. "What America Has to Live Down, V," *New Age* (12 Sept. 1918), p. 314.

53. "Pastiche. The Regional, I," *New Age* (12 June 1919), p. 124.

54. "On the Imbecility of the Rich," *Egoist* (15 Oct. 1914), p. 389.

55. "Studies in Contemporary Mentality, XIX," *New Age* (10 Jan. 1918), p. 209.

56. *Epilogues* [I], p. 13. Quoted in LE, 345.

57. *La Culture des idées*, p. 143.

58. *Epilogues* [I], p. 13.

59. *La Culture des idées*, p. 157. Gourmont contributed to the flowering of the ethnographic and philological study of folklore in late nineteenth- and early twentieth-century France. Under the pseudonym of J. Drexelius he wrote several studies on folk songs and on the identity of myths in various cultures. Pioneer ethnographer and folklorist Arnold Van Gennep was among his collaborators on *La Revue des Idées*. If Gourmont, as we shall later see, preferred *La Chanson de Roland* to the *Iliad*, it was largely because he considered the former a more spon-

taneous expression of popular folk traditions. See Rees, *Remy de Gourmont*, p. 234. This entire area of folklore and comparative myth would of course become a crucial concern of Pound's as he increasingly came to see his *Cantos* as embodying the "Sagetrieb" or "The Tale of the Tribe."

60. *Epilogues II*, p. 33.

61. Ibid., pp. 81, 110.

62. Ibid., p. 131.

63. Ibid., p. 81, and *La Culture des idées*, p. 115.

64. *La Culture des idées*, p. 143.

65. *Epilogues II*, p. 157.

66. *Epilogues III*, p. 153.

67. *Ibid.*, p. 198.

68. See, above all, Gourmont's long essay "Le Paganisme eternel" (*La Culture des idées*, pp. 111-159) in which he discusses Bacchism, Mithracism, twelfth-century paganism, the neo-Platonism of Richard St. Victor and many other topics that would concern Pound in the *Cantos* and in such essays of the thirties as "Terra Italica" (SP, 54-61).

69. Quoted in René Pomeau, *La Religion de Voltaire*, nouvelle édition revue et mise à jour (Paris: Nizet, 1969), p. 378. In addition to Pomeau's study see also Peter Gay's essay, "Voltaire's Anti-Semitism," in his *The Party of Humanity: Essays in the French Enlightenment* (New York: Knopf, 1963), pp. 97-114.

70. "Pastiche. The Regional, XVI," *New Age* (6 Nov. 1919), p. 16.

71. "Pastiche. The Regional, XVII," *New Age* (13 Nov. 1919), p. 32.

72. Ibid.

73. "Studies in Contemporary Mentality, V," *New Age* (13 Sept. 1917), p. 426.

74. T. S. Eliot, "The Theology of Economics" (Letter to the Editor), *New English Weekly* (29 March 1937), p. 575. In Paige Typescript #545, 22 February 1920, to Homer Pound, there is a very revealing passage in which Pound speaks of having arranged a meeting between Major Douglas and John Maynard Keynes (the Mr. Bukos of Canto XXII who proclaims himself "an orthodox / Economist"). Keynes, Pound observes in this letter, "has invented whole Roman Apostolick Church of economics, just as bad as the old Whore of Babylon."

75. "The Revolt of Intelligence, VI." *New Age* (15 Jan. 1920), p. 176.

76. "How I Began," *T. P.'s Weekly* (6 June 1913), p. 707.

77. Paige Typescript #512, 10 Jan. 1919.

78. *Epilogues III*, p. 68.

4. Flaubert and the Prose Tradition

1. T. S. Eliot, "Lettre d'Angleterre," *Nouvelle Revue Française* (May 1922), p. 620.

2. *Promenades littéraires*, 4th series, p. 189. This volume contains not only Gourmont's "Souvenirs du symbolisme" but also five pieces on Flaubert—"Les Deux Flaubert," "La Fécondité de Flaubert," "L'Accoucheur de Madame Bovary," "Les Curés de Flaubert," and "Flaubert et la bêtise humaine."

3. "Augment of the Novel," reprinted in *Agenda* (Autumn-Winter 1969-70), p. 54.

4. Hugh Kenner, "The Poetics of Speech," in *Ford Madox Ford, Modern Judgements*, ed. Richard A. Cassell (London: Macmillan, 1972), pp. 169, 172, observes that "there were never two contemporaries less equipped to understand one another than Eliot and Ford, unless Eliot and William Carlos Williams." Part of the two men's disaffection for each other, he suggests, perhaps derived from

literary politics, for Ford clearly "foresaw the consequences of Eliot becoming literary dictator." Given Pound's warm respect for Ford as both novelist and critic, Eliot's silence vis-à-vis this doyen of "les jeunes" seems worth noting.

5. Quoted in Herbert Schneidau, *Ezra Pound, The Image and the Real*, p. 24. Schneidau's study contains an excellent discussion of Pound's debt to Ford, especially as it concerns the prose tradition in verse.

6. Ibid., p. 11. Modern French prose was of course not Ford's exclusive importation. Walter Pater, George Meredith, George Moore, Henry James, just to name a few, were equally oriented towards the Continental novel. See Mary Neale, *Flaubert en Angleterre* (Bordeaux: Société bordelaise de diffusion, 1966).

7. Schneidau, p. 12.

8. Paige Typescript #251, August 1912. At the Pound Center, Beinecke Library, Yale.

9. *Critical Writings of Ford Madox Ford*, ed. Frank MacShane (Lincoln: University of Nebraska, 1964), p. 141.

10. Ibid.

11. *Epilogues* [I], p. 112.

12. Stephane Mallarmé, *Oeuvres complètes* (Paris: Bibliothèque de la Pléiade, 1965), p. 366.

13. Paul Valéry, *Oeuvres*, I (Paris: Bibliothèque de la Pléiade, 1968), p. 1330.

14. "The Approach to Paris, III," *New Age* (18 Sept. 1913), p. 608.

15. "The Approach to Paris, IV," *New Age* (25 Sept. 1913), p. 632.

16. "The Approach to Paris, V," *New Age* (2 Oct. 1913), p. 663.

17. "The Approach to Paris, VI," *New Age* (9 Oct. 1913), p. 694.

18. Quoted in René Wellek, *History of Modern Literary Criticism*, vol. I (New Haven: Yale University Press, 1955), p. 266.

19. Stendhal, *De l'Amour* (Paris: Armand Colin, 1959), p. 292.

20. Ibid., p. 291.

21. "Tradition and Other Things," *Egoist* (15 July 1914), p. 262.

22. Unpublished manuscript version of Canto IV (?), included in the Beinecke Library's "Ezra Pound and his Contemporaries" exhibit, Fall 1975.

23. *Le Problème du style*, p. 122.

24. "Wyndham Lewis," *Egoist* (15 June 1914), p. 234.

25. Pound often praised "the public utility of accurate language which can be attained only from literature, and which the succinct J. Caesar, or the lucid Machiavelli, or the author of the Code Napoleon, or Thos. Jefferson, to cite a local example, would have in no ways despised" (LE, 409). Napoleon and his Code would later figure significantly in the middle Cantos for precisely these reasons.

26. T. S. Eliot, "Beyle and Balzac," *Athenaeum* (30 May 1919), p. 392. "The exposure, the dissociation of human feeling," Eliot noted in the same article, "is a great part of the superiority of Beyle and Flaubert to Balzac . . . the patient analysis of human motives and emotions is the work of the greatest novelists and the greatest novelists dispense with atmosphere." In Balzac, on the contrary, "the fantastic element" was "an atmosphere thrown directly upon reality direct from the personality of the writer." Although Pound conceded that Balzac "extended the subject" (SP, 153), that he gained "what force his crude writing permits him by representing his people under the ἀνάγκη of modernity, cash necessity" (LE, 300), he shared Eliot's (and Gourmont's) low evaluation of Balzac as an artist. Pound was incapable, for example, of seizing Henry James's complex relationship to the author of the *Comédie Humaine:* "Hueffer says that James belauds Balzac. I cannot see it. I can but perceive Henry James wiping the floor with the author of *Eugénie Grandet*, pointing out all his qualities, but almightily wiping the floor with him" (LE, 308).

27. "Wyndham Lewis," *Egoist* (15 June 1914), p. 234.

28. "What America Has to Live Down, II," *New Age* (29 Aug. 1918), p. 281.

29. "What America Has to Live Down, III," *New Age* (5 Sept. 1918), p. 297.

30. "What America Has to Live Down, II," p. 281.

31. Walter Pater, *Appreciations, With an Essay on Style* (London: Macmillan, 1925), p. 29.

32. *Le Problème du style*, p. 32. One might compare Gourmont's "Le style, c'est de sentir, de voir, de penser, et rien de plus" with Flaubert's quotations of Buffon and La Bruyère: "Bien écrire c'est à la fois bien sentir, bien penser et bien dire;" "tout l'esprit d'un auteur consiste à bien définir et à bien peindre." Flaubert, *Correspondance*, nouvelle édition augmentée (Paris: Conard, 1926-1933), vol. VII, p. 290, and vol. VIII, p. 397.

33. *Le Problème du style*, pp. 34, 122. Page reference to this work will hereafter be given in the body of the text.

34. *Promenades littéraires*, 1st series, p. 17.

35. "Les Traducteurs," *Promenades littéraires*, 5th series, p. 169.

36. *Promenades littéraires*, 4th series, p. 339.

37. Kenner, *The Pound Era*, p. 47.

38. *La Culture des idées* (1964), p. 37.

39. See Herbert Schneidau, "Wisdom Past Metaphor: Another View of Pound, Fenollosa, and Objective Verse," *Paideuma* (Spring-Summer 1976), pp. 15-29.

40. Davie, *Ezra Pound: Poet as Sculptor*, p. 246.

41. Daniel Pearlman, *The Barb of Time: On the Unity of Ezra Pound's Cantos* (New York: Oxford University Press, 1969), p. 74.

42. Ford, quoted in Schneidau, p. 26. In the *ABC of Reading*, p. 65, Pound adduced an anecdote from the preface to *Pierre et Jean* about the pedagogic uses of Flaubertian constatation: "It is said that Flaubert taught De Maupassant to write. When De Maupassant returned from a walk, Flaubert would ask him to describe someone, say a concierge, whom they would both pass in their next walk, and to describe the person so that Flaubert would recognize, say, the concierge and not mistake her for some other concierge and not the one De Maupassant had described." Schneidau, p. 28, relates this passage to Pound's Imagist attempts to "present a complex instantaneously"—"to delineate the concierge in a few essential details that will make her uniqueness leap out at the reader; in terms of art history, a perceptual image must be stripped down to the essences that constitute a conceptual image." As in Joycean epiphany, "the aim is an exactness of registration that will manifest the uniqueness of the object or situation, that Scotistic *haeccitas* which Joyce called *quidditas*."

43. "The Approach to Paris, V," *New Age* (2 Oct. 1913), p. 662.

44. Harry Levin, *The Gates of Horn* (New York: Oxford University Press, 1966), p. 34.

45. *The Confucian Odes* (New York: New Directions, 1959), p. 114.

46. *Impact, Essays on Ignorance and the Decline of American Civilization* (Chicago: Henry Regnery, 1960), p. 238.

47. Quoted in Pearlman, *The Barb of Time*, p. 69.

48. Forrest Read, "Pound, Joyce and Flaubert: The Odysseans," in *New Approaches to Ezra Pound*, ed. Eva Hesse (London: Faber and Faber, 1969), p. 131. I am considerably indebted not only to Read's valuable *Pound/Joyce*, but especially to his incisive triangulation of Pound, Joyce, and Flaubert in this particular essay.

49. Pound had his friend the painter "Christian" (Georges Herbiet) translate some of the "Moeurs Contemporaines" series for Picabia's *Pilaou-Thibaou* (10 July 1921). The same translations appeared in the Dadaist number of *Ça Ira* (Nov. 1921).

50. "Paris Letter," *Dial* (Apr. 1922), p. 403.

51. "Paris Letter," *Dial* (Sept. 1922), p. 335.
52. Ibid., p. 333.
53. "Augment of the Novel," *Agenda* (Autumn-Winter 1969-70), p. 49.
54. "Paris Letter," *Dial* (Sept. 1922), p. 332. In an earlier *Dial* article, writing in response to Middleton Murry's denigration of Flaubert's "small sensibility," Pound similarly observed, "He did however create Charles Bovary, and the creator of this most Russian character in French literature was not lacking in human pity, he disdained to falsify it by slobber." "Paris Letter," *Dial* (Apr. 1922), p. 402.
55. Read, "Pound, Joyce and Flaubert," p. 138.
56. "The Revolt of Intelligence, IV," *New Age* (1 Jan. 1920), p. 139. All subsequent quotes in this paragraph are from this same article.
57. See in particular E. J. H. Greene, *T. S. Eliot et la France* (Paris: Boivin, 1951), pp. 144-161.
58. *The Portable Joyce*, ed. Harry Levin (New York: Viking, 1966), p. 483.
59. *Le Problème du style*, p. 106, and *Promenades philosophiques*, p. 283. Both passages marked by Pound in his own copies.
60. "Studies in Contemporary Mentality, IX," *New Age* (18 Oct. 1917), p. 528.
61. "Paris Letter," *Dial* (Sept. 1922), p. 334. Pound would later apply very nearly the same phrases to Mussolini's feats of social engineering, as symbolized by his draining of the marshlands outside Rome. Pound also noted in *Jefferson and/or Mussolini*, p. ix: "It is possible that the Capo del Governo wants to go slow enough so as not to see, in his old age, an Italy full of fat peasants gone rotten and a bourgeoisie stinking over the peninsula as Flaubert saw them stinking through Paris."
62. Quoted in Mary Neale, *Flaubert en Angleterre*, p. 60.
63. T. Sturge Moore, *Art and Life* (London: Methuen, 1910). See also his essay "Flaubert," *Quarterly Review* (Oct. 1914), p. 336, for a rather negative appraisal of *Bouvard et Pécuchet*.
64. *Promenades littéraires*, 4th series, p. 181.
65. Ibid., p. 206.
66. T. S. Eliot, "Eeldrop and Appleplex," *Little Review* (May 1917), p. 8.
67. "Eeldrop and Appleplex," *Little Review* (Sept. 1917), p. 18.
68. "Studies in Contemporary Mentality, II," *New Age* (23 Aug. 1917), p. 364.
69. "Paris Letter," *Dial* (Sept. 1922), p. 333. In a 1942 essay Pound again explained the Flaubertian intentions of his "Studies in Contemporary Mentality": "Flaubert published his *sottisier*. But half a century later the study of what was actually printed and offered for sale on the bookstalls was considered eccentric on the part of the present writer. I made an analysis in eighteen numbers of the *New Age*, but no publisher has wanted to reprint the series, which was, in any case, cut short by the protests of the readers of the said journal. Yet a whole system is collapsing, and for want of having paid attention to the symptoms of its own defilement" (SP, 332).
70. "Studies in Contemporary Mentality, III," *New Age* (30 Aug. 1917), p. 385.
71. "Studies in Contemporary Mentality, XIII," *New Age* (22 Nov. 1917), p. 69.
72. "Studies in Contemporary Mentality, VIII," *New Age* (11 Oct. 1917), p. 507.
73. "Studies in Contemporary Mentality, V," *New Age* (13 Sept. 1917), p. 426.
74. Ibid.
75. "René Crevel," *Criterion* (Jan. 1939), p. 229.

76. Hugh Kenner, *Flaubert, Joyce and Beckett: The Stoic Comedians* (Boston: Beacon Press, 1962), p. 22. These and the following pages owe a great deal to Kenner's chapter on *Bouvard et Pécuchet:* I have merely extended his argument to make Pound's debt to the techniques of Flaubert's *sottisier* more explicit.

77. "Paris Letter," *Dial* (Apr. 1922), p. 404.

78. "Paris Letter," *Dial* (Sept. 1922), p. 332.

79. Hugh Kenner, *The Poetry of Ezra Pound*, p. 256.

80. Ernest Fenollosa, *The Chinese Written Character as Medium for Poetry*, p. 22, and Flaubert, *Correspondance*, vol. VIII, p. 135.

81. G. F. Thorlby, *Gustave Flaubert* (New Haven: Yale University Press, 1957), p. 54.

82. *Promenades littéraires*, 4th series, p. 181.

83. "Paris Letter," *Dial* (Sept. 1922), p. 335, and P/J, p. 208.

84. Compare Ford's *The Critical Attitude* (London: Duckworth, 1911), p. 29: "Nothing was more true than the words of Flaubert when he said that if France had read his *Education sentimentale*, she would have been spared the horrors of the Franco-Prussian War. For, during the period before 1870, France had drifted for a time into the same happy-go-lucky frame of mind that has always existed in England. And so exactly did Flaubert depict this frame of mind in this his most monumental book, that could France have set itself seriously to the task of reading and pondering upon it, undoubtedly some tightening up of the national character must have taken place. France, however, amiably ignored the masterpiece, just as, in all probability, England would ignore a similar work did it produce one."

85. "Paris Letter," *Dial* (Sept. 1922), p. 333.

86. "Revolt of the Intelligence, VI," *New Age* (Jan. 15, 1920), p. 176. Compare Canto CI/724;751: " 'infini' as measured by Renan / 'la bêtise humaine.' " The reference to the "whole mental structure" of the age comes from "Pastiche. The Regional, XVI," *New Age* (6 Nov. 1919), p. 16.

87. *Le Chemin de velours*, p. 175.

88. Kenner, *Flaubert, Joyce and Beckett*, pp. 1-2.

89. Gourmont had observed that the best of Naturalist literature, such as Huysmans *A Veau l'eau* or Maupassant's *La Maison Tellier* (a favorite of Pound's), was comic in inspiration. He included in this category "Flaubert's enigmatic *Bouvard et Pécuchet*, an achievement which goes far beyond these two perfect but minor works to become high comedy, at once moving and cruel." *Promenades littéraires*, 4th series, p. 145.

90. Colin Duckworth, "Flaubert and Voltaire's *Dictionnaire philosophique*," in *Studies on Voltaire and the Eighteenth Century* (Geneva: Institut Voltaire, 1961), vol. 17, p. 149. See also T. Besterman, "Voltaire jugé par Flaubert, *Travaux sur Voltaire et le dix-huitième siècle* (Geneva: Institut Voltaire, 1955), vol. 1.

91. "Paris Letter," *Dial* (Apr. 1922), p. 403.

92. "Paris Letter," *Dial* (Sept. 1922), p. 335, and P/J, p. 208.

93. "Parisian Literature," New York *Evening Post, Literary Review* (13 Aug. 1921), p. 7.

94. Read, "Pound, Joyce and Flaubert," p. 127.

95. Levin, *The Gates of Horn*, p. 293. Victor Brombert points out in *The Novels of Flaubert* (Princeton: Princeton University Press, 1966), pp. 211-212, "Not only was Flaubert attracted to erudition for its own sake and urged on by the desire to know ('Il faudrait tout connaître'), but he was convinced that all truly great literature is encyclopedic in nature: Homer and Rabelais, he observes, are 'encyclopedias of their time.' "

96. Donald Hall, "Ezra Pound, an Interview," in *Ezra Pound: A Collection of*

Criticism, ed. Grace Schulman (New York: MacGraw-Hill, 1974), p. 27.
97. "Paris Letter," *Dial* (Apr. 1922), p. 403.

5. The Natural Philosophy of Love

1. *La Culture des idées* (1964), p. 70. See also *Promenades philosophiques*, p. 205.

2. *Epilogues* [I], p. 142; *La Culture des idées*, p. 177.

3. Uitti, *La Passion littéraire de Remy de Gourmont*, p. 194.

4. John Espey, *Ezra Pound's Mauberley* (Berkeley: University of California Press, 1974), p. 81.

5. *Epilogues* [I], p. 142.

6. *La Culture des idées*, p. 15.

7. William Blake, "Visions of the Daughters of Albion," *Complete Writings* (London: Oxford University Press, 1966), p. 194.

8. Guy Davenport, "Persephone's Ezra," in *New Approaches to Ezra Pound*, ed. Eva Hesse (London: Faber and Faber, 1969), pp. 145-173.

9. *Epilogues II, 1899-1901*, p. 156.

10. Espey, p. 82.

11. See Burne, *Remy de Gourmont*, p. 41.

12. Ibid., p. 67.

13. Ernest Fenollosa, *The Chinese Written Character as a Medium for Poetry*, p. 28.

14. *Le Problème du style*, p. 132.

15. *Promenades philosophiques*, 2nd series, p. 159.

16. See *Le Chemin de velours*, pp. 87-89.

17. Remy de Gourmont, *The Natural Philosophy of Love*, trans. Ezra Pound (New York: Collier, 1972), pp. 19-20. All page references hereafter included in the body of the text and in footnotes refer to this edition.

18. *Physique de l'amour*, p. 9.

19. Paul Escoube, "La Femme et le sentiment de l'amour chez Remy de Gourmont," *Mercure de France* (1 Oct. 1922), p. 38.

20. Fenollosa, pp. 25, 22, 11.

21. Ibid., p. 19.

22. Typographical rearrangement of this passage suggested by S. W. de Rachewiltz. See also his *Il Paradiso Spezzato dei Cantos* (Urbino: Doctoral Dissertation, 1973).

23. It was something cognate to Gourmont's *luxure* that Pound defined as "luxury" in a 1919 *New Age* article: "Luxury exists as a function; one does not deny that it is abused, but one ascribes the failure of many revolutionary parties to their failure to recognise it . . . as a beneficent part of the social machine . . . The function of luxury is to set a model for living; the luxury of one age becomes the convenience of the next. . . . It is the duty of a sane manufacturing system to overproduce until these things are within every man's reach . . . The function of an 'aristocracy' is largely to criticise, select, castigate luxury, to reduce the barroque [sic] to an elegance." "Pastiche. The Regional, XV," *New Age* (30 Oct. 1919), p. 448. Pound's perspective is not unlike that of Voltaire in his poem "Le Mondain."

24. Kenner informs us that Pound was introduced to Frobenius' *Kulturmorphologie* by Joseph Bard in 1928 (*The Pound Era*, p. 507). He appears to have bought the German ethnologist's seven-volume *Erlebte Erdteile* (1929) shortly after its publication and was especially interested in its fourth volume, entitled *Paideuma*. Frobenius's relationship to Pound's ideogram of Gourmont is indicated by his remarks on Fabre in a 1940 letter to T. S. Eliot: "I know you jib at

China and Frobenius cause they ain't pie church; and neither of us likes sabages, black habits, etc. However, for yr. enlightenment, Frazer worked largely from documents. Frob. went to *things*, memories still in the spoken tradition, etc. His students had to *see* and be able to draw objects. All of which follows up Fabre *and* the Fenollosa 'Essay on Written Character' (L, 336). Although Gourmont makes no mention of Frobenius, he was not unknown in France. His first essays on primitive African art were published in 1895 and, according to Pound, "Guillaume Apollinaire had called Frobenius 'father' " (GK, 203). Davenport suggests that Apollinaire's enthusiasm for African art (shared by Pound's early friend Gaudier-Brzeska) probably led Matisse, Derain, Vlaminck, and Picasso in that direction (see his "Pound and Frobenius" in *Motive and Method in the Cantos of Ezra Pound*, ed. Lewis Leary (New York: Columbia University Press, 1954), p. 44. Pound's use of Frobenius's account of the African legend of Wagadu in the *Pisan Cantos* (LXXIV/430;437) is paralleled by the poet Pierre Jean Jouve's use of the same tale in his novel *Aventures de Catherine Crachat* (1931), the second book of which is entitled *Vagadu* and whose epigraph—"Wagadu est la force qui vit dans le coeur des hommes"—recalls Pound's celebrated "Now in the heart indestructible." André Malraux, too, was interested in Frobenius; according to Armand Hoog ("Malraux, Möllberg and Frobenius," *Yale French Studies*, 18, 1957), he modeled the character Möllberg in *Les Noyers d'Altenburg* on the German anthropologist; Malraux's Spenglerian philosophy of culture (and particularly his concept of the "Musée imaginaire") shares certain traits with the Frobenian *Paideuma*.

25. *Les Chevaux de Diomède*, p. 249.

26. See Daniel Pearlman, *The Barb of Time* (New York: Oxford University Press, 1969), p. 209, for a fuller explication of these lines.

27. See Kenner, *The Pound Era*, p. 311.

28. Pearlman, p. 180.

29. The phrase comes from "Stratagèmes"—"Des femmes, au bon endroit, savent mordre. Elles ne doivent pas être méprisées, ces conservatrices des traditions milésiennes,—mais c'est bien monotone et les artistes sont rares." Quoted in Espey, p. 70. Pound, as Espey notes, used the phrase not only for its sexual connotations (related to the bawdy Milesian tales) but also in the broader sense to signify woman as conservator and inheritor of past gestures. See also Canto CIV/742;767: "Remy's word was 'milésiennes' / William's: monoceros / vide his book plate. / The production IS the beloved." This last phrase of course recalls Goddeschalk's "amas ut pulchram facias."

30. Pound came upon similar distinctions in the works of Frobenius. As Guy Davenport notes: "A culture, in the sense that Leo Frobenius understood it (and hence Pound), has two dominant symbols, the male one of action, the female one of stillness and place (*Ruhe und Raum*). The male symbol is of direction, expansion, intensity, considering space as distance to traverse and measure, and is therefore volatile, unstable, destiny-ridden." Guy Davenport, "Persephone's Ezra," in *New Approaches*, p. 167.

31. Although its context in a Canto dealing with the disorders of Protestant sexuality might lead one to read this passage as a Prufrockian parody, Pound nevertheless used the same terms—unironically—not only in his "Postscript" but also in a letter to Marianne Moore (L, 146) and in "Kongo Roux," his contribution to Picabia's *Pilhaou-Thibaou*. In his essay "James Joyce and Pécuchet" Pound referred to Molly Bloom analogously: "Penelope, la femme . . . vagin, symbole de la terre, mer morte dans laquelle l'intelligence male retombe" (P/J, 208).

32. "The New Therapy," *New Age* (16 March 1922), p. 260. Pound's enthusiasm for Berman was not restricted to his *Glands Regulating Personality* alone.

Pound thought that the new therapy might be especially suitable for his friend Joyce's sundry ailments; Read recounts that while Dr. Berman was visiting Paris in 1922, "Pound persuaded Joyce to submit himself to examination. Dr. Berman proposed endocrine treatment for Joyce's arthritic back and, after one look at his teeth, insisted that they be X-rayed immediately. The teeth proved to be in such bad condition that he advised complete extraction. Joyce accepted the endocrine treatment, but although Dr. Berman must have gained his confidence by comparing Joyce's glaucoma to Homer's . . . Joyce put off the extraction until he had consulted another ophthalmologist, Dr. Louis Borsch, who was to become his longstanding ministrant (P/J, 212).

33. Ibid.

34. Ibid.

35. Ibid.

36. See Kenner, *The Pound Era*, p. 482.

37. Ibid., p. 492.

38. For "dragon world" see Pound's translation of the Noh play *Genjo* in his *Translations* (New York: New Directions, 1963), p. 351. Peter Laurie pointed this out to me.

39. Pound may have been thinking also of another Gourmontian passage devoted to the mating of butterflies: "Butterflies are likewise very fervent, the males make veritable voyages in quest of females, as Fabre has proved. They often fly coupled, the stronger female carrying the male: it is a quite frequent sight in the country, these butterflies with four wings who roll, a little bewildered, from flower to flower, drunken ships going where the sails bid them" (p. 74).

40. Pound's Eleusinian association of light with the act of love finds its confirmation in Gourmont's description of the amorous habits of the glowworm: "The male of this female is a perfect insect, provided with wings which he uses to seek in the darkness the female who shines more brightly as she more desires to be looked at and mounted. There is a kind of lamprey of which both sexes are equally phosphorescent, one in the air, the male, the other on the ground where she awaits him. After coupling they fade as lamps when extinquished. This luminosity is, evidently, of an interest purely sexual. When the female sees the small flying star descend toward her, she gathers her wits, and prepares for hypocrite defense common to all her sex, she plays the belle and the bashful, exults in fear, trembles in joy. The fading light is symbolic of the destiny of nearly all insects, and of many animals also; coupling accomplished, their reason for being disappears and life vanishes from them" (p. 40).

41. Compare Gourmont's comments on the ephemeral existence of the butterfly: "The *purity* of such life is to be admired in many butterflies: the silk-moths, heavy and clumsy, shake their wings for an instant at birth, couple and die. The Great Peacock or Oak Bombyx, much larger than they, eats no more than they do: yet we see him traverse leagues of country in his quest of the female. He has only a rudimentary proboscis and a fake digestive apparatus. Thus his two or three days' existence passes without one egoistic act. The struggle for life, much vaunted, is here the struggle to give life, the struggle for death, for if they can live three days in search of the female they die as soon as the fecundation is accomplished" (p. 24). But if Gourmont construed the butterflies' ephemerality as "a symbol for pure thought" (p. 101), Pound rather saw them as embodying that principle of metamorphosis which is perhaps *the* dominant, unifying theme of the *Cantos* as a whole. It was for this reason that, in a footnote to his translation of the *Physique de l'amour*, Pound quarreled with Gourmont's claim that the insect is "nearly always born adult, and after the death of her parents; she has received from them neither direct education nor education by example, as do the young of birds or mammals" (p. 139). Pound insisted instead on the continuity that might

exist between larval and adult life: "Both Fabre and Gourmont seem to me to go astray in considering the insect as a separate creature, i.e. a creature cut off from its larva or cocoon life. Surely the animal may be supposed to exist while in its cocoon or larva, it may reasonably be supposed to pass that period in reflection, preparing precisely the acts of its desire (as for example an intelligent young man might pass his years in a university under professors, awaiting reasonable maturity to act or express his objections). The larva has its months of quiet, precisely the necessary pre-reflection for the two days' joy-ride of exterior manifestation, amours, etc., its *contemplatio*, or what may be counted as analogous, passing in its cell. The perfection and precision of its acts, being, let us say, proportionate to the non-expressive period. Having spent God knows how long in that possible monotonous nest, it seems small wonder that the insect should know the pattern by heart" (p. 139).

42. Letter to Natalie Barney, 22 Jan. 1954. In the Natalie Barney Archives at the Bibliothèque littéraire Jacques Doucet, Paris. Though Pound had mentioned Agassiz in his 1934 *ABC of Reading* (ABC, 17), it was not until the early fifties that he began to read the American naturalist in depth.

43. Louis Agassiz, *Essay on Classification*, ed. Edward Lurie (Cambridge: Harvard University Press, Belknap Press, 1962), p. 75.

44. Ibid.

45. Ibid., p. 131.

46. Kenner, *The Pound Era*, p. 167. See, for example, the Buffonesque stylistic precision of Agassiz's description of the jellyfish (which to his fellow Transcendentalists seemed but "organized water"): "From the lower surface of this disk hang, conspicuously, three kinds of appendages. Near the margin there are eight bunches or long tentacles, moving in every direction, sometimes extending to an enormous length, sometimes shortened to a mere coil of entangled threads, constantly rising and falling, stretching now in one direction and then in another, but generally spreading slantingly in a direction opposite to that of the onward movement of the animal. These streamers may be compared to floating tresses of hair, encircling organs which are farther inward upon the lower surface of the disk. Of these organs, there are also eight bunches, which alternate with the eight bunches of tentacles, but they are of two kinds; four are elegant sacks, adorned, as it were, with waving ruffles projecting in large clusters, which are alternately pressed forward and withdrawn, and might also be compared to bunches of grapes, by turns inflated and collapsed. These four bunches alternate with four masses of folds, hanging like rich curtains, loosely waving to and fro, and as they wave, extending downwards, or shortening rapidly, recalling, to those who have had an opportunity of witnessing the phenomenon, the play of the streamers of an aurora borealis." Quoted in *The Intelligence of Louis Agassiz*, ed. Guy Davenport (Boston: Beacon Press, 1963), p. 177.

47. See Walter Baumann, "Secretary of Nature, J. Heydon," in *New Approaches to Ezra Pound*, pp. 303-319.

48. In the *Promenades philosophiques*, 3rd series, p. 33 (in Pound's possession).

49. *Confucius*, translation and commentary by Ezra Pound, p. 31.

50. Compare Canto CVI/754;779, "Gold light, in veined phyl[l]otaxis," as well as CIV/743;768, "Hence Webster, Voltaire and Leibnitz / by phyllotaxis / in leaf-grain." Agassiz writes of the Goethean notion of phyllotaxis in his *Essay on Classification*, pp. 128-30: "It is well known that the arrangement of the leaves in plants may be expressed by very simple series of fractions, all of which are gradual approximations to, or the natural means between 1/2 or 1/3, which two fractions are themselves the maximum and the minimum divergence between two single successive leaves . . . Now upon comparing this arrangement of the leaves

in plants with the revolutions of the members of our solar system, Peirce has discovered the most perfect identity between the fundamental laws which regulate both . . ." Agassiz then proceeds to give tables correlating the ratios of planetary revolution with those of leaf phyllotaxis. He concludes of these and other similar analogies: "The same series everywhere! These facts are true of all the great divisions of the animal kingdom, so far as we have pursued the investigation; and though, for want of materials, the train of evidence is incomplete in some instances, yet we have proof enough for the establishment of *this law of a universal correspondence in all the leading features which binds all organized beings of all times into one great System, intellectually and intelligibly linked together*, even where some links of the chain are missing" (my italics). Through Agassiz, then, Pound rejoins not only Goethean *Naturwissenschaft* but also the major currents of American Transcendentalist and French Symbolist thought (compare Baudelaire's "correspondances" and his Swedenborgian notion of "analogie universelle")—blended, in these late Cantos, with neo-Platonism and neo-Confucianism.

51. Léon Vérane, "François Bernouard ou les confidences d'un typographe," *Le Livre et ses Amis*, 4 (1946), pp. 838-846. See also my "Canto 119: François Bernouard," *Paideuma* (Fall-Winter 1975), p. 329ff.

52. Vérane, p. 44.

53. Kenner, *The Pound Era*, pp. 319, 423.

54. Ibid., p. 384.

55. John Peck, "Landscape as Ceremony in the later *Cantos*," *Agenda* (Spring-Summer 1972), passim, and Donald Davie, "The *Cantos*: Towards a Pedestrian Reading," *Paideuma* (Spring-Summer 1972), pp. 55-63.

56. Laurence Binyon's version, in *The Portable Dante* (New York: Viking, 1969), p. 239.

Appendix

1. "Paris Letter," *Dial* (Sept. 1922), p. 332.

2. "Paris Letter," *Dial* (April 1922), p. 403.

3. *Oeuvres complètes*, vol. 2 (Paris: Seuil, 1964), p. 131.

4. *Correspondance*, 3rd series (1854-1869) (Paris: Charpentier, 1891), pp. 268-269.

5. *Correspondance*, 1st series (1830-1850) (Paris: Charpentier, 1887), p. 162.

6. *Correspondance*, 3rd series, pp. 86, 141, 338.

7. Ibid., pp. 364-365, 19.

8. Ibid., 270.

9. Ibid., p. 80.

10. *Correspondance*, 1st series, pp. 181, 171.

11. *Correspondance*, 3rd series, p. 199.

12. Ibid., pp. 121, 164.

13. Ibid., p. 239.

14. Ibid., p. 233.

15. *The Golden Bowl* (New York: Scribners, 1909), pp. ix-x.

INDEX

ABC of Reading (Pound), 62
Adams, John, 115, 156
Agassiz, Louis, 5, 24, 135-136, 151-154
Aiken, Conrad, 73
Albalat, Antoine, 53-56, 59, 103, 107
"The Alchemist" (Pound), 33-34, 36
Aldington, Richard, 4, 11, 13, 20, 23-25, 37, 46, 54, 69
Anacreon, 45
Anselm, Saint, 38
Antheil, George, 15
Apollinaire, Guillaume, 3, 52, 189n24
"The Approach to Paris" (Pound), 29-30, 52
Aristotle, 1, 144
Arnold, Matthew, 106

Babbitt, Irving, 6, 71
Balzac, Honoré de, 109, 127, 135, 184n26
Barney, Natalie Clifford, 15-16, 26, 45, 151
Barrès, Maurice, 7, 23, 57
Barzun, Henri Martin, 16, 97
Baudelaire, Charles, 7, 37, 54, 70-72, 83, 117, 192n50
Bayle, Pierre, 73, 76, 125
Beardsley, Aubrey, 117
Benda, Julien, 71

Bennett, Arnold, 10
Bergson, Henri, 10, 12, 71, 125, 139
Berman, Dr. Louis, 146
Bernouard, François, 24, 156-157
Blake, William, 127, 131-132
Born, Bertans de, 107
Bouvard et Pécuchet (Flaubert), 17, 111, 116, 118-128, 140, 161
Brancusi, Constantin, 153
Brandes, Georg, 5
Brantôme, Pierre de Bourdeille de, 99, 101
Bréal, Michel, 103
Brisset, Jules, 14-15
Brooke, Rupert, 10
Brooks, Van Wyck, 7
Browning, Robert, 56, 110
Brunetière, Ferdinand, 6
Buffon, Georges-Louis Leclerc de, 59, 133, 185n32
Burke, Kenneth, 7, 77
Burne, Glenn, 4, 33
Bush, Ronald, 44
Bynner, Witter, 31

Cantos (Pound), 17, 38, 41-42, 44, 56, 82, 89, 90, 126-127, 132; *Canto* VII, 67; XII, 131; XIV-XVI, 100, 131; XXVI, 138; XXIX, 130, 144; XXX,

193

75; XXXVI, 138; XXXVII, 139; XL, 112; XLI, 138; XLIV, 137; XLV, 33-34, 81; XLVII, 141-143; XLIX, 141; LVIII, 150; LXXIV, 81-82, 147, 150; LXXVI, 149, 151; LXXX, 15-16, 149; LXXXI, 141, 147-148; LXXXIII, 26, 143; LXXXVII, 145; LXXXIX, 166-167; XC, 34; XCII, 154-155; XCIII, 41, 45, 153-154; XCIV, 154; XCV, 81, XCVIII, 42; CVI, 153, 155; CVII, 153; CXIII, 142, CXVI, 128; CXIX, 156-158; CXX, 128

Canzoni (Pound), 8-9, 31

Carlyle, Thomas, 71

Carman, Bliss, 8

Carnevali, Emanuel, 73

Cavalcanti, Guido, 2, 43, 46, 49, 56, 74, 99, 138, 151, 177n37, 177n39

Cendrars, Blaise, 52

Chavannes, Puvis de, 48

Chennevière, Paul, 14-15

Chesterton, G. K., 83

Les Chevaux de Diomède (Gourmont), 10, 16, 47, 73-74, 140

Claudel, Paul, 32, 83, 120

Clayton, T. T., 23

Coleridge, S. T., 63, 165, 173n28

Confucius, 1, 21, 79, 120, 153, 157

Confucius to Cummings (Pound), 39

Corbière, Tristan, 5, 16, 52, 96, 98, 117

Cowley, Malcolm, 7

Cros, Charles, 6

La Culture des idées (Gourmont), 4, 18, 69

Cummings, E. E., 26-27

Daniel, Arnaut, 31

Dante, 2, 7, 40-41, 46, 49, 55, 66, 74, 81, 97, 107, 110, 138, 144, 151, 154, 157, 176n32

Dante, Béatrice et la poésie amoureuse (Gourmont), 43, 177n32m 177n39

Darío, Rubén, 52

Darwin, Charles, 24, 55, 134, 145, 152

Davenport, Guy, 132

Davie, Donald, 29, 32, 53, 70, 106

Davray, Henri, 9, 57

De Cassares, Benjamin, 7

De Rachewiltz, S. W., 188n22

"Deux Attitudes mystiques: Dante et Donne" (Eliot), 176n32, 177n39

Dickens, Charles, 111

Disney, Walt, 120

Divus, Andreas, 38, 103

Douglas, Clifford Hugh, 72, 78, 141, 183n74

Dowson, Ernest, 8, 13

Duchamp, Marcel, 121

Duhamel, Georges, 14, 30

Dujardin, Edouard, 133

L'Education sentimentale (Flaubert), 107, 110-113, 116-117, 122-123, 162, 187n84

"Eeldrop and Appleplex" (Eliot), 67, 119

Einstein, Albert, 141

Eliot, T. S., 2, 4, 7, 15, 23, 26-27, 44, 46, 51, 60, 65-67, 71, 74, 89, 93-95, 101. *See also individual works.*

Ellis, Havelock, 5, 10, 24, 130

Emerson, Ralph Waldo, 153

Epilogues (Gourmont), 18, 68-69, 76, 80-83, 85, 96

Espey, John, 23, 47, 132, 164

Fabre, Jean Henri, 134, 139, 141, 147, 150, 188n24, 191n41

Fenollosa, Ernest, 5, 18, 62-63, 70, 74, 77, 80, 122, 133, 135-136, 189n24

Fielding, Henry, 99

Flaubert, Gustave, 2, 7-8, 24, 28, 47, 52-53, 64, 76, 79, 94-95, 100-102, 105-106, 109, 129, 148, 161-167. *See also individual works.*

Fletcher, John Gould, 31

Flint, F. S., 10-11, 13-14, 16, 173n28, 175n7

Ford, Ford Madox, 5, 9, 17, 28, 53, 95, 98, 118, 180n43

Fort, Paul, 6, 15-16, 52

Four Quartets (Eliot), 35, 66

France, Anatole, 7-8, 10, 13

"Fratres Minores" (Pound), 130

Frazer, Sir James, 87, 141

Freud, Sigmund, 4, 49, 137, 139, 146

Frobenius, Leo, 5, 24, 39, 189n30

Frost, Robert, 98

Galton, Arthur, 69

Gaudier-Brzeska, Henri, 6, 17, 52-53, 64

Gaultier, Jules de, 10, 133

Gautier, Théophile, 5, 28, 44-45, 124, 132

Index

Gide, André, 3, 10, 23, 69
Goddeschalk (Notker Babulus), 12, 38-39, 41-42, 49
Goethe, Johann Wolfgang von, 99, 113-114, 135, 164, 191n50
Goncourt brothers, 10, 52, 96, 101, 111
Goncourt, Edmond de, 117
Gonne, Maud, 91
Gosse, Sir Edmund, 10
Gourmont, Jean de, 24, 26
Grosseteste, Bishop, 146
Guide to Kulchur (Pound), 23, 25, 75, 79, 81, 94, 117, 126, 130, 139, 165

H. D. (Hilda Doolittle), 11, 13
Hanno, 112, 166
Hart, Dr. Bernard, 53
Hecht, Ben, 7
Herbiet, Georges, 185n49
Heydon, John, 154
Homer, 53, 56, 66, 90, 103-108, 164, 187n95
Hugh Selwyn Mauberley (Pound), 4, 18, 23, 44-45, 47, 72, 114, 132-133, 143
Hugo, Victor, 127
Hulme, T. E., 4, 10, 11-12, 59, 62-63
Huneker, James Gibbons, 5-7, 11, 22, 57
Huxley, Aldous, 4, 130
Huysmans, J.-K., 5, 7, 37, 175n5, 187n89

"In a Station of the Metro" (Pound), 105-106

Jakobson, Roman, 105
James, Henry, 13, 23, 47, 74, 83, 111, 113, 117-118, 132, 167, 184n26
Jammes, Francis, 16, 52, 97-98
Jarry, Alfred, 3
Jefferson, Thomas, 78
Jefferson and/or Mussolini (Pound), 25, 139-140
Jolas, Eugene, 95
Jouve, Pierre Jean, 14, 29, 189n24
Joyce, James, 8, 95, 133, 115, 127, 185n42, 189n32. *See also Ulysses.*

Kenner, Hugh, 38, 78, 104, 121, 125, 148, 152, 164
Kipling, Rudyard, 59

Kreymborg, Alfred, 16

Lacharme, Père, 38
Laforgue, Jules, 5-6, 52, 65-66, 96
Le Latin mystique (Gourmont), 12, 36-38, 42, 46, 50, 55
Lautréamont (Isidore Ducasse), 20
Lawrence, D. H. 98, 130
Leconte de Lisle, 103-104
Legouis, Emile, 9
Lenin, V. I., 25
Lettres à l'Amazone (Gourmont), 15, 43-46
Levin, Harry, 109, 172n11
Lewis, Wyndham, 6, 10, 17, 47, 64, 71
Linnaeus, Carolus, 153
Litanies de la rose (Gourmont), 5, 11, 13-14, 23, 29-36, 44, 50, 61, 97
Livre des masques (Gourmont), 4-5, 7, 10, 13, 51-52
Locke, John, 61-62
Louys, Pierre, 22
Lowell, Amy, 20, 31, 51
Lustra (Pound), 44, 111, 130

McAlmon, Robert, 25
Machaut, Guillaume de, 45
Madame Bovary (Flaubert), 102, 111-113, 122
Mallarmé, Stéphane, 3, 67, 96-97, 127
Malraux, André, 189n24
Manning, Frederic, 23
Mansfield, Katherine, 10
Marinetti, F. T., 11
Marx, Karl, 78, 110, 163
Maupassant, Guy de, 8, 95-96, 101, 122, 185n42, 187n89
Maurras, Charles, 71
Mead, G. R. S., 42
Mencken, H. L., 7-8, 16, 20, 84
Mockel, Albert, 26
Monroe, Harriet, 13
Montaigne, Michel de, 68, 99, 101, 126
Moore, Marianne, 130, 189n31
Moore, T. Sturge, 10, 118
More, Paul Elmer, 6
Mozart, Wolfgang Amadeus, 150
Murry, John Middleton, 10, 186n54
Mussolini, Benito, 25, 72, 78, 82-83, 186n61

Nagy, N. Christophe de, 164

Index

Napoleon, 101
Nathan, George Jean, 7
The Natural Philosophy of Love
(Pound translation), 4, 24, 49
134-155
Nietzsche, Friedrich, 6-8, 71, 74, 76,
136
"Night Litany" (Pound), 32

Olson, Charles, 64
Orage, A. R., 10, 20, 72
Ovid, 99, 107, 130, 145, 152

Pater, Walter, 101-102, 184n6
Paul, Deacon, 38
Pauthier, Guillaume, 54
Pavannes and Divisions (Pound), 72-
73
Pearlman, Daniel, 108, 143
Peck, John, 44
Péladan, Joséphin, 8
Pensées inédites (Gourmont), 23
Perse, St.-John, 32
Physique de l'amour (Gourmont), 4-5,
24-26, 49, 129, 133-137
Picabia, Francis, 126, 185n49
Plato, 41, 152
Poe, Edgar Allan, 31, 133
Pope, Alexander, 103, 147
Pound, Dorothy Shakespear, 69
Powys, John Cowper, 22
Powys, Llewelyn, 10
Praz, Mario, 45, 47, 175n5, 177n46
Le Problème du style (Gourmont), 5,
12-13, 17, 43, 53-67, 69, 73, 76, 95,
101-108, 111, 115-116, 118-119, 133,
165
Promenades littéraires (Gourmont),
57, 102
Propertius, 41, 56, 99, 115
Prothero, G. W., 21
Prufrock and Other Observations
(Eliot), 111
"Psychology and Troubadours"
(Pound), 36, 41-43

Quinn, John, 6, 8, 21, 91, 110
Quinton, René, 55, 57, 133

Rabelais, François, 99, 125, 187n95
Rabier, Elie, 53, 76, 139
Read, Forrest, 110, 114, 126
Régnier, Henri de, 11, 13, 19, 22, 52

Renan, Ernest, 73, 124
Ribot, Théodule, 41, 53, 60, 76, 139
Richard St. Victor, 36
Rimbaud, Arthur, 5, 16, 42, 146
Ripostes (Pound), 11-12
Rodker, John, 23
Rolland, Romain, 10, 23
Romains, Jules, 14-16, 29, 97-98,
174n54
Rosenfield, Paul, 7, 181n21
Rousseau, Jean-Jacques, 71, 99, 136
Rouveyre, André, 27
Rummel, Walter Morse, 9
Ruskin, John, 72, 151
Ryner, Hans, 15

The Sacred Wood (Eliot), 1, 50, 53-55,
115
Salammbô (Flaubert), 105, 112, 166
Salel, Hugues, 103
Schlegel, Friedrich, 127
Schneidau, Herbert, 63, 95, 164
Schopenhauer, Arthur, 40-41
Schwob, Marcel, 47, 156
Shakespeare, William, 113, 117, 164
Shaw, George Bernard, 114-115
Sinclair, May, 64
Songe d'une femme (Gourmont), 48
Spire, André, 16
Spirit of Romance (Pound), 11-12, 38,
40, 43, 55, 107, 157
"The Spring" (Pound), 132
Stendhal, 2, 7, 10, 46, 97, 99-101, 135
Sterne, Laurence, 99
Stirner, Max, 7
"Studies in Contemporary Mentality"
(Pound), 119-120
"A Study of French Poets" (Pound), 52
Symons, Arthur, 5, 8, 10, 13, 51

Tagore, Rabindranath, 14, 32
Tailhade, Laurent, 16, 52, 97, 111
Taine, Hippolyte, 64, 103
Taupin, René, 1-2, 13, 31
La Tentation de Saint Antoine
(Flaubert), 112, 128
Thompson, Vance, 6
Thorlby, Anthony, 122
Trois Contes (Flaubert), 102, 108, 113-
114
Trollope, Anthony, 84
Turgenev, Ivan, 96

Uitti, Karl, 4, 40, 130
Ulysses (Joyce), 17, 110-111, 114, 118, 121-123, 125-127, 130, 189n31
Untermeyer, Louis, 72
Upward, Allen, 10, 104

Valéry, Paul, 97, 126
Vallette, Alfred, 22, 26
Van Gennep, Arnold, 133, 182n59
Van Vechten, Carl, 7
Vega, Lope de, 7
Ventadorn, Bernart de, 157
Verhaeren, Emile, 52, 97
Verlaine, Paul, 6, 147
Vildrac, Charles, 14-16, 30, 97-98
Villon, François, 7, 19, 58, 81, 115-117
Voltaire, 17-19, 69-70, 83-90, 98-99, 101, 125, 163, 188n23

Wagner, Richard, 127, 133, 176n20
Wang Wei, 47
Whistler, James McNeill, 47, 72-73
Whitman, Walt, 97, 110, 116, 142
Wilde, Oscar, 22, 73, 106
Williams, William Carlos, 19, 80, 183n4
Wilson, Edmund, 7

Yeats, William Butler, 5, 8-9, 13-14, 28-29, 35, 56, 127, 173n28, 176n20, 181n25

Zola, Emile, 120, 156